SUNDAY NIGHTS
AT SEVEN

SUNDAY NIGHTS AT SEVEN

THE JACK BENNY STORY
BY

Jack Benny and His Daughter Joan

1894 -1974

WITH A FOREWORD
BY GEORGE BURNS

G.K.HALL &CO.
Boston, Massachusetts
1991

Published in Large Print by arrangement with
Warner Books, A Time Warner Company.

G.K. Hall Large Print Book Series.

Set in 16 pt. Plantin.

Library of Congress Cataloging-in-Publication Data

Benny, Jack, 1894–1974.
  Sunday nights at seven : the Jack Benny story / by Jack Benny and
his daughter Joan ; with a foreword by George Burns.
    p.   cm.—(G.K. Hall large print book series)
  Reprint. Originally published : New York, NY : Warner Books, c1990.
  ISBN 0-8161-5192-X.—ISBN 0-8161-5188-1 (pbk.)
  1. Benny, Jack, 1894–1974. 2. Comedians—United States—
Biography. 3. Large type books. I. Benny, Joan, 1934–
II. Title.
[PN2287.B4325A3 1991]
792.7'.028'092—dc20
[B]   91-16905

To my children: Michael, Maria,
Robert, and Joanna

ACKNOWLEDGMENTS

It was a great pleasure to interview the many people who took the time to reminisce and recall stories about my father, many of which were new to me. My thanks for their help to Deedee Bail, George Balzer, Signe Bensen, Francis Bergen, Estelle and Mel Blanc, Sandra Burns, Claudette Colbert, Janet and Fred DeCordova, Leonard Gershe, Douglas Glant, Hal Goldman, Al Gordon, Radie Harris, Dolores and Bob Hope, Artie Kane, Dr. Rex Kennamer, Abbe Lane, Ralph Levy, William Paley, Sam Perrin, Betty Sullivan Precht, Nancy and Ronald Reagan, Isaac Stern, Jimmy and Gloria Stewart, Leah and Larry Superstein, Audrey and Billy Wilder, Jane Wyman, and my children, particularly Mike and Maria who remember him best.

I would also like to thank the many gracious and cooperative people of the Special Collections department in the Research Library at UCLA.

This book would have been impossible without the stories and insights from Irving Fein, who knew Dad better than anyone. It would have been equally impossible without the stories as well as the introduction from George Burns, who knew

Dad longer than anyone. My appreciation, thanks, and love to both.

Lastly, my eternal gratitude to my editor, Joan Pollack, who, in her own words, was "dragged kicking and screaming into the computer age." On our twin Macintoshes she corrected my ghastly spelling and errors in syntax; forced me, a born rambler, to be more concise; and organized my disorderly collection of bits and pieces. In short, she got my act together. More important, she gave me encouragement as well as a great deal of TLC.

FOREWORD
by George Burns

When Joanie asked me to write this foreword, I said I'd be happy to. Why wouldn't I be? I knew her when she was on pabulum—I bounced her on my knee—I let her grab my nose—I gave her her first cigar.

And her father, Benny Kubelsky, also known as Ben K. Benny, and later, Jack Benny, was my best friend for over fifty years. I was going to say Jack was my *closest* friend, but you might think I was making another cheap joke about him. And I wouldn't do that to my best friend.

Anyway, that whole miser thing was a made-up gimmick to get laughs. The Jack Benny I knew threw his money around. Not far—but he threw it.

By now most of you know that Jack Benny was not only my best friend, but he was also my best audience. He laughed at everything I said. That might be one reason why he was my best friend. Jack didn't just laugh at things I said, he'd fall down on the floor . . . on the street . . . in the men's room . . . wherever we were. I still have a bad back from all the times I had to pick him up. But it was worth it.

When Joanie told me she was going to write

this book, I must confess I wondered about it. After all, Irving Fein, Jack's manager and now mine, wrote a book about Jack. One of his writers, Milt Josefsberg, wrote a book about Jack. And Mary wrote a book about Jack. So I asked myself—who could possibly know anything of interest about Jack that his manager, his writer and his wife haven't already told us? The answer is just two people: his masseur, whom we have yet to hear from, and his only child, Joan.

She brings a new perspective to the subject. (How about that? After eight books, I'm beginning to talk like a writer.) What was it like growing up with such a famous comedian for a father? Did he make time for her . . . share her interests? What was the relationship she saw between her parents? Was life in the Benny household all a barrel of laughs? What was Jack like out of the public eye, when he let his hair down? (That's where Jack and I were different. He would let his hair down, I just took mine off.)

The point is, Joan Benny was there. She had a front row seat. And most of all, the great pleasure of this book is that so much of it is in Jack's own voice. So the pages that follow should make for interesting reading.

I miss Jack. He was a nice man.

George Burns

P.S. Yesterday Joanie dropped by to thank me for the foreword, and we had fun together. She couldn't have been more grateful. In fact, she gave me back my cigar. Nice kid!

January 1990

INTRODUCTION

It is perhaps odd to begin a book with an apology, but I must. I must beg pardon for my tardiness and procrastination. This book should have been written long ago. One day in 1984, shortly after my mother passed away, as I was sorting through closets and boxes and file cabinets, I came across a strange bundle of papers. At first glance I thought it was a movie script. Then I realized it was much too thick for that. I started reading and discovered it was a manuscript—an autobiography. Many years before, in the late 1960's, Daddy had mentioned he was writing a book about his life—I remembered the title, *I Always Had Shoes*—but I had long since forgotten about it. I assumed he had lost interest because he never spoke of it again. And there it was, in the back of a file cabinet, almost four hundred pages—a completed book.

Why was it never published? I don't really know, at least not for sure. I recall hearing a story that it had indeed been sold to a publisher, but that Daddy bought back the rights because my mother objected to it. She was offended that he talked about his former girlfriends. It doesn't sound like a good enough reason to me—I mean he could have just cut that section—but then I'm only repeating what I heard.

Some of the facts here have been told before, in magazine articles and in three previous Jack Benny biographies, but never in detail and never by his own account. There are some stories even I had not heard before, particularly about his childhood and his early years in vaudeville. I wish I could say my lateness was due to intimidation, having to follow those other books, but that just isn't true. None of them left you with the feeling of really knowing Jack Benny, the whole person.

But how do you sell a book about a nice man who lived a nice life? Even his autobiography is nice. People don't buy books about nice. To get it published, let alone sell, it would have to be a tale of hardships, deprivations and adversity. You know—the tragic clown. It would have to be gossipy, dishy, salacious and scandalous, or at least one of the above. And my father's life doesn't qualify on any count.

He was married only once, and it was, by and large, a happy union that lasted forty-four years until death did them part. Now there may have been an occasional transgression (though he wasn't John F. Kennedy), but if so, he was certainly discreet (he wasn't Gary Hart), and by today's moral standards that's hardly scandalous. Perhaps worth a little gossip, but not enough to sell a book.

He didn't have a drinking problem. He didn't do drugs. As far as I know he never even tried a joint. Every so often he took a sleeping pill. To my knowledge he never hit my mother, and though there were times when I certainly gave him provocation he never hit or even spanked me. Actually, considering his profession, he was a terrific father. If I had to find a fault it would be that he was self-centered, and by that I mean he was focused on *The Jack Benny Show*, like a horse wearing blinders allowing no peripheral vision, looking only straight ahead down the stretch to Sunday night. The result: occasional absentmindedness and a lack of interest in matters not in his direct view. But without that focus he would not have been as successful for such a long time, so I could hardly consider it a grievous fault. No "Daddy Dearest" there!

He was raised in reasonably comfortable circumstances by loving, hardworking parents. No rags-to-riches tale. From the time he left home at age eighteen to begin a career in vaudeville, he climbed up the show business ladder rung by rung to stardom—no great leaps either—steady all the way. Even in the early days he was rarely out of work. Few misfortunes. Fewer setbacks. No catastrophes. No book!

Yet, in spite of all the negatives, a part of me has been saying, "Do it anyway. Maybe your reminiscences and his autobiography intertwined *would* work. Write about your very special childhood, the memories and anecdotes, the happiness and humor. Do it for yourself and as a legacy for your children. They are, after all, his grandchildren—a part of him. They're so proud to be his grandchildren, but sadly didn't know him long enough, and they deserve more. Hold it! Wait just a minute! How about him? How about writing it for Daddy? He deserves it at least as much as they."

But how and where to begin?

I tried using a legal pad, clipboard, and painstakingly sharpened pencils. That didn't work. Then a few flimsy stabs on my old high school typewriter and the wastebasket overflowed. Start with my birth? That's too banal. Start with Daddy's death? That's too sad. And then one day fate was on my side. On a flight from New York to Los Angeles I was seated next to a gentleman I recognized as a very famous writer. How fortuitous, I thought. I introduced myself, told him how much I enjoyed his books, and tried a little tentative conversation. He seemed to want to talk as much as I, so while we were chatting about all sorts of things, I was trying to summon the courage to ask his advice. ("What chutzpah!" he'll think. "Here's this stranger, this silly woman who doesn't know piddly-squat about writing, asking me, Famous Author, for helpful hints.") Finally, as we were drinking after-lunch coffee I took a deep breath and plunged ahead.

"Tell me," I said, "how do I write a book about a nice man? No dirt, no scandal, just a rather ordinary man—in fact, my father. Where do I begin?"

4

Without that chance meeting with that lovely man, who preferred that I not give him credit, I might still be emptying the trash. "Begin with your most vivid memory," he said.

"The car won't start until you give me a kiss." I can still hear Daddy saying that every Sunday morning, our special time together. He would come to my room early, about 7:30, to wake me up. I'd get dressed and we would make ourselves some breakfast and eat it in the kitchen—just the two of us. On Sundays my mom was still asleep, it was my nanny's day off and the house was quiet. It was wonderful.

I no longer remember what make of car he had, only that it was a convertible and it was waiting for us with the top down under the porte cochere at the side door of our house. We'd get in the car, Daddy would turn the key and press the ignition, but nothing would happen. The engine would only whir, it wouldn't start. He then would push and pull every button on the dashboard, twist all the knobs and pump the accelerator, but still the motor wouldn't budge. At length he would sigh and say to me, "Honey, the car just won't start until you give me a kiss." So I did, it did, and off we went. For a long time I believed there was some kind of scientific connection between kissing and car-starting.

Our routine never varied. We drove to Malibu Beach taking the long way, Sunset Boulevard. (Daddy was not a very good, certainly not an observant, driver, and this was probably the only route he knew on which he couldn't get lost.) The drive took about an hour, curving its way around Holmby Hills, Bel Air, Westwood, Brentwood, Pacific Palisades, Santa Monica and finally turning north on the Coast Highway to Malibu. The morning fog curled into the open car and it got warmer and warmer as the sun cut the haze. Daddy would park near the ocean, we'd take off our shoes and walk and splash along the wet sand with the surf hissing and bubbling and the white foam spraying through my toes. He would tell me all about the radio show he was going to rehearse and broadcast that afternoon. He would describe the guest star, tell me some of the jokes and ask if I thought they were funny. He drew me into his world and, best of all, asked for my opinions. However childish or silly my ideas must have been, he never let on that perhaps he didn't take them seriously. I felt very grown-up and important on those heavenly Sundays.

On the way home we would stop at some coffee shop or diner for lunch and he let me have a hamburger, a Coke (forbidden at home) instead of milk, and a chocolate sundae (also forbidden at home). I don't remember what he had, only that he asked for his coffee boiling hot, and he meant *boiling*. Daddy drank coffee and soup like that all his life.

Then it was a fast trip the rest of the way home because I had to take my hateful nap and he had to get to the studio on time. Later I would sometimes go along, too, but it was when I was very young and had to stay home that Daddy ended every show by saying, "Good night, Joanie."

CHAPTER 1

My father lived the almost perfect life span. Playing it like a game, if you had eighty years to live, when would you like it to be? My answer would be to have lived the eighty years that ended the day after the moon landing in 1969. Perfect! As a show business brat I grew up listening to tales of vaudeville: the Palace, the minstrel shows, Al Jolson. According to George Burns, my dad and everyone else who had been there, Jolson was the greatest entertainer who ever lived. I would kill to have seen him in person in blackface. Eddie Cantor, who also sang in blackface, said whenever he was playing New York at the same time as Jolson, he couldn't go to see Jolson because he couldn't then do his own act.

I would have loved to have been around for all the incredible beginnings, inventions, advances, transitions: from the horseless carriage to automobiles; from the Wright Brothers to the F-15; from crystal sets to television and on and on. How wonderful to have been in New York during the Roaring Twenties with the speakeasies, the Charleston, the whole crazy lifestyle.

I always loved to hear my parents reminisce about their years on the road and in New York.

The colorful Jimmy Walker was the mayor, night-clubs were thriving, and Broadway was represented by such talents as Helen Hayes, the Lunts, the Barrymores, Fanny Brice, Ethel Merman, Ed Wynn, Cole Porter, Jerome Kern, the Gershwins, Rodgers and Hart—in addition to Jolson and Cantor. All that talent, all at one time, in any single season during the late 1920's and early 1930's!

Can you imagine the incredible evenings when they got together at someone's apartment for a party, entertaining and trying out new material for their friends? Can you imagine sitting around the living room listening to George Burns tell jokes, Jolson sing, Gershwin play the piano with Merman belting his latest song? I would give anything to have been there. But I wasn't—not quite yet.

And since my life with Daddy didn't begin until he was forty years old, let's go back to the real beginning of his life. Here it is in his own words, from that fortunately discovered manuscript.

There are a few things you should know in advance. In the first place I was not born in Waukegan. I was born at the Mercy Hospital in Chicago on Valentine's Day, 1894. My parents lived in Waukegan, but my mother insisted on giving birth in Chicago. She believed it was an honor to be born in a big city. "When people ask my son where he was born, I want him to say he was born in Chicago," she told her friends. And she dreamed, with all her heart and soul, that her son should be a famous concert violinist.

In the second place, I should warn you in advance that if you're expecting my book to be like other show business autobiographies, you're likely to be disappointed. I did not triumph over adversity. I did not go through struggles and hardship. My only handicap is golf. I always had shoes and warm clothes. I come from a conventional, warmhearted Jewish family. My father, Meyer Kubelsky, was a hardworking immigrant and his wife, Emma, was an ordinary housewife who was a genius at baking a cake or making cookies. From eating my mother's pastry I developed a desire for sweets that has plagued me all my life. I never had a problem with narcotics or drugs and I am at most a moderate drinker. My sex life was not lacking, but certainly it was nothing sensational to write about.

I love my wife. She is the only one I've ever had and we've been married for forty-five years as I write this in 1972. Had I known, as a young man, that someday I would want to write my autobiography, I assure you that I would have gone out of my way to have at least two or three great love affairs.

I have had very few hair-raising adventures. It is true that once in Stuttgart I was shot at, but the man missed me completely. I didn't even get a flesh wound, so there goes that heroic enterprise.

In the third place, I must disillusion you further. I'm not really a cheapskate. Once, many years ago in the Moulin Rouge, a Hollywood nightclub where the standard tip was a quarter, I tipped the hatcheck girl a dollar. She returned it.

"Please, Mr. Benny," she said, "leave me with some illusions."

And finally, you should know that I am not really thirty-nine.

In the early years of this century Waukegan citizens with sensitive ears avoided the vicinity of 224 South Genesee Street between four and six o'clock in the afternoon. These were the hours when I, Benjamin Kubelsky, practiced the violin. I loved the violin, but I hated practicing. I especially hated scales, but the worst were the Kreutzer exercises, which are a series of hundreds of exercises based on the scales, running up and down the four-octave range of the violin. I practiced in the front parlor of our second floor apartment on South Genesee, the poor end of Genesee—North Genesee was the fancy Genesee. If I looked out the window, I could see Papa's haberdashery store across the street and, beyond that, Lake Michigan.

When Mama went over to help in the store, I stopped practicing. I'd watch the boats. I'd watch the people by the docks. I'd fall into a trance and dream of running away to faroff countries. I would try to keep an eye out for Mama, crossing the street. She was a tall, slender, beautiful woman with sad blue eyes and long dark hair. Usually she was sweet and gentle and patient. Sometimes, seemingly for no reason, she would fall into a depression and be bitter for days and sometimes she would get violently angry. I often aroused her anger. I would get so dreamy that I would forget to watch out for Mama returning home to make supper. She'd come into the parlor and see me with the fiddle on my lap and the bow hanging down on the floor.

"Benny, what are you doing?"

"I don't know, Ma."

"Why ain't you practicing?"

"I finished already," I lied.

"It's only five o'clock."

"I don't wanna practice. I don't wanna be a musician. I can't help it, Mama," I said, sighing.

"Look at Mischa Elman. He's your age and already he's famous. All over the world people know about Mischa Elman. And why? From working hard. From sticking. You got a talent like a Mischa Elman only you must practice to bring it out."

"Yes, Mama."

She went into the kitchen and put a few sticks of kindling on the coal in the coal-burning oven to start the fire for supper. I played another set of Kreutzer exercises—you had to play each one ten times before going on to the next one. When I shifted them from one position to another, the fingers of my left hand began to hurt. As I resumed practicing I cursed Mischa Elman who was only three years older than I but had become rich

13

and famous and had even played for the Tsar of Russia.

Even before Mischa Elman, even before I was born, my mother dreamed of my becoming a musician. She loved music and played our battered old upright piano in the parlor. She always played on Sunday and I was fascinated by her music. When I was three or four I began trying to copy her. Apparently one day I actually picked out a minuet I had heard Mama play, note for note. Mama cried with happiness. She taught me the fingering of the C major scale and I learned how to play nursery rhyme melodies with both hands. I was happy playing the piano. Then along came Elman and I was switched to the violin. My father laid out $100—a huge sum of money for him at that time—for a half-size fiddle. My first teacher charged 50 cents a lesson. Then came Professor Lindsay, the best music teacher in Waukegan, who charged a dollar a lesson. Two years later Lindsay convinced my parents that I should study with Dr. Hugo Kortschalk. He taught at the Chicago Musical College and later founded the Berkshire String Quartet. He did not take many pupils, but thought I had real talent and said he would take me on at fifteen dollars a lesson if I agreed to practice for two hours a day. This was something of a hardship for my parents, but that didn't matter to them. Meyer Kubelsky thought two hours of work a day was a cinch. Papa came over in one of the earliest waves of Eastern European immigration from a ghetto village near the Polish

14

border. This was not the kind of labor that he would call work.

Much as I hated practicing violin, I hated school and homework even more. Mama and Papa, I'm afraid, looked on me as a total failure, a hopeless case. I was inclined to agree with them. There wasn't any subject I was interested in. I wasn't even crazy about sports. I played football and baseball. I was fast on my feet and had good eyesight and coordination and I could have been a professional ballplayer. In fact I played for one season with a semipro team and our pitcher was Bob O'Farrell, who later played in the major leagues. We played other teams for a few dollars a man. But you have to care very much about anything, be it football or violin, to make good and I just didn't care.

When I got to puberty, I became very interested in girls and very much enjoyed what we then called "spooning," but even this I didn't make into a big thing as did some of my friends who couldn't get sex and girls and "art poses" (the latter smuggled in from Chicago at great expense and handed around) off the brain. They would brag about taking girls for walks in the unpopulated areas of Waukegan and what they did with them. I thought vaguely that it might be very interesting to do this myself but then when I thought of having to get up my nerve and persuade the girls and all the trouble of taking them for a long walk—well, it just seemed entirely too much for me.

I played truant from school as often as I could.

15

Mama was called in to get reports of my bad conduct. I talked in class. I made jokes. I broke people up. I was sent to the principal's office so many times I became part of the furniture there. But I didn't even work hard at being a juvenile delinquent. I didn't break windows or unhitch horses from carriages and I certainly didn't steal. I was a dreamer. I couldn't concentrate. I was bad in every subject: English, History, Geography, Arithmetic, Civics. I was only graduated from public school because the principal wanted to get rid of me and let the high school worry about me.

I attended Central High School for one term, at the end of which the principal, Mr. Stebbins, informed my father that I was flunking every course. My father hired a private tutor to help me pass the final examinations. I failed them all.

At last Mr. Stebbins summoned me to his office. "Benjamin Kubelsky," he said, like a judge pronouncing sentence, "we have no place in this school for people like you. It would be better if you left. But I want you to know that forgiveness is part of our philosophy here at Central. If you mend your ways and are prepared to buckle down, we will open our doors to you in the future. I know you are not a fool. Education is a key that opens many doors. I hope you will think this over."

I didn't. I was in 107th heaven.

After I was thrown out of high school, I was also cut off by Dr. Kortschalk. He told Papa if I wouldn't practice he did not want to teach me any longer. Next Papa sent me to a local business school. I took to bookkeeping and accounting like a fish takes to land. Before you could say "double entry" I was kicked out of the Waukegan Business College.

As a last resort Papa said he would teach me the haberdashery business. This was one of the least exciting propositions ever made to me, but what could I do? I was fit for nothing. So I went to work for him. Mornings I opened the store and swept the sidewalk. I pulled up the shades and straightened the merchandise. In winter I put coal in the banked stove to heat the place. Papa taught me how the stock was priced, how to keep the books and how to enter the payments of his debtors (he sold a lot on credit).

Saturday was payday in Waukegan. One Saturday Papa was in the back of the store where there were full-length mirrors, fitting a customer with a heavy overcoat. I was at the cash register when another customer came in. He handed me a dollar. I took it.

"It's on my account," he said.

"Thank you," I said, as he departed.

"What did you sell, Benny?" Papa yelled out.

"Nothing—some man just came in and handed me a dollar on his account."

"So—what was his name?"

"Do you have to know their names?" I asked.

"Dear God," my father said, looking up at the ceiling toward heaven above. "Tell me, what did I do so terrible to deserve this?"

A couple of similar instances convinced Papa I would never be a businessman and he asked me not to help out in the store anymore.

There is a saying that coming events cast their shadows before them. My parents and I saw the shadows and not the events. I'm told that when I was three years old I liked to get a smile out of people by reciting poems and singing nursery rhymes. My best audience was Grandma Sachs and Papa's sister, Aunt Clara. I would collect all the chairs and put them in rows in the parlor. Then I would put on a little show. Sometimes I played the piano and later, when I was learning to play the fiddle, I added a few violin solos. When I was eight years old I performed at the Saturday children's matinees at the Phoenix Opera House. I would be dressed in velvet knickerbockers, a white silk shirt and a black Windsor tie. Grandma thought I was adorable. At one concert I played a medley of Stephen Foster songs with piano accompaniment.

"You should be proud of Benny," Grandma said.

"He don't practice," Mama said. "Without practicing, he'll be a nothing."

"You'll see," Grandma prophesied.

"What'll I see? From this he's making a living? 'Old Black Joe'? 'Way Down Upon a River'? This is music? He ain't fit to carry Mischa Elman's rosin."

"You'll see," was Grandma's answer.

"I should live so long," Mama would say, sighing.

Poor Mama. She didn't live so long. She died of cancer in 1917 when she was forty-seven and I was twenty-three. In the meantime I was a bitter disappointment—a cheap fiddle act in vaudeville and she never came to see me because she thought show business was immoral.

At seventeen I was playing in the pit orchestra of one of the two vaudeville theaters in Waukegan, the Barrison, making $7.50 a week. I was learning about show business through osmosis. One week in 1911 the Marx Brothers came to town. They were then billed as the Marks Brothers and used their real names: Arthur, Julius, Herbert and Leonard. Harpo, Groucho, Zeppo and Chico came later. Their mother, Minnie Palmer, who had a sharp sense of show business values, ran the act. At the Monday rehearsal when we were given the music for the musical acts, Mrs. Marks watched me pick up the notes fast—and she saw how well I played their act. Like all vaudeville acts that had any music, they carried around their own orchestrations in combinations for four, six, eight or twelve instruments; up to a full orchestra for the big theaters in the big cities. Minnie talked to me after rehearsal one day. She was impressed by my playing and sight reading and offered me $15 a week plus transportation and room and board to travel with her young sons. She wanted me to play the violin for their act and conduct the pit bands.

If I had gone on the road then, I might have

become so successful as a pit musician that I never would have become a comedian. Actually, I wasn't thinking about being a comedian—it was the furthest thing from my mind. But I did think how nice it would be to be a straight man in a comedy team because the straight man wore good clothes and carried a cane and a straw hat.

I accepted Minnie's offer. My parents turned it down flat. They wouldn't even discuss it.

Then suddenly one year later the Barrison closed. Cora Salisbury, a lively intelligent woman who had earlier taken me under her wing, decided to go back to work. She had previously played piano in a vaudeville act and was recently widowed. She was a motherly type with an enormous coiffure of black hair and an even more enormous bust. In fact, at forty-five she was a couple of years older than my mother. She asked if I would join her in a piano-violin act, strictly music, no patter.

Again I went to my parents, but with a difference. I was now eighteen. Still, they thought I was ruining my life forever.

Mama cried, "We didn't give you music lessons so you should make a disgrace of yourself."

"But it's a chance to make something of myself," I said. "I have a big future. I'll be making twenty dollars a week and Mrs. Salisbury says I'm good enough to be making fifty dollars or maybe more someday. It's the chance of a lifetime."

"The people in the theater are rotten human beings," Papa shouted. "They got no morals. They got no decency. If you go on the stage, don't come home no more. You ain't got no home as far as I'm concerned. Permission you want? For what? To ruin your life? I seen plenty of these actors. They don't know from religion. They don't sleep or eat regular. They're good for nothing— and the women—hoo, hah—they're worse than the men. In front of Mama I can't tell you my honest opinion of such women. They paint their faces and smoke cigarettes and curse. Such things you wouldn't believe."

I pleaded, but they were stubborn. Finally I said that if I was compelled to make a choice I would remain at home. But I asked one favor: that they talk to Mrs. Salisbury and let her explain about vaudeville. Mama weakened. Not Papa.

Mama spent an afternoon having a heart-to-heart talk with Mrs. Salisbury. It was obvious from the way Cora looked, dressed and spoke that she was a decent respectable lady. She promised Mama that she would take care of me, see that I lived in respectable boarding houses, ate kosher meals and got plenty of sleep. She promised to guard me from the "loose" actresses who, my parents were convinced, were lounging around in hundreds of theaters, waiting for the chance to seduce their son. Mrs. Salisbury coaxed Mama around to the idea that a son with such basic integrity couldn't be corrupted. Then Mama got to work on Papa and coaxed him into giving his consent to a trial period of three months.

So one morning in September 1912, with my violin case in one hand and my satchel in the other,

21

I boarded a train with Cora for Gary, Indiana, where we had a three-day booking at the Majestic Theater. We were in the second spot, opening with a rousing rendition of "The Poet and Peasant Overture" and closing with a fast jazzy version of "Everybody's Doing It, Doing It, Doing What? Turkey Trot, Turkey Trot." Cora would hit a series of thundering chords with her left hand and fantastic arpeggios with her right while I was doing crazy runs up and down three octaves. We were killing the audiences, I can tell you. They thought I was doing something impossible. As time went on I began to pantomime to suggest the terrible struggle I had in playing these numbers. Later, when we added a big solo for me, "The Rosary," for which I was given an amber spotlight, I looked poetic and would play with the pinky finger of my bow hand delicately extended. Actually, though I didn't know it, I was an actor playing the role of a violinist. I looked and acted more like a violinist than a real violinist did.

We were what they called a "class act." Cora wore a blue velvet gown, rhinestone earrings and a rhinestone tiara. I was decked out in a tuxedo, stiff shirt and bow tie. Papa, in a gesture of reconciliation, had taken this finery out of his stock and presented it to me as a going-away present.

A few weeks after we were on the road I had quite a jolt. The concert violinist Jan Kubelík was giving concerts in the Midwest and he had heard about me. His lawyer told me that I would be sued unless I changed my name. He said I was deliberately misleading the public by using the name Kubelsky and playing the violin. I told him that Kubelsky was my real name but they didn't believe me. So I became Ben Benny and the act became Salisbury and Benny. A few years later when I was doing a single, playing the violin and adding some comedy, Ben Bernie was also doing a talking-and-fiddle act—and had been doing it for many years. Again, another lawyer said they would sue. So once more I changed my name— this time to Jack Benny. Why Jack? This happened shortly after World War I. My good friend, Benny Rubin, who was also in vaudeville, was having dinner with me when two sailors came over to our table. In those days all sailors called each other "Jack."

"Hello, Jack," said one of them. "Didn't we meet you at the Great Lakes Naval Station? Weren't you in the show there?"

"Yes, Jack," I answered, "I was." We reminisced about the navy. They kept calling me Jack and I kept calling them Jack.

When we went outside Benny Rubin yelled, "There's your name."

"What name?"

"Jack, I like it. JACK BENNY."

Cora and I played theaters scattered throughout the Midwest. We played split weeks—three days here, three days there, a Sunday someplace else. I spent many lonely hours in railway stations in the middle of the night waiting for a milk train to take me to the next town. No, I don't look back with nostalgia on those first two seasons in vaudeville. It was hard work. It was a constant getting on a train, getting off a train, carrying your bags to the cheapest hotel or boarding house, running to the theater, playing three, four, five shows a day, smiling when you faced the audience, taking your bow and fighting all the time for a better place on the bill (the best position was next-to-closing). In spite of Cora's promise to my mother, I didn't get much sleep during that time. But I learned how to sleep on the wooden benches of railroad stations, on dusty coaches and backstage in a dressing room that was usually shared with the male members of the other acts.

At the end of the second season Cora's mother became seriously ill and she had to return to Waukegan. I went to Chicago to find a replacement. He was a young pianist named Lyman Woods. Tall and handsome with a narrow mustache, he looked very distinguished. He couldn't read music, but he was a natural. He could learn a new number after hearing it only once. We called the act "From Grand Opera to Ragtime," and now I got top billing. It was Bennie and Woods. I changed the spelling from Y to IE because I thought IE had more class. That didn't last long.

We opened as before with the good old "Poet and Peasant Overture" and after playing a few bars of it straight, we did it in ragtime. Then Woods did a medley of a Brahms's "Hungarian Dance" and a Chopin nocturne, playing as if he were Paderewski. Then I did "The Rosary." I played it in the amber spotlight, then got a white spot and went into a fast new number, "When Ragtime Rosy Ragged the Rosary." Audiences for which we played hadn't heard this variation and it slayed them. Then we segued into a medley of currently popular ballads like "You Made Me Love You (I Didn't Want to Do It)" and finished with some ragtime hits. When we came out to take our bows, Lyman was also holding a fiddle and the two of us did a smattering of "Alexander's Ragtime Band" with Lyman making a mess of his fiddle playing. We usually exited to laughter and applause. The act was still straight violin and piano, but we had started to put humor in our music. Lyman was naturally amusing and I was learning to get laughs by playing my fiddle in funny ways and with gestures. We still didn't speak a single word.

Soon the act was playing the better theater circuits and we were getting $350 a week as a team. We were even playing major cities. As I've said, I fancied myself something of a dandy and most of my salary went for the high life. I wore snappy two-toned shoes, high-class suits, a diamond ring and a diamond stickpin. I was a real big shot—a spender!

Lyman and I worked together for five years. In 1917 our agent decided we were ready to play the Palace Theatre in New York. The Palace was the Mecca of vaudeville. Playing the Palace meant you had made it. We played the Palace and fell flat on our faces. *Variety* gave us only a few lines. Had we gone over big, we would have received half a column. We were never able to figure out what had gone wrong. Maybe our songs were stale or we just weren't sophisticated enough for New York. We never found out.

With all the fuss about changing my name, it seemed pretty silly that when I enlisted in the navy I became Benjamin Kubelsky all over again. I didn't choose the navy because I loved the sea. It was a geographical accident. In 1917 the government established a base near Waukegan: the Great Lakes Naval Training Station. I not only owe my first name to the United States Navy, but it was on account of the navy that I became a comedian. If I hadn't been a sailor at Great Lakes, I wouldn't have been cast in a show they put on. I might never have learned to speak on stage. I didn't mind cracking wise with my fellow vaudeville troupers backstage or in a café, but on stage I couldn't open my mouth. At the mere thought of speaking I got the shakes. It took me years to get over my stage fright and I never did completely. Furthermore, if an Irishman, later to be known in movies as Pat O'Brien, had not also been at boot camp I might have refused to be a comedian in the navy show.

The first three months at Great Lakes I went through the usual boot camp training of marching, drilling and learning all the nautical procedures. We marched—not in all kinds of weather, but certainly in the two kinds on the shores of Lake

Michigan that year—sleet and snow. I was not wild about it, but I obeyed orders. I didn't have much choice.

Meanwhile the sailors who had been in show business before the war began putting on impromptu shows in the recreation hall on Saturday nights. Naturally I took part with my fiddle. One evening I made the mistake of playing "The Rosary" straight. You never heard such booing. Pat O'Brien, who was waiting in the wings to do a dramatic sketch, noticed my embarrassment and came on stage. This looked prearranged to the sailors. Pat whispered in my ear while I continued playing as though it was perfectly normal.

What he whispered was, "For heaven's sake, Ben, put down the damn fiddle and talk to 'em." Then Pat stood there with his hands on his hips —grinning.

"Fellows," I desperately ad-libbed to the audience, "I was having an argument with Pat O'Brien this morning . . ."

I paused, not because of any great sense of timing, but because I couldn't think of what to say next.

"Yeah . . . this morning . . . with Pat O'Brien . . . an argument about the Irish Navy."

From out front, sweet sounds of laughter came to my ears.

"You see," I went on, "I claim the Swiss Navy is bigger than the Irish Navy and the Jewish Navy is bigger than both of them put together."

This brought down the house.

My next line, as I remember it, was, "I've heard you sailors complain about the food."

They groaned in agreement.

"Well, I want to tell you that the enlisted men get the same food as Captain Moffett gets." I paused—on purpose this time. "Only *his* is cooked."

Now and then, when I marched with a gun on my shoulder and wanted to forget my tight boots, I thought about why the sailors preferred to laugh at these jokes instead of being uplifted by my interpretation of "The Rosary."

One morning at rehearsal for a show to raise money for the Navy Relief Fund, they needed someone to read two lines in a sketch. The director pointed to me. It was just one of those things— it could have been anybody. I read the lines in my flat midwestern tone. Because the other actors were overplaying their parts, my slow flat delivery sounded funny in contrast. Every day I kept getting more and more lines. I played Izzy There, the Admiral's Disorderly. By the time we opened in Chicago I was the comedy hit of the show. After two smash weeks we went on a tour of the biggest midwestern cities, closing at last in Waukegan in December 1918.

After the Armistice I decided to go back to vaudeville all alone. It was a difficult step to take. To do a single I would have to talk as well as play the fiddle. Where would I get the words? I wasn't rich enough to buy an act from a professional gag writer so I had to make one up myself. I figured out a few jokes. I borrowed some. I stole some. My new act was Ben K. Benny: Fiddle Funology. I worked on it in front of a mirror by myself for two weeks. I paced it, I timed it, I chose the numbers. I tried it on a couple of cronies and when I felt I was ready, I went out on the Western Vaudeville Circuit. I opened with the good old "Poet and Peasant" in ragtime. I told a few jokes. I played a few of the new hits.

I also sang—in a rough baritone voice. One thing you could say about my singing—I was loud. In Chicago I bought two special numbers. One was about the coming of Prohibition: "After This Country Goes Dry, Goodbye, Wild Women, Goodbye." My other aria was a tender romantic ballad entitled "I Used to Call Her Baby, but Now She's a Mother to Me." It was a variation on Oedipus Rex. It worked. Everywhere I went I heard the sweet sounds of laughter and applause. I was still slotted in the second place, the "deuce" spot, but soon I was getting better placements and more money.

By 1921 I had drastically changed my act. I didn't sing. I didn't play violin except at the close of the act when I played myself off with a few bars of "Tiger Rag." I talked. But I held the fiddle all through the act—the fiddle in the left hand and the bow in the right. I was still unsure of myself as a comedian and the fiddle was my psychological crutch. Since I no longer did weird musical effects, I was no longer a "fiddle funologist." Now I called the act "Jack Benny: Aristocrat of Humor." Its essence was low-keyed jokes about topical issues and long stories about my dumb girlfriends. All comedians had dumb girlfriends.

The years went by and I was playing the best theaters and getting a good salary, $350 a week and $450 on the road, which was the best money I ever made in vaudeville. You had to be a Harry Lauder or a Sarah Bernhardt to get the fabulous salaries of $5,000 weekly or more. And yet I was a headliner in a way—that is to say, now I was playing in the next-to-closing spot and I received prominent billing on the marquee. But I was not a star. I did not, indeed, become a star until I went on the radio.

CHAPTER 2

I have always been romantic about women. For many years I thought they were almost a higher species than men and put them on a pedestal. All my life, there have been women I admired at a distance in a sort of heroine worship and there have been other women I have respectfully adored in personal friendships. The women I worshiped —usually from afar, so afar that they never knew it—were tall, statuesque and talented, like Nora Bayes.

In 1927 when she was forty-seven and I was thirty-three, Nora Bayes was making a comeback as the headliner of a bill at Keith's in Washington,

D.C. Even in middle age, she was a stunning woman with a dynamic personality. She just hypnotized an audience. She was a great song stylist, with a soft contralto voice. Some of her songs were romantic ballads and some were comedy songs. She was magical on stage, casting an unbelievable spell on her audience. She never stood still. In perpetual motion, she crossed, turned, smiled, swung her hips and did a recitative in the middle of a song. She had been one of vaudeville's top-ranking stars since 1908 with her husband-partner, Jack Norworth. They wrote "Shine On, Harvest Moon" and featured it in their act.

Modesty was not one of Nora's virtues. Originally the act was billed: *Nora Bayes, Assisted and Admired by Jack Norworth.*

Norworth had a habit of assisting and admiring other girls besides his wife, but he assisted and admired the other girls in their bedrooms. So she divorced him in 1913 and did a single. Then her billing was: *Nora Bayes, The Greatest Single Woman Singing Comedienne in the World.*

People thought she was Irish. She looked Irish and had an Irish lilt in her voice. She was really Jewish and her real name was Leonora Goldberg. She was a crazy temperamental person who had four or five husbands and I don't know how many lovers. On tour she traveled in her own private railroad car. In hotels she sometimes booked a whole floor to accommodate herself, her piano accompanist (George Gershwin for a time, early in his career), her retinue of servants and her rel-

31

atives, friends and sycophants. She fought with her managers and agents, broke contracts and was wildly extravagant. She didn't have a cent in the world in 1927. She was still as beautiful and as talented as ever, but her erratic behavior scared managers and she hadn't worked in years.

However, I found her a wonderful human being and was deeply thrilled to be on the same bill with the actress I had looked up to as the ideal of a vaudeville performer since I'd broken into show business as an adolescent. Except for Jack Norworth, I was the only performer ever permitted to work with her. She liked a little piece of business that I was doing with Willie Burns, George's younger brother, and asked if I wanted to do a bit with her. I suggested that after she closed her act, we could do what was known as an "afterpiece." She loved the idea. I can't tell you how thrilled I was. Me—doing a bit with the great Nora Bayes.

She had a sofa in her act on which she sat to sing some of her songs. After she took her bows, I entered through the opening in the curtain. My hat was on. I was holding my overcoat. The audience stopped cheering.

"I was just getting ready to go home, but you said you wanted to see me about something, Miss Bayes."

"Yes, I did. You know that story that Mr. Burns was telling and you didn't let him finish it?"

"Well, it wasn't a nice story."

"Come sit next to me," she said. I did. "I'd love to hear the end of that story."

"I can't tell it to you, Miss Bayes."

"Oh, please," she coaxed, wriggling her torso in a most suggestive way.

"If I told it to you—you'd slap my face. The audience would hate it. It's a terrible story."

"Don't be silly. Tell the story. We're all sophisticated. I'm sure it can't be that bad."

"It's worse," I said. But I was weakening. I slithered closer to her.

"Whisper it in my ear," she said seductively.

I did, moving closer and closer, almost getting on top of her, as she giggled and laughed. I was practically making love to her as the curtain came down.

The audience went crazy.

Nora Bayes was the first of my heroines. They were women with that indefinable quality of class, that certain something that sets them apart from the whole human race. They are superior human animals in the way that a musician like Pablo Casals is a superior human animal. Such women have a distinctive manner of dressing and moving. Their minds are sharp. Their conversation is interesting. Their emotions run deep. Florence Vidor, whom I met once at a dinner at the home of the silent movie director, Thomas Ince, was such a person. So were Kay Francis, Irene Dunne, Ingrid Bergman, Ann Sheridan, Lynn Fontanne, Ruth Gordon and Helen Hayes. All women are rare and wonderful—but this kind of woman is more. Talent is part of their charm, though these women never permit their talents and ambitions to freeze up their warm femininity. Lucille Ball, one of the most gifted comediennes I've ever known, has beauty—and with it talent, brains and drive—yet she brims over with emotional fire. I have had relationships with these women, and many others, that have been purely platonic. My wife has known I admired them and enjoyed their company. Let me tell you that a man who sees a woman only as an object to quench his sexual thirst has missed out on one of the most inspiring experiences in life. Mind you—I am not arguing that pleasure in bed with somebody you love is not good. I am saying that there is also a pleasure in being with a woman whose company is fun because she is an interesting human being. The fact that she is also a member of the opposite sex gives her those grace notes that make her song more pleasing to hear.

I am not an extrovert. Even as a young man, I could never be aggressive with a girl. In fact, the more a girl excited me, the more tongue-tied I became. I was clumsy at amorous byplay. I wasn't good at that kind of casual teasing and bantering to which girls respond and which leads to infatuation with a guy—often a guy who breaks their hearts. I never had the courage to make an overture to a girl unless I was sure she would accept me. I would begin to sweat and stammer. I didn't know what to say or what to do.

If it wouldn't have looked so ridiculous, I'd have

taken my fiddle along when I went courting, so I could clutch it for security just as I did when I told jokes in a theater.

Greer Garson was one of those platonic secret loves of mine. I had met Miss Garson several times at dinner parties. She was as refined and gracious a lady in a living room as she was playing Mrs. Miniver or Elizabeth Bennet on the screen. Now, one morning, about 8:30, I was taking a walk in Beverly Hills. I love walking. I still walk two miles a day. In Beverly Hills walking is not done. People drive. Walking arouses suspicion in Beverly Hills. The police, driving in prowl cars, have orders to stop and interrogate any person walking. He must explain *why* he is walking. It's assumed if you're walking, you are not only up to no good, but are probably a master criminal. However, by now the Beverly Hills police force knows my idiosyncrasies and I'm not questioned when I'm walking.

Well, as I was walking down Roxbury Drive, I saw Greer Garson. She was driving a long white convertible with the top down. Her hair was streaming in the breeze. A blue scarf was around her neck. She was a vision of loveliness. She saw me and stopped the car.

"Hello, Jack," she said.

"Oh—er—h-h-hello, Greer," I said, my heart beating faster.

She smiled.

"It's a nice—that is, a fine, er . . . day," I said.

"Isn't it, though?"

"Yes, it is," I said.

She smiled again.

If only I'd had my violin I could have played something.

Finally she said, "By the way, we're having some people over to the house this Saturday and if you and Mary are free, Buddy and I would love to have you join us."

"I'd sure love to and I'm sure Mary will feel the same," I said.

In order to get her address, I had to cross the street to where she'd stopped her car. I started across. As I did so, I stepped in the only mound of horse manure seen on Roxbury Drive in fifty years. I slipped. I fell flat on my face.

I picked myself up. I felt terrible. I walked over to the car. To my amazement, Miss Garson was positive I had slipped on purpose, as it was just the sort of thing that could only happen to the radio character of Jack Benny, Schnook Extraordinary.

"You're so funny," she said, "you're delicious. You've made my whole day. I wish I could learn to fall the way you did. It must have taken you years to learn how to fall so as not to hurt yourself."

"I didn't do it on purpose, Greer," I protested. "And besides—I *did* hurt myself."

"You have such an adorable sense of humor," she said.

She never did believe me.

In 1920 I was in the throes of a romance with Leila Hyams, a lovely blonde. She was the daughter of John Hyams and Leila McIntyre. Hyams & McIntyre were stars of vaudeville and musical comedy. Their daughter followed in their footsteps. She was a bright, clever, interesting woman. We were attracted to each other and kept company for a year. I could listen to her talk for hours. We vaguely discussed the possibility of matrimony. We postponed it. She was an ambitious girl. She wanted to be an actress more than she wanted to be a wife. We broke up when she went to Hollywood and became a movie star.

Some men meet the right girl early in life, know it right away and get married once and for all. Some men never find the right girl. Others have to go through several romances until they experience the real thing. That's the way it was with me. And when you come to the real thing you know it, especially after you've had the other kind of romance, which looks like love and feels like love but isn't. It's more like infatuation, but an infatuation that lasts for a long time.

Before I found the real love of my life I had another serious romance with a girl called Mary Kelly. She was tall and had golden blonde hair. Her face was beautiful. Her voice was low and quavered with a kind of delight in everything. She was a talented performer. She played in a big-time vaudeville act, Swift & Kelly. She played the "dumb" girl. She came from Chicago and her family was devoutly Roman Catholic. One of her brothers was a priest. I knew her family and they were wonderful people. She, too, was an ardent Catholic. We didn't think we would get serious when we started going out.

I met Mary through Gracie Allen. Mary shared an apartment with Gracie and another actress, Rena Arnold. Gracie wasn't married to George Burns yet, though she'd recently become his partner in a vaudeville act. Burns and I had been friends for several years. One evening Burns & Allen broke in a new act at a small theater in Newark. Burns asked me to watch the show and give him my opinion. He and Gracie were as nervous as any vaudeville actors were when they tried out new material before an audience. Besides me, they had invited Mary Kelly, Rena Arnold and Miss Arnold's escort.

The new act was sensational. George asked us all to supper—his treat. During supper Mary Kelly looked over at me. I looked into her eyes. Our glances joined. We felt a kind of magnetism pulling us. I began seeing her all the time and dropped every other girl. From being stuck on each other, we went on to become crazy about each other. We decided life was unbearable unless we could be with each other constantly. Like George and Gracie. They were now married. We also would get married, like Gracie and George. We would start a new vaudeville act—Benny & Kelly. Just like George and Gracie.

Looking backwards from the vantage of wisdom, I can see we weren't at all in love. We were infatuated with each other. It was George and Gracie who were in love. We caught their emotion, which was so strong it was contagious. You can catch love by picking up love microbes from being around a man and a woman who are in love. That's what Mary and I caught. A disease. A bad case of love.

I'd like to interrupt Daddy here to let George Burns say a little about my father's love life:

"In the early days Jack was a terrific ladies' man. He went around with all the girls. He played on the Orpheum Circuit and slept with every girl from coast to coast. He and Phil Baker were two of the handsomest guys in show business. As they followed each other from town to town they would leave notes with names and phone numbers. Until he met Mary Kelly. That was serious.

"Jack liked married women, but he was very secretive about it—he really was silly—we were staying in a suite of rooms at a hotel and his current lady had a room very nearby. Every evening he said to me, his best pal, 'I think I'll go make her laugh for a few minutes.' I said, 'Make her laugh for me, too.'"

Mary Kelly and I were in trouble from the start because of our religious differences. Mary oscillated from one extreme to the other. At one moment she was convinced she couldn't live unless we were married. I would say let's do it right now—let's go to Waukegan, meet my father and begin planning our married life. Then, likely as not, she'd fly into a temper. She'd say we could never marry. We were of different faiths. She could never marry a person of my faith. The whole situation was impossible. We had to break it off. We must never see each other again. And she was so dramatic, so convincing—I'd believe her and we'd break it off.

Once, after being on tour for several months, during which time we'd written each other love letters almost daily, I got off the train in New York. I couldn't wait to kiss her again. She was standing at the gate. Her face was angry. She looked like she'd been crying.

"What's the matter?"

"I can't marry you, Jack."

"We don't have to get married," I said.

"Everything is over between us," she said. "I can't stand this torture any longer. We have to forget each other."

We sat down on a bench in Penn Station and talked it over, heart to heart. She showed me why we had to break it up. I promised to put her out of my mind. I would never call her again. I would never write her another letter. We were finished.

Two days later, the phone rang. "I miss you so much, honey," her velvet voice said. "I gotta see you. Just once more. Then we'll break it off for-ever."

So we started all over on the merry-go-round of frustration. I guess maybe she liked tormenting herself and me. Each time we broke up, I'd be heartbroken. I'd go on the road. I wouldn't write to her. Then there would come a telegram from her: CAN'T WE BE FRIENDS? THE LEAST YOU CAN DO IS WRITE TO ME.

I'd write to her. She'd write to me. I came back. We were in love again. Then sooner or later she'd say, "What's the use, Jack? We can't go on like this. We've got to end it. Let's call the whole thing off."

So we called it off.

If I tried to act distant or even tried to be just a friend, she didn't like that either. Once, we had a date. I had just come in from a long tour and was too tired to go out. I called room service. We planned to have dinner in my room. We gave our orders to the waiter. While waiting for the food, we got into a nasty argument. Either I had written to her while away, which was wrong, or I had not written to her, which was equally wrong. One word led to another. By the time the room service waiter wheeled in the wagon, she was nearly in hysterics. The waiter, ignoring us, calmly laid the table and put out the food. He acted as if it was the most natural thing in the world at the Forrest Hotel for two people to be shouting at each other while dinner was being served. I signed the check. He wished us a hearty appetite.

41

We sat down, still arguing. I had lost my appetite, but she was the kind of person that trouble and worry make hungrier. There she was, sobbing and crying, tears running down her face while devouring a bowl of mushroom soup, a filet mignon with hashed brown potatoes, a dish of ice cream and a pot of coffee.

Seeing the absurdity of this, I began to laugh. She got more upset by my reaction. I laughed harder. She was now keening and wailing. I was rolling around on the floor, laughing. She couldn't forgive this.

And I think this cured me of Mary Kelly.

I went to Europe for three months to get her out of my system. She met me when I came back. I couldn't believe my eyes.

"Why didn't you write me?" she asked. She was pouting. She looked enchanting.

"Write you? I thought you hated me. Remember?"

"You could have written me a letter—just one letter."

"We're not in love anymore. Why should I write you letters?"

"You could have at least sent me a postcard," she said. She was smiling. She put her arm in my arm.

I know it's crazy, but our romance started all over. But now I was worried all the time. I was waiting for the fireworks to begin. I never knew what would make her flare up.

Now she said we had to get married. Neither

her family nor her religion was as important as our relationship. I said we'd better wait. She couldn't wait. While playing in St. Louis, I got this wire from her: IF YOU WANT ME, I WILL COME AND MARRY YOU TOMORROW. I NEED YOU. I LOVE YOU. I AM DESPER-ATE. MARY.

I read the telegram a dozen times. I wore out the carpet in my hotel room. Then I made up my mind. If we got married, our life together would be a hell on earth. I couldn't ruin her life as well as mine. I telephoned her and said that we must forget each other.

She married another man. She was as unhappy in marriage as she had been unhappy before. She began eating more and more and drinking heavily. For about ten years I didn't see her.

In 1934, when my radio popularity brought a demand for personal appearances, I was booked on a stage show tour. I took along my orchestra and several acts. I had an idea for a sketch that would satirize girl singing trios like the Boswell Sisters. I told agents I was looking for girls who sang badly. One had to be very fat. One had to be thin and short. And a third had to be homely as sin. In the sketch they would pretend they were real sisters. They would be rotten singers who thought they were marvelous. I would tell the audience that I was always on the lookout for new talent and I was going to audition a young singing trio. The moment these three ridiculous-looking girls came out, I figured the audience would laugh.

One day Mary Kelly came to the radio studio. She asked for a job. I didn't recognize her. Her eyes were still sweet, but her hair was unkempt. Her voice had cracked and become harsh. And her body, once so lovely, was now fat and shapeless. I was touched by the spectacle and didn't know what to say when she asked me to give her the job of the fat girl in the trio. I didn't want to do it.

She pleaded with me.

"How can I do this to you, Mary?" I asked. "We've been sweethearts. Once, we cared for each other. How can I go out and make fun of you now? I can't do it. Please don't ask me. I can't."

But she begged me. "What's past is past," she said. "I gotta have the job, Jack. I'm down on my luck. I need the money."

She got the job.

She was sensational. She still knew how to get laughs. She mugged and sang out of tune and shook her fat body like she was one mound of jelly.

How the audience laughed.

I didn't.

I cried.

They couldn't see me crying because I wore a smile on my face. I'm supposed to be a comedian. They paid their money to laugh. Mary Kelly was sure earning her salary. I was crying inside. I was crying for Mary Kelly and for myself and for all the bad things that can happen to nice people in life. I was lucky. I had found a new love not long after the breakup with Mary Kelly and this time it was the real thing. All the romance that had happened before seemed like shadows on the wall in comparison.

CHAPTER 3

Despite what he's said about liking women who were "ladies" in the old-fashioned sense, I'd like also to point out that Daddy's kind of woman was strong-minded, unpretentious, down-to-earth, funny and at the same time feminine. Daddy liked women in general; better still if they were beautiful, dynamite if they were ballsy: Barbara Stanwyck, Ann Sheridan, Carole Lombard—and, of course, my mother.

I didn't hear love knocking. Like every turning point in my life it came accidentally without fanfares. I didn't realize that here, at last, was my dream girl. I was just going to a party in Vancouver, in British Columbia, a party I didn't really want to go to. It was 1921. I was still a struggling violin act with jokes. I was tired of being compared to Ben Bernie and had just changed my name to Jack Benny. I was twenty-seven years old. I was shy with girls and had never been in love. Lust, yes; love, no. I was playing the Orpheum in Vancouver, working in the deuce spot on a bill that included the Marx Brothers. From their crazy singing act, the Four Nightingales, that had broken me up in Waukegan back in 1910, they had become one of the outstanding rip-and-tear farcical acts in vaudeville. They closed the show—because nobody could follow them. It was about twenty minutes of total insanity.

Zeppo, the youngest brother, talked me into going to this party. He said he knew some fascinating Vancouver girls and it would be wild, with Canadian ale, Canadian rye, Canadian women and Canadian whoopee. I told him I didn't like wild parties and I didn't like wild women. He talked me into going with him.

We drove to a large frame house on the outskirts of the city. When we entered, much to my relief, we were in a nice family home. Zeppo's wild party was just in his imagination. It was his idea of a put-on—I would expect a wild evening and be disappointed. Instead it was Zeppo who was disappointed at my reaction. We were guests at the home of Henry Marks, a distant relative of the Marx Brothers. He was a well-to-do dealer in scrap metals and, like my father, a strict orthodox Jew.

Tonight was the first night of Passover and we had been invited to the family seder. I was introduced to Mrs. Marks, their older daughter, Ethel, who was about twenty, her younger sister, Sadie, and a little boy, Hilliard. Sadie was fourteen with long black curly hair tied in a red ribbon. She was trying to act grown up. She had borrowed her sister's dress and high-heeled shoes on which she wobbled. She hung on my every word. She thought I was a suave handsome Prince Charming. Though I was thirteen years older, she made up her mind she was going to marry me someday. I didn't take her seriously—she was just a cute kid.

The seder was a traditional one and gave me a warm feeling of being at home. During dinner little Hilliard asked the four traditional questions, the first of which I should have heeded: "Why is this night different from all other nights?" It was the most important night of my life, but I didn't know it.

There was the reading of the Haggadah, the long story of the persecution of the Jews in Egypt and their exodus, under the leadership of Moses, to the promised land of Israel. We sang the old songs and then Papa Marks proposed that since I was a violinist myself, he would like me to hear his daughter Sadie play a piece by Bach. To make a confession—I didn't listen. I'd always hated auditioning girl violinists and I whispered to Zeppo to make some excuse so we could get out of there before we had a whole evening of amateur fiddling. Sadie heard me. She finished the piece but her eyes were flashing with anger.

She paid me back. The next day at the matinee she brought three of her friends. The four girls sat in the first row at the Orpheum. During my whole act they stared up with vacant expressions. They didn't laugh once. I didn't recognize Sadie

47

Marks—I had already forgotten her. But I was very upset by four girls in the front row not laughing.

Two years later Sadie moved to San Francisco with her family. I was playing the Pantages. She came to see the show and afterward went to the stage door to say hello. She said, "Hello, Mr. Benny, I'm—"

"Hello," I said, and walked right by her.

In 1926 in Los Angeles I went out on a double date with a fellow vaudevillian, Al Bernovici, his new wife, Ethel, and Ethel's younger sister. Ethel looked vaguely familiar, but I couldn't place her. The sister, my blind date, was a smashing brunette with a vivacious smile and sparkling brown eyes. I remember she wore a simple black dress with a pearl choker and a white cloche hat. I made no connection between this smartly dressed, poised woman and the little girl who played Bach on that first night of Passover. She didn't let on that I had not only ignored her the first time we met, but was even ruder later in San Francisco.

This time it was love. Love at *third* sight.

The four of us had dinner at Musso Frank's in Hollywood. I don't remember many of the details except that I kept staring at her and she kept smiling and I wanted desperately to say clever and provocative things, but I was tongue-tied and embarrassed. Later I learned that Sadie hadn't wanted to go on this date because she was seriously seeing someone else and also because she distrusted actors. At that time Ethel was not having a happy time with Al, and Sadie blamed it on his being a performer. Like my parents, Sadie thought all actors were happy-go-unlucky. Yet she liked me. She didn't know why, but she liked me.

I know why I liked *her*. She was different from most other women I met in show business. She had manners, she listened politely when others spoke, she dressed with style and simplicity. She was exquisitely lovely. She had a way of laughing—like the music of a rippling arpeggio of silvery notes.

I asked her for a date the following evening. She said no. The evening after that? No. Any evening? No.

Well, I just couldn't get her out of my mind. I thought about her and thought about her all through the night. The next morning I went to the Hollywood Boulevard branch of the May Company where I knew she was working in ladies hosiery. I couldn't think of a convincing reason why I should be at a ladies hosiery counter, but I went there anyway. "Well, it's a small world," was my brilliant opening line. And then I just stood there looking dumb.

"Can I show you some silk stockings, Mr. Benny?" she asked.

I nodded. I would have given a million dollars right then to have had a fiddle in my hands.

"These beige imports from Paris are quite nice," she said, opening a box. She made a little

49

fist and burrowed it into the stocking. "You'll notice how sheer they are, Mr. Benny."

"I'll say they are," I agreed, still gazing at her face.

"Then we have this number in a flesh tone suitable for evening," she said. "I'm sure any woman would love them."

"I'll take a dozen of these and a dozen of those," I said hoarsely. I was in a trance.

"What size does she wear?"

"The same as you."

She wrapped the hosiery. I asked her to lunch. She accepted. I went to her counter every day, bought stockings and then we went for lunch. I bought enough French hosiery to restock the May Company. Sadie later told me that she had broken all sales records for that department in the history of the store. It was the only way I could think of as an excuse to be near her. It never occurred to me to simply tell her that I was crazy about her, that I was in love with her and wanted to spend the rest of my life with her. I was too shy and afraid. So instead I bought silk stockings in gross lots.

Sadie broke up with her boyfriend, and although I had to go back on tour, I telephoned her often.

It was around this time I first heard of some crazy new invention—wireless radio. My friend Goodman Ace, who would have a wonderful radio show, *Easy Aces,* told me millions of people were

50

putting earphones on their ears and scratching around with crystal sets so they could listen to bands playing and people talking and it didn't cost a nickel. I told him such people were nuts. The next time I played Kansas City, where Goody lived, he told me even more people were buying "radios." He thought this would finish vaudeville entertainment and I had better get out of vaudeville and into radio. I didn't listen to him. Not then. I was sure it would all blow over. He was already doing an hour show every week on a local Kansas City station making jokes and talking about movies, shows and books. I told him he was wasting his time. I thought he should become a full-time comedy writer. He was the best comedy writer of that time. I bought material from him whenever I could afford it.

In 1926 there was this new thing called a network. It was the National Broadcasting Company of the RCA Corporation. I gave them six months. Will Rogers said at the time, "Radio is too big a thing to be out of." What did a cowboy know, anyway?

I admit I was a little stunned when I heard about the money Sam 'n' Henry were getting paid in the theaters that played movies in combination with stage shows. They had been a small-time vaudeville act at a top salary of $200 a week. Then they concocted a silly little fifteen-minute radio program about a taxi cab company with characters named the Kingfish, Amos and Andy. They even had Pepsodent Toothpaste for a sponsor. They were on five nights a week. I remember you could walk down a street on a warm evening when the windows were open and hear their voices. When the blackface team of Sam 'n' Henry returned to the theaters they changed the name of the act to Amos 'n' Andy and got $5,000 a week. Their listeners were in the millions and these fans wanted to see Amos 'n' Andy in person.

I still thought it would blow over as soon as people got tired of the novelty. Who would want to hear disembodied voices from a speaker when you could see real entertainers in the flesh on a stage?

Besides, I had other things on my mind.

I was in love. I was dying to marry Sadie, but I was afraid of marriage. I couldn't live without her, but I was afraid of marriage.

For about a year our romance was of great value to the stockholders of A.T.&T. I telephoned Sadie three or four times a day. Sometimes we talked for an hour. At the end of the tour I rushed back to Los Angeles to resume buying hosiery. Now we went for dinner and drives as well as lunch.

Then I returned to New York and a show called *The Great Temptations* in which my aim was to prove to Jake Shubert that I was a comedian and not a fiddler. The phone calls resumed. I still could not muster the courage to tell her I loved her. Not only was I shy, but my reservations about the responsibilities of marriage continued. I took marriage seriously, as a lifetime proposition. I didn't share the easy come, easy go marital attitude of many people in and out of show business.

Meanwhile Sadie decided that since I had never mentioned love or marriage to her, I probably wasn't serious after all. While visiting in Vancouver she met a young real estate man who fell in love with her and proposed marriage. They got engaged. She didn't break the news to me. Her sister did. I ran into Ethel (by now and evermore called Babe) in Chicago when *The Great Temptations* moved there.

"You can't let her do this. She'll ruin her life. She's too young to get married," I told Babe.

Babe said, "You tell her yourself."

She called her sister and put me on the phone.

"Listen," I cried, now so worked up I forgot I was shy, "what's this I hear about you getting married? YOU'RE TOO YOUNG TO GET MARRIED! Come to Chicago and talk to your older sister . . . and me."

Sadie came to Chicago to talk it over. First she talked it over with Babe and on Sunday we drove out to Lake Forest, where my father was then living. She talked it over with my father. We drove to Waukegan and I showed her the sights. Later that evening she talked it over with me.

"Are you really in love with this man?" I asked.

"I thought I was," she replied, looking me straight in the eye, "but now I'm not so sure."

"Are you really going to marry him?"

"Yes."

I hesitated. I cleared my throat. "Well," I said

53

nervously, "I wasn't planning to get married. I mean—never in all my life, but if I ever were to get m-m-married, I certainly would plan to marry you and if you should say you would marry *me*, I would marry *you*."

"I don't know what you mean, Jack."

"I think we ought to get married."

"Why?"

"My father likes you."

"Really?"

"You could join my act."

"That's a silly reason to get married."

"I'm going to use a girl in the act. Look at George Burns and Gracie Allen. They're married. They work together."

"I'm not an actress."

"You could be."

"Oh, Jack," she said.

I finally blurted out, "What I mean is, I love you and I want you to be my wife."

"You said I was too young to get married."

"To him maybe, but not to me."

She accepted.

We were supposed to get married the next Sunday because there were no Sunday performances, but I was afraid if we waited until Sunday, Sadie might change her mind. We got married on Friday, January 14, 1927. We used my mother's ring because there was no time to buy one. It was an intimate affair at the Clayton Hotel in Waukegan attended only by my father, Babe and Al Bernovici, the rabbi and one family friend. It was an orthodox wedding. When I stepped on the wine glass at the end of the ceremony, Sadie fainted dead away!

It had been snowing heavily all week and I had to drive back to Chicago to give a performance that night. It was a long hard drive. We all had dinner after my show and that was it. Not even a honeymoon.

A few months later Sadie suddenly asked me if I remembered a seder in Vancouver with Zeppo Marx.

"I'll never forget it," I said. "There was some silly little girl who played the fiddle and she was ridiculous—all dressed up in her sister's clothes."

"That silly little girl is your wife, Jack," she said, grinning from ear to ear.

The first year of marriage was tough on Sadie. If she hadn't been patient and sympathetic, it wouldn't have lasted six months. You see, I was thirty-three years old and I didn't think of myself as a married man. Mentally, I was still a bachelor. Shortly after our marriage I decided I wanted to go out on the town with "the boys" after the show. Jack Waldron, an old buddy, was in the show and we planned to make the rounds. Sadie said she would like to join us.

"No," I said. "Just because I'm married doesn't mean I can't see my old friends alone."

"You're right," she said.

I met Waldron in the lobby of the Sherman Hotel where we were staying. We phoned George

55

Jessel. He couldn't join us. He had a date. We tried Benny Rubin, who was headlining at the Orpheum. His phone didn't answer. We went to a restaurant where actors hung out. Nobody was hanging out. I returned to the hotel and was too ashamed to go upstairs after such a short absence, so I sat in the lobby for an hour.

"Did you have a nice time?" Sadie asked sweetly.

"It was great," I lied.

But I still didn't learn. Later in New York I got that old restless feeling, the urge to be free and on the loose. I told Sadie I was going over to the Friars Club where I watched some vaudeville actors playing rummy. Then I went over to the Lambs Club and watched some stage actors shooting pool. I was very bored. I wandered along Broadway and looked into Lindy's and Dave's Blue Room and I saw some guys I knew and sat around with them and I felt empty. Something was missing, but I didn't know what. Suddenly I knew. I wanted to be with Sadie. I was bound to her not just by a legal document and a religious ceremony. I was linked to her by love.

Soon our best friends were other married couples in show business and we went around with them every night when we were in the same cities. Our group included Burns and Allen, Benny Fields and Blossom Seeley, Jane and Goodman Ace, Fred Allen and Portland Hoffa, Eddie and Ida Cantor, Jesse Block and Eve Sully and Jack and Flo Haley. We all remained married to our original mates. I know that people assume actors and actresses are bad marriage risks, yet not one couple in that group was ever divorced.

Sadie never wanted to be in the act. She hated performing. Even though she was born with an instinctive gift for comedy and she is a good critic of material, she only wanted to be Mrs. Benny. In 1928 I was breaking in a new act and using a "dumb girl" for about a four-minute routine. I was working the Orpheum Circuit when the girl took sick and had to go to the hospital.

So I asked Sadie to help me out for a few weeks till she recovered. Sadie did it. She was as nervous as a cat on a hot stove, but she forced herself to do it. She shook so much she had to hold on to my arm while she spoke. I knew about stage fright. I wrote the book on stage fright. I assured Sadie that you could be scared to death inside but an audience would never know it. As long as you looked sure of yourself outside, it didn't matter. Sadie was a natural as a comedienne and the first time she walked out on a stage she was a professional.

A comedian is not necessarily someone who cracks jokes or makes funny expressions and does wild pieces of business. Sometimes he or she is a subtle interpreter of lines and situations. Sadie knew instinctively that she must not read comedy lines as if they were hilarious and she was waiting for laughs. She believed in her lines when she said them. She let the audience discover the humor.

The trick in playing comedy is to make an audience believe what is going on and for this you have to believe it first yourself. This is why I think a comedian is basically an actor. The art of comedy is like the art of acting—except that in comedy, the actor has to be able to believe the most preposterous and exaggerated things.

Sadie became part of the act in Seattle and was she ever a hit! Much later on my radio program the name of her character was Mary Livingstone. This became her name in everybody's mind and finally she changed it legally. She's been Mary in my mind for so long that, frankly, it's been an effort to call her Sadie here. Anyway, after Seattle we played a week in Oakland and a week in San Francisco.

Then in Los Angeles the original actress recovered and rejoined the act. After opening day, the manager of the Los Angeles Orpheum told me, "I can't understand this, Jack. I got reports from Frisco and Seattle that you had a terrific new partner. But I got to tell you honestly that your new partner stinks and the act is dying. You'd better get rid of her. What I don't understand is how she got such raves in Frisco."

"Well, you see, the managers in Frisco and Seattle—they saw me with a different partner."

"Who was this partner?"

"That was my wife."

He advised me to pay off the girl and put my wife back in the act, which I did. It was a hit again.

One evening some executives from Metro-Gold-wyn-Mayer came to take a look. They had been looking for a suave master of ceremonies for Metro's first all-talking, all-singing musical motion picture. Hollywood was going through the sound revolution. Irving Thalberg, Metro's executive producer, had decided to make *Hollywood Revue of 1929*. There would be musical numbers, comedy skits, drama sketches, singing and dancing. A big chorus number to a new song, "Singin' in the Rain," would be included. Such stars as John Gilbert, Norma Shearer, Joan Crawford, Lionel Barrymore, Laurel and Hardy, Marion Davies and Buster Keaton would make cameo appearances. They wanted someone sophisticated to tie it all together.

My agent, Sam Lyons, told Thalberg that he knew of a witty, handsome, dapper emcee and all he had to do was catch my act at the Orpheum in downtown Los Angeles. He did and I was hired. After he saw the first day's rushes, Thalberg was so excited that he signed me to a five-year contract starting at $850 a week, with raises every six months.

Imagine—me a movie star! I couldn't believe it.

After a while I did believe it. I dreamed of a career in the movies. Let other vaudevillians mess around with this silly radio business—I wanted to be where the glamour was.

Mary and I rented a mansion with a swimming

pool. I swam, got tan, took long walks, reveled in the sunshine and improved my golf. Sure, I missed Broadway, the action at Lindy's and seeing friends at the Friars Club. But soon I got used to going to bed by ten o'clock and rising at six to report for makeup at 7:30 in the morning.

Hollywood Revue was completed in three months.

My next picture for Metro was *Chasing Rainbows*, which was such a box office flop that the exhibitors renamed it *Chasing Customers*.

Nevertheless Thalberg still loved me. He picked up my option. My salary was raised to $1,000 a week. But I didn't make any movies. I was told there were no vehicles for my talents. Every week I received my check and was told to report the following Friday when I received another check. I had nothing to do but swim with Mary and play golf and go to a lot of fine parties and give a lot of fine parties.

Every studio in town wanted to borrow me, but Metro would not loan me out. I told Thalberg I was getting bored and I hated not working. I pleaded with him to loan me to another studio. He wouldn't. Then Earl Carroll called me from New York. He was preparing a new edition of his *Vanities*. He wanted me to co-star in his show for $1,500 a week. I accepted and after some haggling with Thalberg was released from my contract.

Earl Carroll fascinated me. He was a man of contradictions. He had brains, talent and the most refined taste in costumes, scenery and lighting.

During the 1920's his shows were the finest of their kind and the girls were all ravishing. His instinct was perfect when it came to selecting show girls and dancers. But his comedy was filthy and obscene. He always played for notoriety. Of course it was all worth millions in publicity. The more his shows were indecent, lewd and pornographic, the more popular they became.

Mr. Carroll and I had problems from the start. I refused to play in the dirty skits and spent more than a few sleepless nights waiting to be fired. But he gave in. Those skits went to another comic, Jimmy Savo, and I was allowed to do my regular monologue in the second half of the show.

When we opened on Broadway the first scene showed seventy stunning girls sitting on a fence while the overture played. Everyone agreed that not even Ziegfeld offered such a riot of color and beauty. But some of the comedy material was so smutty that even sophisticated New Yorkers were offended.

Robert Benchley of *The New Yorker* found 50 percent of the show "cheap filth." He suggested that all the dirty material be put in Act I so people could have a leisurely dinner and arrive to enjoy the good things that would all be in Act II. I'm happy to say that I was included in the 50 percent he liked. He said, "Mr. Benny has long been a weakness of mine. Probably the straightest player of all our revue comedians, he can, by drawing in his cheeks ever so slightly or changing the angle of his hat a fraction, or even simply by pausing before reading a line, give an invaluable grace to the clumsiest witticism, and he has plenty of chances to work this miracle in some of the sketches in which Mr. Carroll has placed him."

One night the police came backstage to arrest Carroll along with Jimmy Savo and two of the showgirls. The grand jury didn't indict them, but the raid, the charges and the countercharges gave the 1930 *Vanities* the kind of publicity money can't buy. We ran 247 performances—longer than any previous *Vanities*. It was SRO every night.

All this time my agent, Sam Lyons, had been urging me to get into radio before it was too late and all the prime time and prime sponsors were taken by other comedians. He said dozens of advertisers, agencies and networks were after me to do a program. When the *Vanities* went on the road, I decided to listen.

Earl Carroll released me from my contract. I was now free and available. But suddenly all those sponsors and networks who had been fighting over me declared an armistice. Nobody wanted me in radio after all. I couldn't even get an audition. The weeks went by and by and by. Christmas of 1931 was a cold holiday.

Finally in January 1932 I was offered a four-week engagement at a nightclub. Back then I hated playing nightclubs and this would have been in Miami. A week before I left I happened to run into Ed Sullivan. "Doing anything tomorrow night?" he asked.

"No," I replied.

"You could do me a big favor. I'm starting a radio program—mostly gossip and interviews—and I'd appreciate it if you would come on my show and do a few minutes. Just kind of wing it. I can't pay you any money."

I had always liked Ed and he had been kind to me in his newspaper column. I said I'd do it.

I didn't wing it. I came well prepared with a five-minute string of little jokes. *The Ed Sullivan Show*, which forever changed the course of my life, began. After reading some items about Hollywood movies and romances, Ed introduced me as a star of vaudeville, motion pictures and Broadway.

My very first radio spiel began: "This is Jack Benny talking. There will be a slight pause while you say, 'Who cares?' . . ." My five minutes didn't rise much above that level.

But someone did care. The president of the advertising agency representing Canada Dry Ginger Ale thought I was funny. His client wanted to be in radio with a variety program and he talked them into making me the star. He called my agent. My agent called me.

Mary and I celebrated by washing our dinner down with vintage Canada Dry Ginger Ale, that magnificent exhilarating beverage. It was better than champagne. "Mary," I asked, "do you think the American people realize what a wonderful, refreshing drink this is?"

"I love you, Jack," she said.

But radio was not the soft touch my agent had promised. Even with a full-time writer, it was a ten-hour job five, six or even seven days a week.

After Canada Dry our next sponsor was, briefly, General Tires. I made an agreement with them: I wouldn't tell them how to put treads on their tires and they would let me tell jokes and do comedy commercials my way. I found a wonderful announcer, Don Wilson. Don was not as round and fat as he later became, but he was plump even then. He had a warm voice, he could read a commercial with laughter in his throat and he proved a great foil to play against. It was now that my radio character who was the butt of the jokes began to emerge.

I made an important discovery one evening, thanks to Mary, while listening to *The Ed Wynn Show*. We were trying to analyze why one joke that got a big laugh from the audience was funny, when another that we liked much better got only a titter. Mary said, "You know, Jack, Ed is playing the show to a studio audience. He must be doing sight gags that get laughs, but it doesn't mean anything to us at home."

She was right. The radio audience totaled approximately thirty million, but it really consisted of small family groups. I felt that now I understood the medium. I would play to those family groups and get them to know me and my family (the cast) as real people with real problems. Exaggerated people, yes, but fundamentally honest and true to life.

General Foods became my sponsor in October 1934. They had introduced a gelatin product that they called Jell-O. It came in six delicious flavors, all of them totally ignored by the consumers. Knox was the best-known gelatin then and Jell-O couldn't seem to make a dent in the market. From coast to coast, stores were stocked with mountains of unsold Jell-O. The board of directors considered scrapping the entire product, but as a last-ditch stand, they hired me. They were so desperate that they gave me a completely free hand with the commercials as well as the format of the show. I warned them that I wouldn't make ridiculous claims about Jell-O. I intended to make fun of it and predicted I would sell a lot of Jell-O.

They gambled. The risks were increased because they owned a Sunday evening time and in 1934 the Sunday evening hours were considered undesirable. Mondays through Thursdays were the big radio nights. I was given thirteen weeks to prove myself and off we went, on the NBC Blue network, Sunday nights at seven.

CHAPTER 4

Something much more important than Jell-O entered my life in 1934. Mary and I decided to adopt a daughter. Joanie was about two weeks old the first time I saw her. She was long and skinny and wrinkled all over her face and tiny arms. Her little legs looked crooked and were wrinkled all over, too. Her skin was puckered, there were big red blotches on her cheeks and her eyes were very blue. She was bawling so loud and she looked very mad. The only reason she didn't wake up the other newborn babies lying in the row after row of cribs in the hospital was that they were all yelling, too.

I couldn't believe my eyes.

"Is this the one you picked?" I asked Mary.

Mary was smiling a secret smile. "Yes," she said. "Isn't she darling?"

"How can you want to adopt a funny-looking thing like that one?"

"I can't help it," Mary said. "I just love her."

She became very beautiful and I fell in love with my daughter before she was living with us even two days. She completed our lives. As she grew older, she came to look like me and Mary. She has my blue eyes and my love for music and she has Mary's face and figure and manner of talking and smartness. Anybody would take her for our natural daughter. I feel as though she is ours and always has been ours. We told her she was adopted from the very beginning when she was too young to understand because we wanted her to get used to the idea of what it meant to be adopted. We did not rear Joanie in the permissive style that was fashionable then in Beverly Hills. Mary and I firmly believed that every child must be guided and disciplined and that the children of show business celebrities were more vulnerable to temptations than other children. For example, she wasn't allowed to use makeup until she was sixteen, although most of her friends were already putting on lipstick and eyeshadow at thirteen. She wasn't allowed to date until she was a senior in high school.

Being the softie that I am, it fell upon poor Mary to do the dirty work of disciplining little Joanie. As a child, Joan was always coming to me and complaining about her mother making her do this or do that. Once, at seven, she was seething with fury.

"I'm so mad at Mama," she said, "I'm just never going to talk to her again. I hate her, I hate her."

So I put her on my lap and told her about how when I first saw her I thought she was so ugly and how it was Mary who had wanted her so and how much Mary loved her and that these rules she hated were for her own good and necessary for her own happiness. Not long after I had this little heart-to-heart talk with Joanie, one morning she said suddenly out of a clear sky, "Daddy, I love you very much."

I said, "Joanie, you don't love me as much as I love you."

And then—mind you, she wasn't more than seven or eight—she, remembering our little talk, answered, "Yes, I do. I love you *more* because I loved you all my life and you didn't love me until the second day."

That story of my arrival was a family favorite for years. Today I am often asked what it was like to be adopted. How would I know? I've never been anything else. A silly question and a glib reply. The truth: I consider myself one of the most fortunate people in the world.

My adoption was hardly a secret. How could it have been when in 1934 my parents were well on their way to stardom? "The Jack Bennys Adopt Baby Girl" hit many of the fan magazines and newspapers of the time. No, I couldn't read then, but I knew even before I was able to understand that I had been adopted. I knew it just as I knew I had blue eyes and blonde hair. My parents handled it very matter-of-factly, never making it an unusual or mysterious occurrence, and since my best friend, Sandy Burns, as well as her little brother, Ronnie (George and Gracie's children), were also adopted, it must have been five or six years, or at least until I was questioned about it by outsiders, before I learned there was an alternate way to have babies. I thought if you wanted a baby you went to an orphanage and picked one out.

Later, of course, I became curious and asked the obvious questions: Who were my real parents? Why didn't they want me? Where are they now? I received what I thought and still believe were wise answers—in short: "We don't know who they are; we don't know where they are now; and they couldn't keep you because they couldn't afford a baby and wanted you to have a good home.

Adoption records are sealed so there's no way you can ever find out. Besides, you're luckier than other children—most parents can't pick the child they want, but we *chose* you and we wanted you very much."

I was a born pragmatist, and even then I reached the conclusion that since the records were sealed and it would be impossible to find the answers, to say nothing of the fact I couldn't have more wonderful parents, or indeed have been luckier, it hardly seemed worth my while to worry about it.

Did I say lucky? In an interview with the man of a thousand voices, Mel Blanc, a few months before he died, I discovered from his wife, Estelle, whose family had known my mother's family way back before the turn of the century, something my parents never told me.

"Your mother and father were set to adopt another baby, but that baby was late. It wasn't born by its due date. Your mother went to the synagogue in New York—the adoption agency—and she saw you, Joanie, and you looked like you needed care and attention. You were so skinny. Your mother had already decorated the nursery and hired a nurse and was paying her, so she said she would take this little malnourished baby home and fatten her up and care for her until the other baby arrived. So you came into their lives and then they didn't want the other one, they wanted you. They'd fallen in love."

69

Dad was famous for his timing, but I topped *him* that time. How lucky can you get?

It was in September of 1934, at age three months, that I became legally a member of the Benny family. My parents had been settled in their first real home, an apartment at the Essex House on Central Park South, for about a year and a half. After all the years of being on the road in vaudeville they finally had a sense of permanence, of living like normal people. My mother became a housewife —or so she said. Word has it that she tried her hand at cooking, but I have to assume it was not a successful endeavor since as far back as I can remember we always had a cook and I don't recall ever having seen her in the kitchen. She also tried pregnancy but gave up after two miscarriages.

My sojourn at the Essex House was short-lived. I always say I come from New York, but I'm not sure if just nine months counts. We moved west —to Beverly Hills—before my first birthday. There my parents rented a succession of houses, a different one for each of the following three years. The first belonged to Charlie Chaplin. It stood and, oddly enough, considering the current tear-down craze, still stands on North Beverly Drive, but I have no memory of it at all. I don't remember the next one either, though I know it was on Benedict Canyon and its claim to fame was that it belonged to the woman who owned the Hope Diamond.

Next came a house one block up the same street.

That one I recall mainly because of its large swimming pool. By then I was three and had learned to swim, or at least dog paddle and, like most Southern California children, I was a water rat. I couldn't get enough. I can still hear, as I heard for all the years of my childhood, my mother calling, "Joanie, get out of the pool . . . *now* . . . okay, five more minutes. This time I really mean it. *Out!* . . . All right, just one more lap . . . No, you can't dive in again . . . *Get out now!*" It wasn't that I was being particularly disobedient, it was just that I loved the water more than I feared being sent to bed early or not being allowed to listen to the radio.

My parents enjoyed swimming, too, but since they had never had formal lessons, their styles were not exactly regulation. Daddy did his own personal version of a breaststroke combined with a dog paddle and Mom managed a regal sidestroke. Daddy swam every morning. I think this was because his best friend, George Burns, told him it was healthy. George had adamant opinions about health—certainly well-founded ones. Daddy waded in from the steps at the shallow end, swam laps for about ten minutes and got out. This was a morning ritual. Mother didn't listen to George. She swam only in the summer, only when there were friends to join her, and even then it always took some cajoling.

At about the time we moved to the third rented house, my parents bought a lot at 1002 North

71

Roxbury Drive, and during the following year our new and permanent home was under construction. We moved in shortly after my fourth birthday.

Our white brick Georgian house soon became my sanctuary, the center of my world. All of my memories, at least until I was married and had a home of my own, revolve around it in some way. That house remains alive for me even today. I can still picture every detail—every room, hallway, nook and cranny, as well as the furniture and fabrics. Although I don't recall my dreams often, when I do they always take place there, and everything looks exactly as it did. The dreams are always happy dreams, and for just that fleeting moment between sleep and waking I'm home again . . . touching my childhood.

It seemed majestic; a perfectly proportioned two-story home on a city acre of land. In front spread an expanse of emerald green lawn separated from the sidewalk by multicolored seasonal flowers—pansies, gladiolus, marigolds, phlox and others. In the center a red brick path from the sidewalk to the front door was bordered by double rows of hedges enclosing red and pink rose trees and more flowers. At the north edge a driveway led to the five-car garage and the backyard.

In 1938 Beverly Hills was a rural community, and what is now the commercial center or triangle that includes the famous Rodeo Drive was then a quaint village. Today there isn't ten feet of space in all of Beverly Hills that hasn't been built on, but then, although there were houses standing on either side of us, looking out from the front across the street, three large vacant lots ranged all the way to Sunset Boulevard. For a treat when I had been good, my nanny, Signe Bensen, known to all as Bens, would take me for a walk across those lots up to Sunset to buy me an ice cream. Every day at three the Good Humor Man parked his truck there. I could hear his tinkly music from my bedroom and I remember hoping that I had been good enough. I also remember that after you ate your ice cream if on the empty stick it said "Good Humor" you were given another one free.

One of the many quirky health ideas of the 1930's was that ice-cold milk was bad for a child (and cod liver oil was good!) so my milk was always served lukewarm. One afternoon when I was three Daddy took me to a local soda fountain and ordered us each a chocolate ice cream cone; my very first. When the soda jerk handed me mine I tasted it and gave it back to him. "Warm it, please," I said.

Signe Bensen came to work for my parents when I was still in diapers. I remember that I liked her a lot. I recently discovered that she lives in the Los Angeles area and went to visit. It was the first time we had seen each other in over forty years. She's now in her seventies but still as tall and statuesque as I remembered her. We had fun reminiscing, and, of course, some of her stories were ones I had never heard. Here are a few of the things she said:

"You were lucky. Your mother and daddy really wanted you. Not for just publicity.

"You had your own ideas, even at that tender age—and you would disappear on me. That would terrify me. You'd hide in the house or in the garden outside—and you were tiny—you could disappear. And you wouldn't answer when I called.

"You and Sandra Burns saw each other every day when you were little. You two stuck together. There was one time when I really got mad and I spanked Sandra and you at the same time. You had an idea—you were going to that ice cream wagon, and I didn't want you to go without me. But you were going—you started out so I took the two of you—smack, smack! You were so surprised you didn't even cry! And I remember your big eyes—both of you. The way I found finally that I could discipline you so you *knew* you were disciplined was I'd sit you on a chair and wouldn't let you get off. The inactivity just slayed you. But your mind was working 100 percent all the time. You used to look up with those big eyes and you'd say, 'But you didn't tell me I couldn't do that.' How did you think of those things?

"I remember the Bing Crosby boys because at one of the birthday parties—I guess their nurse had taken her eyes off them and I turned around and there they were washing their hands in the punch. They were full of the devil.

"Many times we had our meals upstairs in your playroom—because your parents were going out. But a lot of times both Mary and Jack would come

74

in—and how Jack managed to sit on those little chairs, I'll never know. But he did. And he would converse with you and that was fun. He would get down and play with you. You had a toy train with wheels that were hard to push. He'd push and you would help. A couple of times when you had a cold he came in—oh, he felt bad that you were sick, and so he told you a story or read to you from one of your books. You were so enthralled. You sat there leaning against him, just kind of looking. He would have spent more time with you, but he either had the writers there or was going out to play golf. And when you were ill your mother would also come in and spend time with you. She would talk to you. You said you were scared about something—or that something happened—but you never told what it was. You kept your own counsel about a lot of things, which is unusual for a child that young. Usually you blurt it out to whoever—your mom or whoever. But you kept things to yourself.

"Your parents disciplined you sometimes. They talked to you, that's all they had to do—very serious talking. You were a little high-strung and if they had sharpness in their voice, you kind of shriveled up and got small. They'd sit you in a chair and talk. That was enough.

"Your mother and father were always telling you you were a pretty girl. You were a good girl. I thought you had a lot of love, you really did. They might not have spent as much time as they

75

would have liked, but whenever they did, you were full focus."

Bens was tall and blonde and Scandinavian and she always wore a nurse's uniform. Of course it was Bens's job to eat with me when I was very little. And I didn't like to eat. I pushed the food around on my plate and occasionally took a small mouthful, which I chewed slowly. My parents were smart—they didn't eat with me then. But poor Bens had to. I can still see us sitting at the breakfast room table and hear Bens in a very bored and sometimes desperate voice saying, "Eat . . . eat . . . eat, Joanie, eat . . . Joanie, eat . . . please, another mouthful . . . Joanie, please eat." And on and on. I no longer remember whether there was a punishment for not finishing, but I do recall vividly having to hear repeatedly—like most American children of my generation—"Don't leave anything on your plate. Think of the poor starving children in Europe!"

When I was little Daddy would do silly things to make me laugh. When I ate dinner with Bens he put on impromptu shows for me. From where I sat I could see straight through the dining room to the main hallway. Pretending he didn't know I was watching, he would slowly march back and forth across the space between the doors as if he were crossing a little stage. He would glue pieces of paper to his eyelids with spit and make funny faces as he walked by in profile. Then he made believe he was going down a flight of stairs by kneeling lower and lower and crouching down as he went across until he was out of sight. Then, seconds later he returned, starting in a crouch and then getting taller and taller as he went up the invisible stairs. It may have been ridiculous, but at age four or five I thought he was hilarious.

Later when I was a bit older, dinners were frequently family affairs. If my parents weren't going out, we ate together, which was wonderful, except on Tuesdays when we had liver and Fridays when we had fish—liver was *good* for you and the fish was freshly caught only on Friday.

When my best friends, Sandy or Deedee LeMaire (the daughter of Rufus LeMaire, an ex-vaudevillian, then studio executive), came to dinner we discovered we could open the window next to the table in the breakfast room and dispose of any unwanted delicacies directly onto the hedge and flower bed below. I never knew what effect this had on the snapdragons, but if Mother was right and liver and fish were good for humans, they must have been good for flowers, too. We also used to practice this art with milk and brussels sprouts. Bill, the gardener, never ratted on us. Perhaps he never noticed.

I come from a very small family. So small, in fact, that I once remarked, "For Thanksgiving dinner we can split a capon in the breakfast room." Facetiousness aside, in truth we celebrated birthdays and holidays with our "extended" family: my maternal grandparents, Momma and Poppa, Mother's sister, Babe, and her husband (first Myrt, then Clem—Al came and went before I was born), her brother, Hilliard, and his wife, Harriet, and later their two children, and Bens. Hilliard was known as Hickey, a name I gave him as a baby..

Christmas was the most exciting event of the year—not only because of all the presents, but because it was the one occasion in which I was allowed to fully participate. About a week before, my parents and I went to pick out the tree. It had to be a nine- or ten-foot-tall silver-tip and it had to be green. Given those facts I could pick the one I liked best. It was delivered to our house and placed in the bay window in the library, looking out on the front lawn, and could clearly be seen from the street.

When I was about five I made up my mind I wanted a red tree. Red was my favorite color. Daddy and Mother and I were at the Christmas tree lot looking at the green silver-tips and I begged and begged, "Couldn't we have the tree sprayed red?" Mother's answer was a very definite no—our tree had to be green. "That's final!"

Then Daddy had an idea (yes, he spoiled me terribly), "Let's get Joanie a little red tree for her room." And they did.

Each year for the next few, until I outgrew my penchant for things red and switched to blue (no, I never got a blue tree), a two-foot red Christmas tree sat on a table in my bedroom. I was allowed to trim it with the leftover balls and tinsel from the big tree.

The trimming of the big tree was a major production; the butler strung the lights, Bens stood on a ladder decorating what I couldn't reach, I did the bottom. The most beautiful of the ornaments was the top one—a large silver star with small flame-shaped light bulbs at the five tips. A light hidden inside the center shone through the cut-out words: "Merry Christmas."

When the tree was decorated the gifts that had already begun to arrive were placed underneath. By the day before Christmas they fanned out to cover at least half the room—most of them for me. I think in those early days I must have received at least a hundred presents. It took more than an hour to unwrap them. (I thought that was a lot until I read Shirley Temple's autobiography. In her heyday she received over 500,000!) Some were from my friends and some were from my parents' friends—but many came from business associates to show how much they "loved" me. Of course I couldn't tell which were which, but I didn't much care. A present was a present. Some were lavish, some were trinkets. Some came from people who didn't know what to buy for Daddy —he had everything—so they bought a gift for me instead.

At this point you may be wondering why the granddaughter of Meyer Kubelsky had a Christmas tree—or in my case, two. At that point in time and in Beverly Hills it wasn't very unusual. My memory may be faulty, but I seem to recall that most families, Jewish or not, had trees and celebrated Christmas then. It wasn't really a religious thing, more like just an excuse to celebrate and exchange gifts.

In the early 1940's the Jewish population of Beverly Hills was perhaps 50 percent. I remember at El Rodeo Elementary School we had a Christmas program wherein each grade from kindergarten through eighth grade sang all the traditional carols—two per class, and groups of us would go caroling the night before Christmas Eve. Somewhere between high school and motherhood all that changed, because by the time my own children started at El Rodeo there was a "holiday" program, and no mention of Christmas. Each class now sang "holiday songs" from around the world—many of which just happened to be Hanukkah songs. But what really amused me was that although it was supposed to be nondenominational there was no mention of Christ at all. The school orchestra played "Silent Night" (no lyrics) and the eighth graders sang "Adeste Fideles" (in Latin). Our public schools had become parochial. They even had days off on Rosh Hashanah and Yom Kippur. Probably because the Jewish population by 1960 had grown to about 90 percent.

What did my parents think of all this? Not much, since they didn't think much about religion. They thought about show business—that was their religion. With my children I've always celebrated Christmas, too. And taught them carols and read the related stories in the New Testament. To me, it isn't important whether or not one believes in Christ as the saviour—the Christians do,

I as a Jew don't—but the story of his birth is lovely, nonetheless, and for children, what with Santa Claus and the tree trimming and the festivity and the presents, the most exciting event of the year. Besides, it's important to one's education to know about all the world religions and beliefs, not just your own.

Another highlight of those early years was summertime. Plink, plonk, plink, plonk, bounce, hit, bounce, pause—missed! Plink, plonk—those were the sounds I heard from my bedroom in the afternoons when we first moved into the house. Until I was six and began first grade I was sent to my room to nap every day from one to three. I loathed it violently, fervently. Of course I never slept. But I had to stay in my room anyway. In the summers the sounds coming from the direction of the pool drove me crazy: the splashing, the laughter, the incessant Ping-Pong. I wanted to be where the action was—where the glamour was—with Mother and her friends, like George Raft and Betty Grable, and Bob Taylor and Barbara Stanwyck. Those two hours stretched endlessly until I was allowed to join the party.

Pools in those days were built quite differently. No such thing as Dig-a-hole-and-spray-with-Gunite. And either we had ritzy friends or 1930's pools tended to be larger. I don't remember any 12 × 25's then. Ours was 30 × 60, the Burnses' was about the same and some, like one across the street and Jack Warner's, were Olympic size.

Like most of the others, ours had all tile sides, tile gutters and tile stripes running the length of the bottom. Some pools had mosaic designs such as fish or flowers scattered along the sides or bottom. Not ours—we had an octopus! Not just a cute little plaque with an adorable representation of an octopus. Nothing so trivial. Our octopus was fifteen feet in diameter. Set in a pastel blue tile octagon, "Ollie" had great black eyes and enormous blue and green tentacles with little brown suckers at their tips. The tentacles undulated and rippled with the movement of the water. As much as I loved to swim and as difficult as it was for my mother to get me out, that *thing* terrified me.

Fortunately, the pool was large enough for me to avoid Ollie by swimming close to the edges, looking straight ahead or down. Sometimes when I was feeling brave, I managed to swim over him with my eyes closed. But he was always there. I complained a lot. Finally, in desperation, my parents decided to do something about it. They didn't want poor little Joanie to be frightened, and so, one winter (I must have been about seven), at great expense the pool was drained, the black tiles in the eyes replaced with pastel shades of green and tan, the pool refilled and the problem solved. "There now, you won't be scared anymore, will you, sweetheart?" Daddy said.

"No," I replied, "I guess not."

What Mom and Daddy didn't realize was that I had never minded the black eyes—it was those ever-waving, menacing tentacles that had me

82

panic-stricken. But what could I say after they had gone to so much trouble? They thought they had done the right thing, and now I simply had to learn to live with it. As I grew up, I got used to it—in fact, throwing and diving for coins on Ollie became a favorite sport. Today I think of our octopus with nostalgia.

CHAPTER 5

I think you could safely say my young life was special. I remember Daddy taking me to Chicago when I was seven—just the two of us. How thrilled I was to have him all to myself. It was summertime and we stayed right on Lake Michigan at the Edgewater Beach Hotel. We spent the mornings playing golf—that is, he played, I walked with him and watched. We spent afternoons on the beach, swimming and sailing. It was a blissful few days until I almost ruined it.

Daddy decided to take me to the Riverview amusement park. I could hardly wait. I had never been to an amusement park before and it sounded very exciting. There were all kinds of rides and we went on most of them. We ate hot dogs and cotton candy and Cracker Jacks. When I wanted more he said okay. I could have anything I wanted. Quite naturally he was recognized, and people stopped him frequently to ask for an autograph or to take his picture. I loved every minute of it.

I was so proud to be with him. This wonderful man was my very own daddy.

And then we came to a ride called shoot the chutes or something like that. You went up an elevator to the top of a structure where you entered a small boat. The boat hurtled down a very steep chute, like the downward path of a roller coaster or ski jump, splashing into water at the bottom. Daddy wanted to try it and I didn't. I was terrified and started to cry. The more he insisted, the more I cried, and the more I cried, the more adamant Daddy became. He wanted to go on this ride and he wanted me to go with him. He lost his temper completely and called me a crybaby. I don't know what triggered his anger—but angry he was— even furious. Finally, he said, "If you won't go, we're leaving." And he meant it.

I realized I had no choice. I wasn't about to be taken home in disgrace and ruin my whole day with Daddy, and maybe even the rest of the vacation, so I dried my tears, pulled my small self together, and off we went. Up the elevator and into the boat. We sat side by side, he put his arm around me, and told me not to be scared. I screamed on the way down the chute, but by the time we hit the water I had decided this was the best ride in the park, and wanted to do it again. And again . . . and again. By the end of the ride Daddy had forgotten his anger, forgiven me, and was in high spirits. And we went on it again . . . and again . . . and again.

I adored my grandparents, Momma and Poppa. My father's mother had died long before I was born, and his father, Poppa Two, went to his reward when I was six, so I have only hazy memories of him. I called him Poppa Two because I had known my mother's father first and called him Poppa; when I was later introduced to my other grandfather, Daddy said, "Joanie, this is Poppa, too." So, Poppa Two he was.

Momma and Poppa lived on Third Street near Fairfax. I loved going to their apartment with Bens in the afternoons and with my parents on Friday evenings for dinner. It was kind of dark with old furniture: warm and comfortable and cozy. It looked like what you would expect a grandparent's home to look like. I was never bored there. They always had some activity planned: walks, games, music, and lots of food. Momma was a great cook—the kind you read about in stories of Jewish mothers, and Poppa made kosher dill pickles. He was famous around Hollywood for them. They were the best in the world, juicy and extra hot. I can still taste them and feel the fire in my mouth afterward. They were in great demand among my parents' friends, from Claudette Colbert to Clark Gable, and every year he put up hundreds of jars of them. Later, when I was first married and lived in New York I still had cupboardsful!

I remember taking walks with Poppa in the afternoons after my nap. He would hold my hand as we headed east to Fairfax. There, on a huge field, on the acreage now known as Park La Brea, sat a blimp. Sometimes it took off or landed while we watched. The Goodyear blimp, perhaps. I don't remember. I only recall my childlike delight in watching this huge thing float off the ground or, better still, be pulled down with mooring ropes. On the way home Poppa bought me an ice cream cone—by then I knew not to ask to have it warmed!

Poppa, I have been told, taught me how to walk. He would get down on all fours, put a card on his head (I was always fascinated by cards and today play almost every known card game) and coax me to walk to him to get it. Many years later he taught my older children, Michael and Maria, to walk using the same method. It worked.

Perhaps we lit candles at those Friday night dinners—I can't really remember. I do remember that Momma and Poppa weren't particularly religious, although Poppa, who had emigrated from Romania, read *The Daily Forward* in Yiddish and played pinochle with his male friends at a Jewish club. Momma's parents had been immigrants, but she was one of four sisters and two brothers, all born in Denver. Her family, the Wagners, were a colorful lot. One of her sisters, Aunt Eddie, who lived in Seattle, could have been the prototype for Auntie Mame. One of her brothers had been a World War I hero; the other was an alcoholic who tried to commit suicide by jumping out of a second story window. Unsuccessfully. Then there was Momma's Uncle Younkel—she loved to tell the story about how he had been a horse thief back in the "old country" and continued to practice his trade in Denver. When caught, he would plead not guilty and defend himself by saying in his thick Jewish-German accent, "I don't know what happened. I'm not a thief. The horse just followed me home."

Momma and Poppa had a fantastic gramophone along with the latest pop records. This was when records were made of glass and broke easily. Contained in a large console with storage space in the bottom, the player sat on top under a hinged lid. Along one side of the turntable was a bin for extra records, on the other, another bin, this one slanted and felt-lined. The machine played one record at a time and when it finished, its strange arm moved to the edge of the record and, by some odd mechanism, gave it a little shove, pushing it into the felt bin. Usually it worked pretty well, but because its technique was not always to be trusted, the record sometimes got hurled instead of shoved, overshot the bin and landed on the floor in pieces. I don't recall the manufacturer of this marvel.

My best childhood friends were Sandy and Deedee. We were truly the Terrible Trio, always thinking up ways to get in trouble. On weekends and after school we played together constantly, frequently at my house, in the courtyard at the back of the driveway. A white trellised fence ran the length of the property almost to the back alley. The trellis was covered year-round with rambling lavender and pink sweet peas and it divided the driveway and courtyard from the main backyard. In the early years the courtyard doubled as a badminton court, but the games were infrequent, the lines eventually disappeared and the net post holes were filled in. This was where I first learned to ride a bicycle, going alongside and grabbing on to the trellis. Later it became my home playground —perfect for hopscotch, team jump-rope and pogo-sticking. I was an expert, but my pogo-sticking ended abruptly many years later. While showing off by doing it in high heels I fell and sprained my ankle. It was the finish of a promising career.

One of the TT's favorite activities was climbing over the wall into the neighbor's garden. We stole fruit from their trees, rearranged their potted plants, and occasionally left the hose running into their pool. We eventually got caught, or to be accurate, the neighbors complained to my parents. That ended that! But with our fertile young minds we found bigger and better substitutes. Usually harmless, but one time . . .

Zachary Scott, the movie star and a friend of our parents, had moved to Beverly Hills, and he had a daughter, Waverly, our age. We were informed that she would be coming over one afternoon to play with us, and we were to be gracious and friendly. And so we were. We welcomed her, played games with her and had milk and cookies in our kitchen with her. We were very, very nice. But we had surreptitiously added two tablespoons of milk of magnesia to her milk. We never had to play with her again.

In the 1930's and even up until the 1960's, most people weren't particularly security conscious. Certainly not as they are now. Today most movie, TV and rock stars live in houses hidden from view behind heavy gates and iron fences, with armed guards, hidden cameras and television monitors. When they emerge from their lairs it's in limousines with darkened windows. (Perhaps soon they'll have moats, alligators and drawbridges!)

The only security we had were burglar alarms next to each of the access doors and behind the beds in each of the main bedrooms, all of which were hooked up to the local police station. And then there was Frank, the night watchman, who came at nine at night and left at seven in the morning. He was a sweet old man who spent most of his time asleep at the kitchen table. Although he had been a cop at one time and carried a gun he was hardly ominous looking. As far as I know he only used his gun once, and that was when, in the middle of the night while making his rounds, he entered the powder room, saw himself in the mirror and shot it. What precautions my parents took were because of the Lindbergh kidnapping. If there were any such threats aimed at my family I was never told about them. I rather doubt there were.

We were on easy terms with the sightseers clutching their maps of movie stars' houses and the tour buses cruising the street. Eddie Cantor, Jimmy Stewart, Hedy Lamarr, Jack Haley, Agnes

Moorehead, José Ferrer and Rosemary Clooney, Polly Bergen, Lucille Ball and Desi Arnaz, all lived within two blocks of us. The 900 and 1000 blocks of Roxbury Drive were a Mecca for the curious. In those days movie stars were relaxed and friendly and so were the tourists. They frequently came to our front door, rang the bell and asked for an autographed picture. Sometimes they asked if they could meet Mr. Benny. Usually a maid answered the door and gave them each an autographed photo. A stack of pictures was kept in a drawer in the foyer table. Sometimes I answered the door, had a short chat and handed out a photograph. It was also perfectly normal for Daddy, if he was nearby, to answer the door himself. He enjoyed—or rather loved—meeting his fans.

The house next to ours (1000) belonged to a family named Burr. It was also a white Georgian, two-story brick, so of course the two houses were frequently confused by the fans. During their first few years as our neighbors, the Burrs dealt with the constant picture-taking, ringing doorbells and interruptions with some equanimity, but eventually it got to them. One day a large sign appeared in their driveway: JACK BENNY DOES NOT LIVE HERE. HE LIVES THERE. Under the "there" a huge arrow pointed to our house.

I don't know whether or not we were responsible for the Burrs' finally moving, but move they did and the house was bought by Lucy and Desi, who moved in with their two small children, Little

90

Lucie and Little Desi. A perfect solution. Now the fans could choose either house and not make a mistake.

When it came to entertaining, my parents were no slouches. Their parties were frequent and lavish. During the late 1930's and early 1940's—the years when my parents held their spectacular New Year's Eve parties—I was sent off, usually with Deedee, to spend the night at my grandparents'. It was normally a treat to go there, but a party night was the one time I wanted to stay home where the action was, but I was told I was too young. By the time I was eight, I was finally allowed to remain at home and even invite a friend over.

I loved to watch the frantic preparations: the tent for dinner and dancing being erected over the patio, the caterer's truck arriving with giant boxes of ingredients for the extravagant meal, the rental company truck with the chairs and tables and table settings, the florist with magnificent centerpieces for the tables and vines to decorate the pillars, the dance floor being nailed together, and on and on. The place was a madhouse. I tried to help and not be in everyone's way, but I probably didn't succeed.

Those glittering parties—I remember how beautiful the women were in their evening gowns and jewels and how handsome the men in their dinner jackets. I was taught always to say "evening gown" and "dinner jacket," never "formal" or "tuxedo." A party was "black or white tie," never "a formal." After a full day of "helping" the crew I scurried upstairs, not wanting to miss watching Mom get dressed. There was as much commotion in her dressing room as downstairs. I had to stay in a corner to be out of the way of her hairdresser, maid, and dressmaker. Then into Daddy's room to help him choose his cuff links and studs. What would they have done without me?

Mother and Daddy went downstairs just about the time the doorbell began to ring. And there was Barbara Stanwyck, slim and elegant with her husband, Robert Taylor. Then . . . Frank and Nancy Sinatra, Van and Evie Johnson, George and Gracie, Stewart Granger and his wife, Jean Simmons, George Montgomery and his wife, Dinah Shore, Tony Martin (later with Cyd Charisse), Jimmy and Gloria Stewart, Ray and Mal Milland, Gary and Rocky Cooper, the Edward G. Robinsons, the Robert Montgomerys, the Humphrey Bogarts, Keenan Wynn, Danny and Sylvia Kaye, the Henry Fondas, Ronnie and Benita Colman, Bob and Dolores Hope, Al Jolson, Ronald Reagan and Jane Wyman, Ann Sheridan, Betty Grable—and on and on.

The casts changed as the years went by—different pairings reflected the occasional divorce and remarriage and new faces appeared as they also did on Hollywood movie screens, but the format of the parties remained the same. It began with cocktails, followed by dinner and dancing under the tent, and always ended with the best part of all and what made a Hollywood party unique:

impromptu entertainment in the living room. A professional pianist hired for the evening would be noodling on the Steinway as guests drifted in. He would soon be displaced by Sammy Cahn or Johnny Green, neither of whom could wait to take over. Entertainers love to entertain—particularly when they are with their friends and colleagues and feel they can let their hair down and be silly or risqué. It didn't seem at all extraordinary for Dinah to start things rolling with a Sammy Cahn song. Then George Burns would get up and tell the stories that made Daddy literally fall down and pound the floor. Jane, Van, Tony or Betty might sing, Danny Kaye do a doubletalk routine accompanied by Sylvia—Frank would knock 'em dead with a ballad or two or three.

When I was old enough to invite Deedee or Sandy to spend the night, we worked out our own routine for these galas. By the time the party began, we would be dressed for bed in pajamas and robes. We would go to the upstairs landing, lie flat on our tummies and peer through the railings to watch the guests arrive.

Our front door opened directly into the foyer, a large circular entrance room that rose two stories high. To the left as you came in was that table with the drawer full of Daddy's autographed pictures and to the right was the door to the living room. Just beyond the table the impressive staircase began, circled the room and ended on the landing where we were keeping vigil. The walls were covered with a pale green Oriental wallpaper, painted with climbing flowers and vines. From the high dome of the ceiling hung a three-tiered, perfectly proportioned (it didn't look enormous, but it was) crystal chandelier. During the two major earthquakes I remember, it swayed back and forth precipitously, just missing the banister.

Certain we couldn't be seen or heard, my friend and I gossiped and giggled on the landing with our perfect view of the front door. We were as excited as any young fans anywhere. I remember that the woman I thought most beautiful of all was not a movie star, but the wife of one: Mal (Mrs. Ray) Milland. She had prematurely gray hair (she was only in her twenties then) that was stunning against her creamy skin and lovely face. She had a penchant for shocking pink gowns. I always thought her elegance put the bleached-blonde glamour girls to shame.

Mother, of course, knew we had been watching, but she didn't mind as long as we went straight to bed after all the guests had arrived. Naturally, we were not allowed to join the party, but she devised a plan for us to at least briefly enjoy the festivities in my room. When the party was in full swing she would come upstairs and ask which three guests we would like to meet—any three we wanted. She would then bring them up for a visit. My first choice was always Van Johnson. The other two varied, but he was my favorite. I had a terrific crush on him. All my life I've been attracted to dark-haired, dark-eyed men. Van was the one exception. He looked outdoorsish, sporty, and always wore red socks (his trademark). All-American with crinkly blue eyes, blond hair and the cutest smile around, he was one of the biggest stars in Hollywood during the war years. He was the bobby-soxers' delight, mobbed by his fans wherever he went.

Although I was not a very pretty child, I had a good brain and tended to observe the people around me rather acutely. I separated my parents' friends into two categories: those whose attitude to me was a pat on the head and a "Get lost, kid," and the few special ones who treated me as though I mattered and who genuinely seemed interested in what I had to say. Van was in the latter group. No wonder I adored him so. He talked to me about his art and listened to my opinions. He was doing a lot of painting then and even gave me one of his pictures, which I hung over my bed.

I had no talent in art. None. Zip. I may be the only child who ever got an F in art—in the first grade! So I was fascinated by someone who was good at it, someone who could draw something and make it look like the thing he was drawing. Not only was I interested in Van Johnson, he was interested in me. What are you learning in school? Tell me about your friends. What do you do in the afternoons? I showed him my treasures and we talked about music and shoes and ships and sealing wax . . . He was wonderful!

There are other people I remember with great fondness—who treated me as an intelligent person, not like a dumb kid—people I could talk to.

Barbara Stanwyck was one of my favorites. She was then married to Robert Taylor and they were maybe my parents' closest friends after the Burnses. I always admired Barbara for her talent and I loved her looks. Later in the evening after dinner and dancing we would return to our stakeout to listen to the entertainment. We were caught from time to time and sent to bed, but as soon as the coast was clear, back we went.

Going to the studio with my parents to watch the show on Sundays was another special part of my life. It wasn't like "going to see where Daddy works." I used to go to Daddy's office and it was just an office. The radio studio was glamorous. But even more glamorous were the motion picture studios, and during the years Dad made pictures I was allowed to visit him on the set. I remember particularly Paramount and Warner Brothers. I couldn't get enough of it. In one of his movies there was a chorus line of girls wearing gorgeous white tulle and silver spangled costumes. They had big, puffy sleeves, sweetheart necklines, tight bodices and ballet-length skirts with layers of petticoats and yards and yards of material. I wanted one so badly. I must have been about five years old and I had a little wind-up Victrola in my room and my favorite activity was playing music and dancing to it. To be able to dance in that costume was my idea of bliss. So I asked Daddy, he asked Paramount, and sure enough, they made the costume for me. I even went to the wardrobe department to have it fitted properly. I danced in it and wore it to breakfast, lunch and dinner. It was a struggle to get me out of it at bedtime. I may not have been much of an actress on the stage, but alone in my bedroom there has never been, in the history of the theater, a more beautiful, more graceful, more regal fairy princess.

Some years later Daddy was doing a film at 20th Century-Fox. Carmen Miranda was then one of their biggest stars. I had gone about as far as my untrained feet could go as Odette/Odile and was entering my Latin/Xavier Cugat period. You guessed it! A Carmen Miranda costume, complete with platform shoes, ruffled orange satin skirt, bare midriff, blouse with big ruffled sleeves and high orange satin hat, bananas and all.

My life was special, too, because when we went out we were treated differently. Daddy was recognized, I was fawned over. People were a little bit nicer to me because I was Jack Benny's daughter. We traveled more than the average family, mostly to New York. I remember being there when I was seven or eight. Danny Kaye, one of my parents' closest friends, had just opened in *Let's Face It!*, and Mom took me to a matinee. It was my first Broadway musical and I was thoroughly enthralled, hanging on every dance step, every lyric. Included in the many songs was one of Danny's famous patter numbers. I think it must have been Cole Porter's "Let's Not Talk About Love," because it's full of different names of then famous people. Knowing we were in the audience,

97

he changed one of the names as written and sang "Joan Benny" instead. When I heard it I promptly jumped up in my seat, turned around from my third-row seat to face the audience and yelled excitedly, "That's me, that's me!"

But being recognized, being special was something I had to learn to deal with. As a young child it's easy to get confused about who is famous and who isn't. It's easy to fall into the trap, to think because you have famous parents that you're famous, too. I was lucky—I learned my lesson about fame at an early age. Mom and Dad were and I wasn't. Yes, I shared in the glow when I was with them or when I was singled out for an interview, but on my own I soon discovered I was "nobody." How interesting to observe that people who fussed over me when I was with my parents ignored me when I wasn't. I don't recall that it upset me—it was simply a fact of life. "So that's how it works. I get it. And now that I get it I can handle it." Understanding made it easy. I separated people I liked and those I didn't by how they treated me as *me*, Joan.

I also learned to separate the me, Joan, and the me, Jack Benny's daughter. I remember going to Hollywood premieres, arriving in a big black limousine with my parents. Klieg lights blazed, bleachers were full of fans, an emcee announced arrivals on a loud microphone and crowds of autograph seekers peered into the cars as they pulled up. "That's Jack Benny and Mary Livingstone and their daughter, Joan," someone would yell to the horde. Later, as a teenager, I attended a few premieres with a noncelebrity date or with noncelebrity friends. The same crowds, lights and brouhaha, only now that same someone stuck his head in the car and yelled, "That's nobody!"

Many years later I found the perfect opportunity—or so I thought—to teach one of my children the fame lesson. It was on a Sunday evening at Trader Vic's in Beverly Hills. We went there as a family almost every week: my parents, my husband and I, and my four children. Bobby, my younger son, was about six and his sister, Joanna, a year younger. This particular night the maître d' was showing us to our table and making a more than usual fuss over my father. As we were walking down the hallway Bobby turned to me and asked, "Is Granddaddy famous?"

"Yes, Granddaddy's famous," I replied.

He thought a minute. "Are we famous?"

"No," I said. "You're not famous." Good, I thought. Now he knows. But I was wrong— Bobby had the last line.

"Well," he added, "we're pretty well known for our age!"

CHAPTER 6

The Jack Benny Show was the focal point of our family life, and since the scripts and recordings were kept in Daddy's room and the show was written in the library, they were my two favorite places to be.

Daddy's room smelled good. I can still conjure up that distinct masculine aroma of cigars and old leather. It was inviting. Not all clean and neat like Mom's bedroom and mine, but strewn with magazines, newspaper clippings, books and scraps of scribbled-on bits of paper. The tones were beige and brown, the side pieces English antiques, and on the walls hung English hunting prints.

At the far end of the bedroom French doors led to a balcony overlooking the lawn and pool; one window faced the patio, and another looked down on the Arnazes' driveway. On either side of the French doors built-in bookcases contained, on the left, his favorite books (biographies) and reference books; on the right, the radio show recordings and leather-bound volumes of all the scripts. Two volumes held one year's shows. Printed on the spines were the dates and sponsor's name for that season. I was fascinated by the ones that read Chevrolet, General Tires and Canada Dry Ginger Ale because they were from a time before I was born, or at least before I was old enough to understand. I couldn't comprehend the idea that Jell-O hadn't always been Daddy's sponsor. After all, every week of my still brief life he told people to buy Jell-O. How could he have told them to buy something else?

The summer of 1940, when I had just turned six, we vacationed in Honolulu. We stayed at the Royal Hawaiian Hotel, then one of the only three hotels on Waikiki. I went outrigger canoeing, learned to surf and do the hula, and sat on the beach with Mom watching her get tan. Cursed with pale, albino-like skin, I spent most of the time covered in zinc oxide, looking grotesque.

I remember we sailed there on the *Lurline*—it was my first sea voyage and I spent most of it being seasick. As we docked at Aloha Tower, Mother, Daddy and I were showered with leis—so many I couldn't see above them. Daddy was presented with one made entirely of Jell-O boxes connected by flowers. How many of *you* recall, "Jell-O comes in six delicious flavors—strawberry, raspberry, cherry, orange, lemon, and lime"? Can you say it fast?

Because of their weight, the recordings of the shows took up all the space on the lowest shelf and eventually spread to the cupboards below. Each huge volume contained five shows, two records per show. Made of black acetate, they measured sixteen inches in diameter (today's LP's are twelve inches) and turned at 16½ rpm, half the present standard commercial speed. The original, unrecorded surface looked like smooth glass, and the needle cut the grooves as the recording was made. When I went to the studio I was supposed to stay in the sponsor's booth, but I used to love to sneak down to the sound booth directly below to watch the recording engineer huddle over his equipment, turning dials and, at the same time, with a little brush, constantly sweeping away the dross, those little ribbons of acetate that accumulated as the grooves were cut.

There was a time when I was not allowed to listen to the Sunday night shows. I could watch them at the studio, but they aired after my bedtime. The records were delivered to our house on Monday mornings, so on Monday afternoons when Daddy was out playing golf I would go to his room and listen to the records of yesterday's show. He had a special extra-large turntable to accommodate those extra-large records, and it played only at 16½ rpm. I was allowed the privilege of opening the sealed package, playing the records, and then filing them where they belonged in the current album. I remember listening to them all alone in his room and, even though I had seen and heard the show the day before, laughing out loud at the jokes, and waiting impatiently for the end to hear him say, as he did every week without fail, "Good night, Joanie."

When I was in college I was introduced to a fellow student who, when he heard my name, said, "Every Sunday night my whole life my parents and I sat at the kitchen table to listen to *The Jack Benny Show*, and way back in the early days I remember he used to say, 'Good night, Joanie,' and I always wondered who Joanie was."

As you walked into Daddy's room his bed stood against the middle of the wall on the right. At its foot, a bench sagged under the weight of the aforementioned clutter. I don't recall anyone, including my father, ever sorting through the mess. It just grew. To the right of the door, a large table held more jumble; mostly scripts—some read, some unread—and a pile of *Liberty* magazines and *Saturday Evening Posts*. On the other side of the bed in front of the bookcase was a huge tan armchair, facing catty-corner. That was my chair when Daddy and I had our "talks," or listened together to the fights. Daddy was a great fight fan, and because it was a way of spending time with him and a way to share something with him, I became a fight fan, too. I remember almost all of Joe Louis's fights. Daddy loved him and rooted and yelled and screamed at the radio the same as people do today at the TV set.

A beautiful antique leather-topped English desk with a tufted leather desk chair took up most of the area on the other side of the French doors. The special phonograph sat on a little table right next to the desk. When I listened to those records I would sit in the leather chair and swivel around. I probably looked like Lily Tomlin's Edith Anne. One day I overdid the swiveling and when I left the room, instead of walking through the door, I walked into it and cut my nose and forehead. Mother screamed when she saw the blood and off we flew to the emergency room for stitches. I don't really remember the incident, but she told that story many times later, particularly at family dinners when she and Gracie talked about how *difficult* their daughters were.

As I've already said, Daddy was a pussycat

where I was concerned, so I remember clearly the few times I made him angry. When he came home in the late afternoon I would follow him around like a puppy, tailing him wherever he went. From my room I could hear his car drive up to the side door. I would rush down the back stairs, open the door for him, get my hug and kiss, and then wait while he and Mom spent their private time together. As soon as he left her room there I was, waiting to follow him into his dressing room because I knew he was about to empty his pockets of scraps of paper and change and I was allowed to collect all the pennies.

This became an almost daily routine, until one day when I thought he wasn't looking and in a moment of greed, after pocketing the three or four pennies, I threw in a nickel as well. At first I thought I had gotten away with it—he didn't say a word. But then a few minutes later as I was about to leave, he said, "Joan, honey, please return the nickel—you know our agreement." Well, I was crestfallen. As soon as he uttered the word "Joan" I knew that in spite of my nonchalance and innocent expression I had been caught. I was never called Joan unless I was in trouble. And the idea that I had done something to displease him immediately made me cry. (I didn't cry easily, even as a child, but a sideways look from Daddy and I dissolved into a pool of tears. This and later at the amusement park are the only times I remember.) Chastised and chastened, I said I was sorry, and returned the nickel. He said he was sorry, too, hoped I wouldn't do it again, and gave me a kiss.

Although the incident hardly set me on the path of righteousness, I never again succumbed to greed, that is, when it came to pennies and nickels.

A sofa with a butler's table in front stood along the left wall opposite the bed. Along with the armchair and desk chair, it provided seating for the writers when Daddy was sick and had to stay in bed. He didn't get sick often, although a glance at his nightstand would belie that statement. His nightstand was a large double-tiered affair with a hollowed section inside and a lamp on top. Though as filled with clutter as the other tables, it was a different kind of clutter: his telephone book, the book he was currently reading, scraps of paper with telephone messages, scraps of paper listing things to do, scraps of paper with ideas for routines, scraps of paper with jokes, file cards with more of the same and forty-seven bottles of pills!

I don't think he took pills very often—maybe an occasional aspirin or nose drops and cough medicine when he had a cold, but he was an admitted hypochondriac. The pills were there—just in case. He worried about his health constantly, had regular checkups and even when his doctor gave him a clean bill, still worried that there was something wrong with him. In fact, he was a very healthy man and until his final illness never looked his age.

Daddy's physician for over twenty years was Dr. Rex Kennamer. He recently told me, "I once took care of a very wealthy countess who had moved to Los Angeles from Texas and wanted to have her face done. I'd taken care of her for some time when she told me she wanted to have 'the same plastic surgery that Jack Benny had had.' I kept telling her, 'He's never had any work done.' Do you know, she finally left me as a doctor because she said I didn't care enough about her to tell her who did Jack Benny's plastic surgery! I could never convince her. She was determined to believe that no one could look that good naturally. She just got mad at me and left."

Our library was across the hall from the dining room, at the front of the house. Beautifully paneled walls, a blue and white Delft-tiled fireplace and a dark blue Chinese rug gave the room its warm and cozy character. (That carpet covers my living room floor today.) A big bay window looked out on the front lawn. The sofa and chairs were blue and white and a big Queen Anne winged leather chair where Daddy always sat dominated the room. A round table and four chairs stood in the bay, replaced every Christmas with our ceiling-high tree. Two large closets, one for silver and the other for junk, were hidden in the paneling on the side of the room opposite the fireplace.

One of the many activities that took place in the library was the writing of the show. (This was early on—by the late 1940's Daddy and the writers, Sam Perrin, Milt Josefsberg, George Balzer and John Tackaberry, used an office in Beverly

Hills.) I remember coming home from school, grabbing some cookies, and quietly sneaking in to listen. I was always welcome and my laughter and comments were greeted positively, but I was certainly considered too young to contribute. I'm sure they were quite right. There they would be; one of the writers stretched out on the sofa, the others in various chairs, Jeanette, the secretary, furiously writing at the round table, and Daddy in, of course, the winged chair. I loved to hear them going over each sentence, each line; discussing whether it was funnier to emphasize this word or that word, whether a line should read "the" something or "that" something. The attention to detail, to fine points, was amazing. They all laughed a lot, but they were serious, too. Someone would come up with a great punch line and you would see a bunch of heads slowly, quietly nodding. Then one of them would say—almost grimly, "That's funny."

Let me digress. Some years later when I graduated grammar school I—and my parents—were honored when I was named class valedictorian, but along with that honor went the responsibility of delivering an address to the parents and class at the graduation ceremonies. I was terrified. My forte was math, not writing, and now I had to write a really important speech. So I had an idea. I would ask Daddy's writers to write it for me. And they did. The trouble was that I wanted portentous and serious, but they only knew how to be funny. The speech they presented to me was hilarious. It sounded like a Jack Benny monologue. I wish I had had the nerve to use it—it certainly had more pizzazz than the vapid, boring one I finally wrote myself.

Goodman Ace once said, "Jack Benny is like a Swiss watchmaker with a joke. Each word must be in its proper place. He takes a joke apart word for word, before putting it together. He may make one small alteration. When he does, you can be sure it will improve the joke.

"I'll give you an example of how methodical he is, of his craftsmanship. In 1963 Jack was about to open at the Ziegfeld Theatre. There was a newspaper strike in New York and all the papers had shut down. Many people, trying to keep up with foreign news, were reading *The Christian Science Monitor*. Anyway, Jack called me from Toronto and asked, 'Do you have a good newspaper strike joke?' I said I just happened to have one and I told him he could go out and say, 'I was reading *The Christian Science Monitor* today. The news is just as terrible, only you *think* it's better.' Jack laughed when he heard it. Then he said, 'Wait a minute.' He went and got a pencil and paper and wrote the joke down word for word as I had said it. He knows how important this is. I'll show you what I mean.

"I remember once I was down in Miami Beach at the Roney Plaza Hotel. Walter Winchell was staying there also. So was Jack Benny. One morning on the beach, Winchell and I got to talking and he said, 'You know Jack Benny very well, don't you?' And I said that I did. So Winchell asked me, 'Tell me, why does he always look so worried?' I said, 'I don't know, Mr. Winchell—maybe it's because he's afraid he'll drop all the way down to second place.' Well, Winchell wrote that down. I looked at his writing and he had left out 'all the way.' I urged him to put back this phrase, but he didn't so it came out 'he's afraid he'll drop down to second place.' Jack would have known that each word was important—and would have placed them properly in the sentence."

I no longer recall exactly the hows and whens of getting the show on the air, but fortunately George Balzer did when I asked him about the details of writing the show each week:

"When we went off the air on Sunday night, we had no idea of what we were going to do the following week. And we usually didn't settle on anything until Tuesday evening. We took Mondays off, and we really didn't work Tuesdays—although when you say you don't work, you're really working all the time. You're always thinking.

"Tuesday evenings we would start checking by phone—anyone have any thoughts or ideas? Then from those thoughts we would select what we thought had the best possibilities. Then we would get in touch with Jack and say, 'How about if we go to a department store to exchange a gift or something?' Jack usually said, 'Well . . . [pause] . . .

that could be something . . . [pause] . . . why don't you write it?' So on Wednesday and Thursday we would write the show. Two teams: Sam Perrin and I, and John Tackaberry with Milt Josefsberg. We each wrote one half. Early Thursday evening we called each other to find out how whoever wrote the first half ended—what line of dialogue—so that the team who wrote the second half knew how to pick it up.

"The script then went to the script girl [Jeanette] and she would make six copies. Friday mornings we all went to Jack's house at ten where we met in the library. We all had positions—chairs —and through the twenty-five years I worked for Jack, we never changed those positions. Even when we traveled, wrote in hotel rooms, we always sat in the same relative places—don't ask me why. More than once it happened that I would sit down in a chair and Tack would say, 'Hey, get up, you're sitting in my chair'—in a hotel room!

"Fridays, with your dad, we went over the script word by word, sentence by sentence, and cleaned it up. It then went to the studio for mimeographing, and Saturday mornings at ten we all, with the cast, met at the studio for the first reading, at which point we timed the show. We were usually from two to four minutes too long. After that first rehearsal, we (the writers) and Jack went into a conference room where we spent the next two or three hours—sometimes longer—again going over the script right from the top, word by word, shortening a line, putting in a new joke, cutting and refining.

"Sundays, again at ten, we'd meet for another reading, then go on mike—then in the afternoon a little more rehearsing, not much, and then we were set for air time, four o'clock to go east for seven o'clock."

Cleveland Amory once made the following computation of the division of time on a typical program:

"Benny delivers twenty-seven minutes and forty seconds of entertainment . . . two minutes and twenty seconds being taken up by individual station identification and by opening and closing commercials over which he has no control. Benny's time is further tailored by a middle commercial, which he does control, and by a Dennis Day song. Actual dialogue, with sound effects, usually runs about sixteen and a half minutes, and the 'spread' of the show—the time consumed by transitions and by studio, and presumably home, laughter—averages about seven minutes, usually including some thirty-five individual 'boffs' as they are called, or 'yocks.' "

George Balzer remembers some funny and endearing incidents while working on the show:

"He was unbelievable in this business for his attitude toward the show and his writers, for the performers. There was no one like him—he had complete respect for everybody. I never heard him say anything to anybody that might be overheard that could be embarrassing—never. He was easy to work with, always ready to listen and never insisted on doing anything if there was someone who didn't feel it was right.

"One time we had finished our reading on Saturday and were then working together in the conference room. We reached a page where Jack said, 'Fellas, I don't like this joke. I gotta have a new joke here.' . . . silence . . . 'What I need is something really good' . . . silence . . . 'something really funny, that will get a really huge laugh' . . . silence . . .

"Then I leaned over to him and said, 'We'll get you a new joke.'

"And he said, 'Oh, so you agree with me, huh?'

" 'No,' I said, 'but it's possible that the four of us could be wrong!'

"He looked at me, and then broke into a laugh, slid down off his chair, and sat there on the floor laughing. Then he got up, and said, 'I wouldn't change that joke now for a million dollars.'

"And he didn't. It went on the air as written, got a big laugh, and he looked up at us sitting in the control booth as if to say, 'You cocky SOBs!'

"Another time we were working in his bedroom—I think he had a cold. Anyway, he was reading our script when his bedroom door opened. There wasn't anyone there—it just opened all by itself. With the script in his hand, still reading, he got up, walked over to the door, shut it and without missing a beat, still reading, went back to bed. Now he's reading . . . reading . . . reading . . . again the door opens. Again he shuts it. This happens a third time. Finally, I went over to the door, unscrewed the plate, and with my pocket knife cut a sliver of wood off, screwed the plate back on, and returned to my seat. Jack continues reading, but now glances every so often at the door, which is no longer opening. Suddenly he stops, looks at me, and says, 'George, what did you do to that door?' So I described to him what I had done.

"He said, 'Well, how about that? I paid a lot of money for this house, and every night for the last year my door keeps opening and I keep on closing it.'

"So I said, 'Why didn't you call someone? The night watchman? The gardener? Anyone could have fixed it.'

"He said, 'I didn't want to bother anybody.' So there you are. There's the man."

In 1942 my parents celebrated their tenth anniversary on radio. Daddy did a special broadcast to commemorate the event, and I was allowed to be on the show, playing myself. It was my public debut and, needless to say, was very exciting. The show was recorded in the late afternoon in the library at home. Later in the evening at one of the local hotels NBC hosted a white tie gala for the cast, production crew and my parents' family and friends. I was considered too young to attend. That was okay—at least I could sit in Mom's dressing room to watch her get dressed. She wore a long white crepe skirt with a white and silver-sequined tunic top and white satin shoes. Her hair was swept up in a typical 1940's style pompadour, her jewels glittered, and I thought she looked more glamorous than any movie star.

When she had put on the finishing touches, Daddy, as handsome as she was beautiful, came in for her inspection wearing his white tie and tails. She adjusted his tie and straightened his pearl studs. I then accompanied them down the grand staircase, got a hug and kiss, and watched as they sailed out the front door to the waiting limousine.

Two or three times each year my parents went to New York. Dad always did a few of the radio shows from there. Those trips allowed him to have meetings with sponsors and network executives and to use different guest stars, the most memorable of whom was Fred Allen. If it didn't interfere with school, and sometimes even if it did, my governess, Miss Vallance, and I went along, too.

We took the *Santa Fe Chief*, never the *Super Chief*—Mom thought the *Super Chief* was too fast. (It left a few hours later and three days later arrived in Chicago a few hours earlier!) All transcontinental trains left from Union Station in downtown Los Angeles and forty-five minutes later stopped briefly in Pasadena. We always left from and came back to Pasadena. There was less commotion and it was less crowded. I loved Pasadena station because you could watch the train arriving. (At Union Station it was already there.) I would get as close to the tracks as I was allowed and wait to feel the vibration that signaled its approach. A minute or two later you could hear the sound of the clanging bell. Then this awesome monster came into view, giant wheels chugging and steam hissing as it slowly screeched to a halt. How exciting! A few years later the sleek diesel engines replaced the steam ones—less impressive, but prettier.

When the cast, writers, director and producer went along, we took one entire Pullman car just for the Benny show. Mother and Daddy each had their own drawing room. Mother always traveled with special pillows and linens. Miss V and I shared another. I slept in the upper berth because there was a window up there and I loved to watch the scenery, the little towns, and the engine up ahead as we snaked and curved our way through the Rockies. Best of all was the rush of sight and sound as one of the other Santa Fe streamliners passed, going in the opposite direction. The morning of the second day the train made its longest stop, a half hour, in Albuquerque, where the Indian vendors sold jewelry. I always managed to cajole Daddy into buying me a small turquoise ring or bracelet. Over those train years I developed a taste for Indian jewelry.

For two days and nights we ate our meals in the dining car—the food was terrific—stood outside on the observation platform watching the tracks disappear in the distance, talked and joked and played cards in the club car. Daddy loved gin rummy, and taught me to play at about the time I learned to talk. It wasn't long after that I got used to hearing him say to me, "Shut up and deal, Joanie!" I could riffle the cards and deal off the bottom of the deck by the time I was eight. After crossing the Mississippi about 5:00 A.M. of the third day, we arrived in late morning at the Dearborn Street station in Chicago. There, a line of taxis waited to transport our troupe to various destinations. Mother and Daddy and I always went directly to the Pump Room at the Ambassador East Hotel for lunch and then to Marshall Field for shopping. In the late afternoon another line of taxis pulled up to the LaSalle Street station where they disgorged our motley group. I can still see the jumble of passengers, red caps and luggage carts, everyone rushing down the platform to board the *Twentieth Century Limited* for the overnight trip to New York's Grand Central Station.

There was a period of time . . . I don't remember exactly when or for how long, when I appeared weekly on the radio shows. It must have been during my senior year in high school because I know I was living at home. Over the twenty-year run of the show Mother had become increasingly nervous and apprehensive about appearing in front of an audience. She had long since passed stage fright. Panic-stricken was more like it! You didn't have to hear what she said to know when she was nervous—you only had to look at her hands. Her palms would become fiery red. In 1950, after eighteen years on the show, she had reached a point of near hysteria. By noon on Sunday her hands looked as though they would burst into flame. She told Daddy she simply couldn't face it any longer.

I think he knew this would happen one day, but her statement came as a thunderbolt nonetheless. Fortunately, it occurred at a time when the switch to TV was imminent. Although he still needed Mary Livingstone because she was such an integral part of the radio show, perhaps on television he could develop a slightly different format and gradually write her out. So he made a deal with her—she would continue to do the radio shows for the next year, but he would work out a way for her not to have to go to the studio or perform in front of an audience. She could then do the TV shows as frequently or infrequently as she chose. But he reserved the right to renegotiate when the time came. (He never did.)

By that time the technology had reached a point so this plan was feasible. On Saturdays, recording equipment was brought to our house and Mother could read her lines, Daddy feeding her the cues. On Sundays I went to the studio in her place, read at the rehearsal and did the show. After Daddy explained to the studio audience how and why this was happening, I played Mother's part live— trying to imitate her voice, her timing, and, the most challenging: her easily recognized laugh. Of course when the show was aired, her voice had been spliced into the tape, so the listening audience heard the real Mary Livingstone and not me.

This was my first stab at professional performing, not like school plays and pageants with only parents and friends to watch. Okay, so in a way it was only pretend, but this was *The Jack Benny Show* and I was a part of it. Unlike Mother, I felt completely at ease with the audience. I enjoyed performing then, and still do. After the show, at the stage door, I was even asked for an autograph or two. Wow, I was a celebrity—for five minutes. I ate it up!

Of course the following day I returned to my normal routine of school and homework, and I was nobody once again. Until next Sunday.

CHAPTER 7

In the same way I recall the old train, I also remember the radio years with nostalgia. Television can never take its place. It seems somehow a shame that we can't have both—just a little opportunity to use our imagination once again. My father made the transition in the early 1950's gracefully and far more successfully than many others, but I always thought radio was truly his metier. And quite frankly, when I look at the old TV shows and listen to the old radio shows, radio holds up better. The radio shows seem less dated. Many of them are still as funny as they were forty years ago.

The vault where Carmichael the polar bear guarded Jack Benny's money was funnier in imagination than in reality. Hearing the echoing, hollow footsteps going down, down, the running water, the chains dragging. You could picture this dungeon-like place. Duplicating it visually didn't have the same impact. This was also true of the coughing and sputtering of the Maxwell, Jack Benny's ancient automobile. By the time the TV show began, Dennis Day was in his thirties and my mother, even though she didn't appear often, in her forties; yet they were supposed to be much younger. It didn't work as well. Also, over the years the audience had a mental image of what the cast looked like, and it was a shock to finally see them as they really were.

On the other hand, I must admit that most of it worked beautifully. Rochester, Don Wilson, Frank Nelson (the rude man who said, "Ooooo!") and Mel Blanc in his many roles did look, I think, as one imagined. The fact that so much of the radio show could be duplicated was the major reason for Dad's long and successful sojourn on TV.

I grew up on radio. I loved it. Although forbidden, I did my homework to it. I never missed *Suspense, The Whistler, Inner Sanctum, Mr. District Attorney* and more. I even hid a portable model under the covers so I could listen to *I Love a Mystery* after lights out. There has never been a mystery or suspense show on TV that could compare in creepy or frightening effects to those old radio shows. The sounds: footsteps, echoes, wind and thunderstorms, creaking doors—you felt as though you were there yourself in that haunted house, alone—in the dark with candles flickering—the big wooden front door slowly opens—some amorphous creature stealthily climbs the stairs . . . terrifying! On television that creature is just an actor with makeup. On radio he's real. Your imagination made it far more chilling and scary than the visual could ever do. Television is wonderful entertainment. But I still miss radio.

The real story of the radio days, those Sunday Nights at Seven, is Daddy's.

"Jell-O, folks, this is Jack Benny speaking," was my opening line as week after week I poked fun at Jell-O. Everybody loved it. Except the sponsor—at first.

From a rating of 22.9 we climbed to 35.3 in a few months. Jell-O was the talk of the country. It became so famous that from being only a trademark for a type of gelatin powder, it became the generic name for all gelatin desserts. The mountains of unsold Jell-O disappeared. Even the warehouses ran out of supplies. People liked it. They kept buying it. The more we kidded it, the more they bought. The Jell-O campaign was the greatest success story for radio as a selling medium.

By 1934 we had been on NBC for more than a year. By 1935 our show was in third place in the ratings. In 1936 it was second. In 1937 *The Jack*

Benny Show was first, where it remained for many years.

From the very beginning I was creating new characters and situations constantly. On one particular night we were going to do a bit with a seventeen-year-old girl from New Jersey who was the president of the Jack Benny Fan Club of Plainfield. We invented the name Mary Livingstone for this mythical girl. She was crazy about me. She would come on the show and read a poem that she wrote herself. It was a poem telling how much she loved me. Then she would reveal that as much as she adored me, her mother hated me!

The NBC casting department sent over a young actress who played little girls' voices. She wasn't bad as Mary Livingstone. She had sounded good at our first rehearsal, the line-reading rehearsal, but it was now time for the dress rehearsal and where was she? We called her apartment. We called the radio registry office. We couldn't get her. So my wife read Mary Livingstone's lines at dress. And when the actress still didn't show for the performance, my wife had to do the bit for the actual broadcast. She was simply fantastic. She did a smart bit of business. When she had a joke, she did a cute laugh before the line, then said the line and then did a cute laugh after the line.

We used the same character on the next show. Then we forgot about Mary Livingstone. But the listeners wouldn't let her go. Suddenly we were blitzed by an avalanche of letters:

"What happened to that adorable Mary Livingstone from Plainfield, N.J.? We *love* her."

"We miss the girl with the wonderful laugh."

"Why don't you put on that girl again—the one whose mother loathes Jack Benny?"

"Please bring back Mary Livingstone."

So we did and she remained on the show for over twenty years. And that's how my wife became a permanent part of the program and my fictional secretary. She went to court and had her name legally changed to Mary Livingstone and that's who she's been ever since. At first she played a dumb girl, but soon the character became sharper—in fact, sophisticated. She needled me constantly. She punctured my boasting. She saw through my little hypocrisies. Usually she would read a letter from her mother. And her delicious rippling silver laughter was always there.

Since I'm often asked about the characters and bits on my dad's radio show—what was real and what wasn't—let me interrupt for just a moment to clear up a few things. "Mary Livingstone came from Plainfield, New Jersey." False. Through the years, Plainfield became so firmly established as Mary's hometown that she often received fan mail from people saying they had known her in school there or that they were friends of her Livingstone family there. As you already know, though born in Seattle she grew up in Vancouver and her maiden name was Sadie Marks. She had never even been to Plainfield.

Another running character, although infrequently, was Mary's sister, Babe. True. Not only did my mother really have a sister named Babe, but my Aunt Babe played herself on the show. She reinforced the letters from her mother in putting down Jack. In real life, she was a great character, a real "babe"—one of Daddy's kind of women.

According to George Burns, Daddy and Babe had a short romance before he met my mother—that is, before Sadie "grew up." Maybe so—I only know that they were close and loving in-laws. She was the one he told his troubles to, the one he visited when he wanted to relax and let it all hang out. She served a similar role for me. She was a good listener, turned a sympathetic ear and had a wonderful, bawdy sense of humor. Daddy told her things he felt he couldn't tell my mother. I did the same.

The letters from Mary's mother told about the husband-hunting adventures of her sister, Babe; her father's problems; and her mother's own adventures. She had many strange jobs—for example, she was the leading bookmaker in Plainfield. Her slogan was: "We Pay Track Odds." Mother Livingstone never stopped despising me. She wished Mary would leave her job with me and get married. She wished Babe would get married. Babe was always getting engaged, but somehow her romances never blossomed into matrimony.

"My darling daughter Mary," she once wrote, "I hate to start this letter with bad news. I thought your father was on the wagon, but last week he lost his job as Santa Claus in the local department store. It seems he breathed on some kids, and their hair turned gray.

"However, am happy to say your sister Babe is engaged again. This time to a very nice man. He's working at the Acme Iron Company as a steam fitter. But Babe had to quit working. You see, the foreman at the Acme Iron Company won't allow husband and wife on the same job. They invited me to go with them to Niagara Falls on their honeymoon, but it was too expensive for three people. So Babe and I are going alone. The reason I'm so anxious to go back to Niagara Falls is because it will bring back those wonderful memories of 1912. Just think, Mary, NO OTHER WOMAN HAS GONE OVER IN A BARREL SINCE THEN."

Once there was an erroneous publicity story that I won a lot of money. Mary's mother wrote: "The whole family listened to Gabriel Heatter's program the other night and was so thrilled to hear about Jack winning all that money. Please send us the details as we didn't hear the finish of the program. The owner came back and made us get out of his car."

Once Mary went shopping with me when I was

returning a pair of shoelaces. I had bought them as a present for Don Wilson. I didn't know whether to get ones with plastic tips or metal tips and finally I had chosen metal tips, but Wilson didn't like metal tips. I went to the laces counter. A saleswoman came over. I asked for the man who had originally sold me the laces.

"Oh," she said, "you must mean my husband. He's in a sanatorium now."

"What happened?" I asked.

"Some awful person came in here to buy laces," she answered. She began crying. "He couldn't make up his mind whether he wanted plastic tips or metal tips. He drove my husband insane." She was sobbing. "All week my husband was lying in bed, staring at the ceiling, and screaming, 'Plastic tips, metal tips, plastic tips, metal tips.' Once he moaned, 'I've got rubber tips, too, but I won't tell him, I WON'T TELL HIM, I WON'T TELL HIM.' I'm sorry, sir, for breaking down like this. I hope you'll forgive me. Now what can I do for you?"

"Hmmmmm," I said.

"Go on," giggled Mary, "tell her."

"Please, Mary."

"Tell her, you coward."

"No," I said petulantly, "Don will just have to take the metal tips and *like it*. He's not going to drive people crazy over some ridiculous shoe-laces!"

Once in a while, Mary would get her lines scrambled. She wouldn't realize she'd done it and she got bigger laughs than with her unscrambled lines. Once we did a scene in a restaurant. Mary and I were giving our orders and all this was building up to a big joke and I had a great payoff line. I couldn't wait for my cue to say it. Mary had the last line of the buildup, which in this case was literally a feeder line. The line was, "I'll have a swiss cheese sandwich."

That's all. "I'll have a swiss cheese sandwich."

On the air, the waiter asked, "And what will you have, miss?"

She said, "I'll have a chiss sweeze sandwich."

The studio audience roared.

Mary couldn't understand it. She thought she had read the line correctly. Was she getting laughs with a straight line? And why?

I knew my big joke was ruined. I forgot it. From then on, I improvised. I repeated "chiss sweeze." Like I wasn't positive, but maybe chiss sweeze was a fancy food.

"What is a chiss sweeze sandwich?" I asked.

They roared louder.

Mary was getting mad. "I didn't say that, and you know it," she cried.

"You did too," I said.

The audience knew we were playing it on the level. We had thrown away the script. They loved it.

"I distinctly said chiss sweeze sandwich," she said—making the same mistake.

The rest of the program we just fooled around

with chiss and sweeze and I destroyed our carefully developed and rehearsed script, but I think our real dialogue was funnier than anything we could have prepared.

Once I did an opening monologue in which I sneered at the Academy Awards. (This was after my film, *The Horn Blows at Midnight*, had opened to terrible reviews.) I said comedy pictures never got Academy Awards. Why was it that dramatic movies always got an Oscar, I wanted to know? —"Yeah," I cracked, "about the only way to win an Academy Award is to make a picture with absolutely no laughs."

"Jack, your last one darn near made it," Mary was supposed to say.

What she did say was: "Your darn one last near made it."

Now there is a line that makes absolutely no sense. But the audience saw she hadn't deliberately twisted her tongue. They loved the mistake.

Another time she had the line: "I couldn't because my automobile was up on the grease rack."

Instead of "grease rack" she said "grass reek."

"My automobile was up on the grass reek." She looked baffled when the audience exploded.

You can never write a mistake joke and get laughs. You can't rehearse it. You can't plan it. It's got to be spontaneous. It's got to be unexpected. It's got to be true.

The following week we did a show from Palm Springs and we opened with my bawling Mary out for her mispronunciation of grease rack. During the first twenty minutes, I didn't miss a chance to remind her, "Mary, the word is grease rack. It couldn't possibly be anything else. In fact, there is no such expression as grass reek." I harped on this, and every time I harped, I got a laugh.

Our guest star that week was the Palm Springs chief of police—the authentic one. We did a routine around his experiences as a crime sleuth. Then I asked him whether he had recently had any unusual emergency calls.

"As a matter of fact," he replied, "I had one only last evening. I went out on a call. There were two skunks fighting on somebody's front lawn."

"Two skunks fighting on somebody's front lawn?" I said.

"Yeah, Jack, and let me tell you—did that grass *reek!*"

Now Mary turned on me. How ignorant I had been all along.

I had to make a coast-to-coast apology for being so ignorant as not to know there could be an expression "grass reek."

By our second year we'd evolved a loose framework for the show. We had three "spots." The opening spot was hung on a topic, sometimes a seasonal topic like Christmas. The second spot would be about the casting of the sketch, if we had a sketch. Then we had the satiric commercial and the tenor sang his solo. Then in the closing spot we did the sketch—usually with a well-known guest star.

Our sketches were the first real satires in radio. We did takeoffs of best-selling novels, hit plays and the new motion pictures. Our very first one was a travesty of the scene in the MGM movie *Grand Hotel* (which we called *Grind Hotel*) where Lionel Barrymore, playing Baron Geigern, makes love to the aging ballerina, Grusinskaya, played by Garbo. The scene opened with sound effects of knocking on a door.

"Who's there?" the dancer asked.

"It's me—the Baron."

"Baron von who?" she asked.

"Baron von two three . . ." I said.

"Four five six . . ." she added.

"Seven eight nine . . ." I said.

"Oh, do come in, my dear Baron."

Grind Hotel went over so well that we repeated it a few months later by popular demand. We changed the opening.

"Who is it please?" the dancer asked.

"It's me—the Baron."

"Which Baron?"

"The one from Wilkes-BARRON, Pennsylvania."

"Oh, that one—come in then, dear Baron."

It was also in the show's second year when my character as Jack the Miser was being built up. I was sick in bed and Mary came visiting.

"Mary, will you take my temperature? You'll

find the thermometer over there on the night table."

"Where?" she said. "Oh, I see it. Well, gee, I'll try—but I don't know— Now open your mouth."

"Aaaaah," I said.

"Wider," she ordered.

"Aaaaaaaaaaaaaaaah."

She paused. "Well, Jack," she said, "I'm afraid it just won't go in your mouth."

"Are you sure?" I asked.

"Not unless I tear the thermometer off the calendar," she said.

The belief in Jack Benny, all-American Miser, was so widely implanted in the public that once the following advertisement appeared in the classified section of a Sacramento paper:

Two women, about Jack Benny's age, would like small unfurnished house. Would like to pay what Benny would like to pay.

One summer I played the Oakdale Music Tent in Wallingford, Connecticut. I was living at the Yale Motor Inn, which is right off the parkway near Exit 66. The assistant stage director of the Oakdale Music Tent came to the inn to give me driving directions to the theater the first time I went over. He got in the car. I was at the wheel.

"Now, Mr. Benny," he said, "the simplest way of getting there, you see, would be to get right back on the parkway at Exit 66, and then you drive until Exit 64 and you're right at the Music Tent."

"Sounds nice and easy, son," I said, revving up the motor and pulling the lever into drive.

He coughed nervously. "But there's one thing I better mention."

"What's that, son?" I asked, smiling. "Be glad to give you an autograph anytime at all."

"Well, thanks, but what I wanted to tell you is that about one mile down the parkway there's a toll booth." He hesitated like he was going to break the bad news and hated to do it. "It's a fifteen-cent toll, Mr. Benny. But I could show you a route where you drive down some of these side roads so you don't get on the parkway and have to pay that fifteen-cent toll."

"I appreciate that, son," I replied, "but I think with my reputation I better pay the toll."

When Mary and I saw *Sunrise at Campobello*, we went out into the lobby at intermission. As I was smoking a cigar, I noticed a newly minted penny shining on the floor. I showed it to Mary.

"Pick it up, Jack," she said, "it's good luck."

I shook my head. "I should stoop to pick up a penny in front of so many people, Mary? I wouldn't do that for a million dollars."

Sometimes, when I get exhausted from overwork and crave a rest, I check into Cedars of Lebanon Hospital to get away from it all. I find hospitals relaxing. Naturally, I knew most of the nurses, but this time there was a new nurse who came to my room as soon as I was ensconced.

She handed me an empty bottle. "We'll be wanting a specimen of your urine, Mr. Benny," she said briskly.

"But that won't be necessary," I said. "There's nothing the matter with me except nervous exhaustion."

"I have to have it," she said firmly.

"I didn't know that, nurse. You see, I went already, just a few minutes ago."

"Never mind the excuses, Mr. Benny. Just do the best you can."

When she came back for the specimen and saw the small amount of liquid, she looked at me with a withering glance and then, giving the line a perfect reading, she said, "You never give *anything* away—do you?"

A few years ago I gave a concert with the San Francisco Symphony Orchestra. The head of the committee arranged to drive me to the airport the next morning. I checked out of the Fairmont Hotel and waited for him in the lobby with all my bags. Suddenly I felt nature's call. I went into the lobby washroom and, as they say, washed my hands. The man arrived. We began driving. Feeling for a cigar in my inside pocket, I realized my checkbook was missing. The checkbook had some important messages in it. Did we have time to go back and not miss the plane? The chairman said I had about ten, fifteen minutes to spare. Back we went. First I went to the room and ransacked it. No checkbook. What about the men's room? I hustled down to the lobby. Maybe it fell out of my coat? Maybe it was still there? I kneeled down at the booth I had occupied and sure enough, there it was, lying on the tiled floor. I stretched my hand under the door. The damned thing was just out of reach. The toilet was one of those greedy operations in which you have to put a dime in a slot to turn the knob and enter. I searched my pockets. No dimes! I didn't want to miss the plane. If I went up to the lobby and changed a quarter at the cashier's, I would surely miss the plane.

What the hell, I thought, *nobody's around—I'll crawl under the door.*

I bent down and crouched and began sliding under the door. I was just squeezing my head under when I heard footsteps. I yanked my head out. I looked up, still on the floor. There was a great fat man, staring at me.

Then he recognized my face. And he believed what he saw. He thought I was trying to sneak under and get a free bowel movement. He had the silliest smile on his fat face.

Some people know I'm not a miser. These are the professional confidence men who specialize in begging letters. We had some seventy-five letters a month from such characters. I remember one from a party who described himself as a farmer. His wife helped out with their little farming enterprise in Iowa. They asked me for a loan of $50,000 with which to buy tractors—a lot of tractors. They wanted to mechanize their farm. To prove they were using the money for this legitimate purpose, the farmer proposed sending me pictures of the tractors. Meanwhile, he enclosed snapshots of himself and his wife in dungarees plus several sad pictures of the old-fashioned and sickly-looking horses which were all they had to pull their plows and harrows and threshers.

I mentioned this letter to George Burns. And, would you believe it, he had received the same letter from the same couple with the same pictures of the tired horses?

I asked him, "What do you think we ought to do about this?"

"Well, they seem like a nice couple."

"Yes, and agriculture is the backbone of our country."

"And not only that, Jack, but it's farmers like these who are helping to feed the starving millions in the underdeveloped countries, so I think as long as they're willing to send us pictures of the tractors, we should send them pictures of two checks, one from me and one from you, each for $50,000."

Usually, you don't answer such letters because begging letters are written by professional moochers who con enough suckers to get by. But one I couldn't resist answering. It was from a man in Utica, New York. His demands were reasonable. He only wanted to borrow $10,000—a mere bagatelle. He started his letter "Dear Sir," not even "Dear Mr. Benny." Some beggars pretend to love your program and say they have long been your greatest fan, but this one didn't waste time on the amenities. He got right down to business. He was a garage mechanic. But he had loftier aspirations. There was a flying school in Houston, Texas. If I sent him $10,000, he could go to this school and become a pilot. He added:

I do not know when I can pay you back, but will remit payment as soon as am earning large salary flying for Pan American or TWA. I am known around Utica as a man of good character, do not drink or smoke or fool around with wimmen, go to church, pay bills promptly, have never been in debt. You will be proud of me someday.

Yours for aviation,
Orville Smikely

I replied:

Dear Mr. Smikely,
    I received your letter and noted its contents. I immediately fired my four writers because evidently my character isn't coming through to you.

In my opinion (which I value highly) the finest joke I ever did on radio was this one. Walking home at night. Sound effects of my footsteps.

Then somebody else's footsteps—behind me. Holdup man shoves a gun in my ribs.

He snarls, "Your money or your life."

There was a pause while I mulled over the question.

He got impatient. "Come on, hurry up," he says.

"I'm thinking it over," I reply, obviously burned up by this thief's haste.

This line clocked over two minutes of laughter. It built and built—stopped—and went on again. On a thirty-minute comedy show, this spread is as carefully budgeted as the salaries of performers.

Two of the four writers (Milt Josefsberg and John Tackaberry) I mentioned in my letter to the would-be aviator wrote this gag: They were working on a transition in which I am going from Ronald Colman's house to my house on foot. Josefsberg thought it would be interesting to have my promenade interrupted by a robber.

(I have always looked for good "butt-ins" or "interruptions" to lend variety or the unexpected to a scene.)

Josefsberg said, "John, I think I got a funny thief line. There's this holdup man, with a gun, and he says to Jack, 'Your money or your life.' But I can't come up with a funny answer."

"Neither can I," replied Tackaberry.

Josefsberg began repeating the feeder line over and over: "Your money or your life. Your money or your life. Your money—"

"Stop nagging," yelled Tackaberry. "I'M THINKING IT OVER."

Josefsberg pounded his partner on the back and said, "That is the best line you ever wrote in your life!"

"What line?" Tackaberry asked.

When I read the scene I felt it would play for a good solid laugh. Perhaps one of a comedian's hardest jobs is to recognize when the material is good and to be able to anticipate the reaction of his audience. Of course, it's just as hard to know how to play so that the lines are not ruined in performance. Playing comedy is often as delicate an operation as taking apart the springs and wheels and levers of a fine Swiss watch—and putting them together again.

Usually I don't rush a good punch line. At rehearsals I told Eddie Maher, who was playing the crook, that after he said "Your money or your life" he was to wait and wait. He was not even to move. He was not to react with a facial expression to whatever I did or the audience did. (We played to a studio audience and I had to consider their reaction.)

"Now, Eddie," I said, "when you feed me the straight line and I do a take and stare at the studio audience, I think I'll be able to make them laugh as long as I want. I think I could keep them laughing for hours. But you have to keep a straight face like you don't hear them. And don't say your next line until I touch the lobe of my left ear."

I demonstrated the lobe cue I'd give him.

When I did this during the broadcast, he gave me the next line, about hurrying up and then I came in with the joke . . .

Though this is my masterpiece of stingy jokes, there were many others that I liked.

Rochester is sharpening a pencil. "Roch," I request, "would you mind sharpening that in the fireplace?"

Rochester is baking a cake. "Boss," he calls out from the kitchen, "we're fresh out of flour."

"I'll go over to the Colmans' and borrow a cup," I said. (Benita and Ronald Colman played my next-door neighbors.) You hear me getting a cup, leaving the house, walking across, then clink-clink, coins dropping in the cup. "Thank you," I say gratefully and continue walking. You hear a bicycle. A Western Union messenger hands me a telegram. You hear a bill crackling.

"Oh boy, a dollar, gee thanks a lot, Mr. Benny," the messenger says. He returns a few seconds later. "Oh, Mr. Benny, I forgot my bicycle."

"You didn't forget it—I BOUGHT IT . . . I sure hate people who make deals and don't stick by them."

On one television show, I am serving dinner to a young man who is courting my daughter. All I know about him is that his father is connected with the banking business. You can see me piling the roast beef high on his plate. "So your father works for a bank," I say pleasantly.

"Yes, Mr. Benny, he's the janitor."

The camera moves in for a close-up of my hands. You see me taking away all the meat except one mingy slice from the young man's plate.

Driving home from the country club, I look morose. "Rochester?"

"Yes, boss."

"Maybe we ought to go back to that golf course and look for my ball some more."

"We ain't never gonna find it. Why don't you give up?"

"Give up? Give up? Rochester, suppose Columbus gave up? He never would have discovered America. Then what would have happened?"

"We'd be looking for that ball in Spain, boss."

My French violin teacher observes: "Monsieur Benny, you 'aven't pay me for your violin lesson today."

"Ah, yes, how thoughtless of me, professor. Have a chair."

"I had a chair last time. Today I want the money."

Mary and I are dining with Gloria and Jimmy Stewart. The waiter brings the check. "I'll take it," I say reluctantly.

"Oh, no," Jimmy says, "I'll take it."

"I couldn't let you do that, Jimmy."

"I'd feel better if I paid the check."

"Oh, well, Jimmy, if your health is involved . . ."

"I don't know what to give Rochester for Christmas," I wonder. "What do you give a man who's got nothing?"

One Christmas, Rochester was shopping for a tie to give me. "Here is one," the salesman said. "It might be a little too plain for your employer, though. Is he a young man?"

"No," said Rochester.

"Is he middle-aged?"

"No."

"Is he elderly?"

"Wrap it up!"

The following Christmas, Rochester decided to give me cuff links. "What type of man is your boss?" the salesman asked.

"Well, he's medium tall, medium weight and rather conservative."

"By conservative, do you mean he's penurious?"

"Well . . ."

"Parsimonious?"

"Well . . ."

"Frugal?"

"Well . . ."

"Thrifty?"

"You're headed in the right direction, but there's a *long, long trail a-winding.*"

"Boss," Rochester once said apropos one of my more extreme avaricious acts, "you can't take it with you."

"If I can't take it with me, I won't go."

At Caesars Palace, Las Vegas, I explained that I wanted to see my doctor before playing this engagement and he checked me over and said it was not advisable for a man of my years to go on tour. "Why do you work so hard, Mr. Benny, surely it can't be the money?" the doctor asked me.

I fold my arms and look at the audience awhile. I take them into my confidence. "Now there," I say, "is a man who is a brilliant surgeon—but the minute he takes off his rubber gloves he's an idiot."

On one television program, you saw me wheeling a cart in the supermarket. As I'm sauntering along the aisles, I see a display of an enormous and taste-tempting chocolate layer cake. Above it a sign says FREE. It's on a big table, there's a knife and fork and you're supposed to cut yourself a little slice. The display is a form of advertising for a new cake mix. I stop and look over the cake. I look at the sign. Then I pick up the entire cake and gently place it in the cart. I wheel down the aisle. Then I stop. I push the cart back to the display table.

Have I been conscience stricken?

Am I going to return the cake?

No, sir. I return for the knife and fork . . .

The vault, where I stored my hoard of money, had one of the best sound effects in radio. It was located deep in the subbasement of my house. This was where Carmichael resided.

(Carmichael was a gift from an Alaskan admirer. He came one day in a wooden crate. He was a big, white, ferocious, man-eating polar bear, so I had to keep him in the basement. Rochester was afraid of him. One day an inspector from the gas company went down to read the meter and was never heard from again. After that whenever I told Rochester to go down and feed Carmichael, he would reply, "I don't want to go down there. What happened to the gas man?" So we had to throw chunks of raw meat down to satisfy Carmichael's appetite.)

Can you imagine? I've actually been asked whether we kept a polar bear in our basement. Over the years 1002 North Roxbury was home to a variety of animals: dogs, birds, rabbits, turtles, goldfish and even a duck, but never a polar bear. Carmichael's growl (he never actually said anything) was the voice of the versatile, incomparable Mel Blanc.

Below Carmichael was where I had the burglarproof vault. (No, that wasn't true either. We didn't even have a wall safe.)

One of the miracles of radio was its power to suggest anything by ingeniously using sound effects. With a few noises, your imagination would paint the whole picture. When I had to go down to the vault, you heard my descent, step by step. You heard steps, steps, steps, steps. Then the steps ceased and the audience knew I was resting. Then the steps, steps, steps, steps continued downward. You heard chains clanking, whistles screaming, bells ringing, tumblers turning, iron doors groaning . . .

I employed a man who had been down in the vault for many years. He was the guardian of the vault. He never came up. During my visits we had many conversations. He was rather like the 2,000 Year Old Man played by Mel Brooks. My little old vault guardian remembered Abraham Lincoln and the Civil War, Andrew Jackson and the War of 1812, George Washington and the Revolutionary War. On his birthday, I always brought him a little token of my esteem. Once I brought him a kite for his birthday.

"Thank you," he piped in his cracked voice, "I always wanted a kite."

Can you imagine—bringing a kite to a little old man down in the depths of that vault?

When we went into television, many thought we would never be able to project the drama of the vault when it was actually shown. We did have to be a little more outrageous. There was one sketch in which a government man calls on me. He works for the Treasury Department. He's in charge of security at Fort Knox. He followed me down the steps to the dungeon. There was a moat with alligators swimming around. On the other side was a huge plant with floppy leaves. I pressed a secret button and a drawbridge was lowered. We crossed over.

Then the Treasury man asked, "But what would happen if a burglar got this far?"

A guillotine came down and almost whacked off his head.

"But just suppose," he asked nervously, "it was a gang and they put the guillotine out of order?"

Suddenly the plant started moving and two branches came out and clutched the T-man around the neck. They started choking him. It was a carnivorous plant, a monster-size Venus's-flytrap. Just when the man was beginning to turn purple, I said to the plant, "All right, Irving, that's enough—this is just a demonstration."

No other phase of my image has the longevity and the laugh-arousing power of the stinginess. It makes no difference whether I'm playing to a sophisticated audience in Las Vegas or to an old audience or a young audience. I've wondered what it is about a miser that they find so humorous. I used to get tired of stingy jokes—in fact, of any gag we kept doing too much. I'd sometimes complain to the writers that they were getting into a rut. I'd say, "Let's cut out these tired jokes about the Maxwell, being thirty-nine, wearing a toupee, the lousy violin playing and for heaven's sake, guys, enough with the stingy jokes."

I found we could get away with leaving out Phil Harris, Rochester, the fiddle, the Maxwell, Mary Livingstone—but the listeners wanted stingy jokes. So I tried rationing them. I wouldn't allow more than one stingy joke a program. I couldn't control other comedians, however. They kept on making Jack Benny stingy jokes. When my daughter got married, Bob Hope said, "The reason Jack Benny is looking so sad these days is that he's not only losing a daughter—but losing a deduction too."

When I was nominated as honorary chairman of a March of Dimes campaign one year, Fred Allen sneered: "The dime hasn't been minted that could march past Jack Benny."

Once I got so sick and tired of being a miser on the show that I told the writers: "Fellers—no more stingy jokes for two months. They're out. I've had it up to here. Let's figure out a twist where for a change I get laughs with kindness, being generous, giving away money, saying—"

"But Jack," they interrupted me, all together.

"No buts about it, fellers. I've made up my mind." I spat my cigar butt into a wastebasket to show them I was tough. "That's the way I want it, see? And that's the way it's gonna be."

So we framed up a sequence in which I'm seen taking inventory in my kitchen. A large economy-size can of tomato juice falls on my head and knocks me out. It does something to my brain cells so when I recover consciousness I become a spendthrift. We planned to sustain this situation for eight weeks. It didn't even last three weeks! The writers couldn't write a generous Jack Benny. I couldn't play the lines they wrote. I didn't believe it myself. I couldn't go against everything I had built up for thirty years. The second week of this running gag I had another brain concussion.

Since then I have resigned myself to being a hard man with a dollar.

Every now and then I find myself unconsciously becoming the character I'm playing. There's a street in Beverly Hills—Camden Drive. The part of Camden Drive between Santa Monica and Wilshire Boulevard is a business area with many shops and office buildings. The parking spaces there are diagonal and the meters charge ten cents for thirty minutes as opposed to a one-dollar minimum in the parking lots. Now it is damn near impossible to find an unoccupied space on Camden. I know because I always take it coming home from the Hillcrest Country Club. Well, one afternoon I was cruising up Camden Drive on my way home when I suddenly saw a Jaguar convertible pulling out. I got into position and waited until the space was clear. Then, with a feeling of triumph, I whipped into the space. Not only had I found a parking place, but there was still twenty minutes on the meter! I sure felt good.

I got out of my car, looked around and suddenly realized people were staring at me. I knew they were thinking, "That Jack Benny, isn't he something? To be so happy about some free time on a meter." Then I realized something else. I had absolutely no reason to park! I was on my way home—I didn't have to see anybody in the neighborhood, I had no errands. Had the imaginary spirit of Benny, the Pinchpenny, taken over? It was a disquieting thought.

With people still staring at me, I couldn't just get back into my car and drive home. I noticed a tobacconist's store up the block, so I went in and bought twenty-five Upmann Perfectos.

As I laid the luxuriously wrapped package of cigars on the seat, I congratulated myself. I smiled at my cleverness. I had outwitted the passersby, I had found a free parking space on Camden Drive and I hadn't let myself be intimidated into driving away. "Not bad, not bad at all, Jack," I said to myself.

Then I remembered something. I had given up smoking last week!

Could it be that the love of money, the urge to get it and the instinct for hoarding what we've acquired is basic to people? I think it is. I think that at heart we are all as prudent and parsimonious as the imaginary "Jack Benny." Most of us would be as stingy as "me" if we had the courage. We're ashamed to show how much we value every nickel and dime of the money that we've had to work for, scrounge for, suffer for. The stingiest people I've known have been wealthy persons who inherited their wealth. They know they're filthy rich. They don't have to impress strangers by throwing their money around with reckless abandon. I've seen multimillionaires study a restaurant bill. They add up every item. They confirm the total. Then they compute *to the penny* 15 percent of the sum and leave that for the tip. The same tycoon might buy a painting for $150,000—but he wouldn't think he was being reckless because in his mind the painting is worth $200,000.

Even when I'm generous—*especially* when I'm generous—I almost feel guilty about it. Having lunch with Edgar Bergen at the Brown Derby, I demanded the check. The waiter did the usual silly take I've come to expect. He said, "Mr. Benny, I'm surprised to hear you ask for the check."

"So am I," I said, "and that's the last time I'll ever eat with a ventriloquist."

CHAPTER 8

Before we get to Rochester, let me clear up another character—the most important one: Daddy. In real life he wasn't cheap, not ever in any way, shape or form! That portrayal was a total myth. It's amazing to me that so many people believed it to be the truth. Even today I am still asked if he was really cheap. Did the public think Lou Costello was really dumb and zany or that Fanny Brice (Baby Snooks) was really a child?

Radie Harris, a longtime friend of the family, recently told me two typical stories. She was once in London at the same time as Daddy:

"Jack had just passed through the lobby of the Dorchester Hotel. I was standing off to the side and overheard a woman talking to her friend, 'But he's so cheap—do you think he's really staying here?'

"Then we were in a restaurant, about to have dessert. Jack had brought his special cookies—he was on a diabetic diet so he carried his sugarless sweets with him. When the waiter served the rest of us Jack reached in his pocket and brought out his foil-wrapped cookie. From the next table we heard, 'Boy, he really is tight—he won't even pay for dessert!' "

A friend of mine, Leah Superstein, who through our friendship also knew my parents, remembers an anniversary party that Daddy once gave at Chasen's. Her husband, Larry, noticed that when the check was presented, Daddy gave it back to the waiter and said, "Put whatever you want on it." Larry said, "Don't you feel uneasy about that?" He said, "No—whatever they put on is less than they would expect me to give. If I sign the bill, no matter what I do, it's not enough—if they sign the bill, whatever they put on is fine with me and they're happy and I'm happy."

He was certainly never cheap with my mother or me. Nor with anyone else for that matter. Mother tended toward extravagance—and that's perhaps the understatement of all time! Daddy indulged her almost every whim. She had gorgeous jewelry and closets crammed with furs, designer clothes, shoes (she was the Imelda of her day), bags and accessories. Whenever he went on a trip, even for just a couple of days, he brought her a gift—and one for me, too. Some were lovely, some were silly trinkets. I remember once he brought me six muumuus from Hawaii. He said he couldn't decide which I would like so he took them all! I had souvenirs from Australia to Africa to Podunk.

Nor did he forget birthdays, anniversaries, Valentine's Day (which was his own birthday), Easter or any other excuse to buy a gift. I can't imagine a man more generous and thoughtful than my father.

His material generosity was matched and maybe even bettered by his professional generosity. My favorite and certainly the most definitive story was told to me by Abbe Lane:

"My fondest recollection of him was when we were going to do our first date together at a theater-in-the-round just outside of Houston. My husband, Perry, was with me, Irving was with Jack, and we drove in a limousine from the airport to the theater. I have to preface this: I've worked with every major comedian, great and not so great, and most of them are seriously insane. I mean a lot of them belong in a home. They're funny, but there's something strange that separates the person they are backstage from the person on the stage.

"In my contract it says '100 percent billing,' referring to the size of the letters on the marquee, but of course with a man like Jack Benny his name comes first—and why not? Anyway, we drove up to the theater. The marquee read 'The Jack Benny Show' in 100 percent and underneath in, I would say, 75 percent it said, 'and starring Abbe Lane.' So Jack looked up at the marquee and said, 'Oh no, no, no, that will never do.' Perry looked at me and I looked at him with expressions that said, 'Oh my God, here's your idol, and the same thing is happening to you that happens with all the other comics you've worked with. He's going to want your name in smaller type. What a disappointment.'

"The second line out of Jack's mouth was, 'I want this changed. I want it to read "The Jack Benny and Abbe Lane Show." ' I almost fainted. I didn't even want that—but it was an insight into the man.

"Now I knew I was dealing with a secure human being. He didn't care about the billing. His name could have been in three-inch letters. It didn't matter, because the audience decides what's important. Jack Benny was Jack Benny—the billing was trivial.

"Opening night came. I did the first half, then came intermission, and your dad did the second half. I always do a little patter between songs, and since we were in Texas, I had worked up a short bit about shopping at Neiman-Marcus. I finished my act, and after intermission Jack came on, and I listened to him over my dressing room speaker. About five minutes into his act I heard him doing stuff about Neiman-Marcus. 'Oh my God, I should have never done this, but I didn't know, I hadn't heard what he was going to do.' After the show I went to his dressing room and said, 'Jack, I just feel awful, because if I make any reference to Neiman-Marcus, it's going to take the edge off what you do.'

"He said, 'Don't be silly. I have lots of other things that I could say, so you do it.' And then he improved on what I had to say. I can't think of another performer in the world who would do that. It was the most wonderful engagement. I felt that I had finally arrived and was working with the best of the best."

Most of the radio stars, except Fred Allen, moved out to Hollywood around the same time we did. We rented homes first, then built our own homes, joined country clubs and became hopeless golfers. Some of us, like Hope and Crosby, became movie stars. Mary and I moved baby and baggage to Los Angeles, not only because we liked the climate and thought sunshine was healthy, but because studio facilities were better and movie stars were available for guest appearances and all of us were deluged with movie bids. Suddenly radio personalities were in heavy demand at the studios.

I made pictures for MGM, Paramount, 20th Century-Fox and Warners. I made movies with radio broadcasting as the theme, like *The Big Broadcast of 1937*. I made such B pictures as *Man About Town, The Meanest Man in the World, Love Thy Neighbor, Artists and Models Abroad* and *Buck Benny Rides Again*. I made such A pictures as *Charley's Aunt, George Washington Slept Here* and *To Be or Not to Be*. I also made *The Horn Blows at Midnight*. This was neither an A picture nor a B picture. There is no known alphabetical letter under which you can classify *The Horn Blows at Midnight*.

Our first radio program in Hollywood was a show describing my trials and tribulations in moving from New York. One scene took place on the *Santa Fe Chief*. My new writers, Ed Beloin and Bill Morrow, wrote the character of a Pullman porter. He was a traditional Negro dialect stereotype. He had a molasses drawl and he *yassuh-bossed* me all over the place. He was such a drawling, lazy, superstitious stereotype that even the original Uncle Tom would have despised him. However, in those days we were not aware of these racial aspects of comedy. I hired Benny Rubin to play

153

this porter. Usually Rubin played all the dialects on the show. In vaudeville, Rubin had been famous for his Jewish dialect routines, but he never played Jewish characters for me. I used Sam Hearn, Patsy Flick and Artie Auerbach for Jewish characters. Rubin played black characters as well as German, Italian and Irish bits. He was also strong on gangster dialect.

So here was Benny Rubin playing a black porter and he sounded as good as Bert Williams. Only he didn't look like Bert Williams. Not only did he have a white face, he had a very *pale* white face with a long hooked nose. Whenever he said, "Yassuh, Boss," during rehearsal, I went into one of those spasms of hysteria in which I pound tables and roll on the floor.

Then Morrow said, "Jack, the studio audience will not laugh at a white man playing a Negro. Rubin is fine, but it won't work here. We won't get our laughs and we need our laughs in the studio to get the timing right."

"So Rubin can put on blackface," I said.

Morrow shook his head. "Benny Rubin can put on six layers of burnt cork—but with his nose and mannerisms he'll still look as Jewish as Willie Howard. We have to hire a Negro actor."

We hurriedly sent out a call for black character actors. Five came to our audition. They had played in nightclubs and on the black vaudeville circuits and some had done bits in movies. We heard all of them and the one we hired for the scene was the least impressive in the reading—

but he had a deep husky growl in his voice and his words came up through his larynx like there was a pile of gravel down there. Once during the reading he modulated into a high-pitched squeal that was marvelous. It sounded like "Hee, hee, HEEEEE."

His name was Eddie Anderson. He had worked in a two act with his brother in vaudeville. He played Noah in the movie version of Marc Connelly's play, *The Green Pastures*. He got this permanent laryngitis when he was a little boy in San Francisco. He had to support his family by selling newspapers and he had to shout louder than the other boys because he had to sell more newspapers than they did. He ruined his voice forever—or so he thought. But then he became the highest-paid black performer until Sidney Poitier came along and Anderson wouldn't sell you his hoarseness for a million dollars.

We put him on for just the one program. He got $75 for two or three minutes. It was a transition sequence. He was supposed to be a regular porter on the *Santa Fe* run from Chicago to Los Angeles, which goes through Des Moines, Kansas City, Albuquerque and many other places. Whenever I mentioned Albuquerque he wouldn't believe there was such a town. He had never heard of Albuquerque even though he had worked this route for years and there was a thirty-minute stop there for passengers to walk around and stretch their legs, see real Indians and purchase Indian souvenirs from the real Indians.

Whenever I'd ask him, "Porter, what time do we arrive in Albuquerque?" he let out his squeal and growled, "There you goes agin, boss, with dis yeah Albee Kerkee. Now you know there ain't no sich place, boss."

On this first program he was sensational.

About five weeks later we did another Pullman porter scene, mainly because we wanted to use him again. Then we decided to make him a permanent part of our little family. We converted him into my butler.

Within two years, he was making $150,000 a year and lived in a gorgeous mansion with his charming wife, Maymie, and his family. He diverted himself with such hobbies as raising thoroughbred horses. One of them ran in the 1945 Kentucky Derby. Another one of his pastimes was road racing in custom-built sports cars.

Now I don't blame a stranger in a washroom who sees me crouching under the door of a pay toilet for thinking I'm miserly—but how do you figure this? Twenty years ago a Cleveland lawyer wrote to me on his legal stationery. He stated it was outrageous that a man in my income bracket should pay a servant the measly stipend I was paying Rochester. (Imagine! Here is an educated and intelligent man, an attorney-at-law, and he thought that Eddie Anderson, the well-known Negro actor playing Rochester, was *actually* my valet, butler, cook and chauffeur.) It was bad enough that I underpaid him, said the lawyer, but to be weeks behind in what I owed him was disgusting. I ignored the letter. I even thought, maybe the man has a sense of humor and this is irony. I was wrong. He was dead serious. In subsequent letters he accused me of being a reactionary, an enemy of poor people and a racial bigot. Then he had the nerve to write Rochester a letter. This got me so mad that I answered the lawyer:

I have received your many ridiculous letters regarding Rochester. You write that you do not like the way I treat him and the salary I pay him. I would like to know if you see any humor in my treating him with consideration and sweetness? (By the way, Mrs. Benny and I have eight servants and none of them is Rochester. All of our help has remained with us for more than ten years—which is some indication that I treat my employees well.)

I would also like to say, though I'm taking a gamble on this as I do not know your income, but I'll bet you that Rochester in a week earns what you earn in a month, or even more. He gets a tremendous salary. If I told you how much you wouldn't believe it. Well, I'll tell you anyway and you won't believe it. He receives $1,600 per week, regardless of whether or not he appears on my program. As you may have noticed on some of our shows there is no "spot" (as we call it in radio) for Rochester, or Mr. Anderson, to give him his right name. Mr. Anderson is a fine professional actor. For your information, "Rochester" lives in a ten-room house, he has two servants serving him, he *has three cars, a stable of horses and is now in the market for a cabin cruiser. I will thank you not to write me any more of your foolish letters. Thank you.*

Why doesn't a lawyer have the brains to figure out that if I were really such a stingy bastard, would I broadcast it to the whole world? Sometimes you feel you're just not getting through to some people. You think you're playing comedy and then you learn that some people think it's true life documentary.

To show you how I exploited this man, he once had a custom-built sports racing car model built to his own design. It cost $20,000. It was a sleek, white, low-slung automobile. It was a real beauty. I never had a car that great. It was able to go over three hundred miles an hour—without even breathing hard. Around 1951 it won a prize at the Chicago Sports Car Show. They interviewed Rochester when he won the prize. He was asked what he was going to do with this car.

"Well," he said, grinning, "I won't turn it into a taxicab like Mr. Benny would do."

His name on the original program was "Rochester Van Jones." He became Rochester forever. Even his wife and children and friends knew him as Rochester. Everybody called him Rochester except one person. The very British Benita Hume, who was often on our program with her husband,

Ronald Colman, could never remember his name. She always called him Manchester.

Rochester was a good name for a butler because it does sound kind of English and it was incongruous for me to have an English butler. Also the word has a good hard texture. It's a name you can bite in to. If I was mad at him, I could yell, "RAH-chester." It was an ideal name when I lost my temper.

Rochester became one of the greatest assets on the show. He was a master of the slow take. His timing became as sharp as a razor. Rochester appeared more often on my radio and television shows than any other single character. He became more than a butler. He was my housekeeper. He did the shopping and fixed the meals. He washed the dishes, vacuumed the rugs, waxed the floors and made the beds. He did the laundry. Sometimes I made a little money on the side taking in laundry from the Ronald Colmans and other neighbors. Rochester drove the Maxwell. He drew my bath and when I was immersed therein, he handed me my soap, washrag and celluloid duck. Afterwards, he massaged me with baby oil. When I suffered a spell of insomnia, Rochester switched on the motor that gently rocked my bed and he sang, "Rock-a-bye, baby, in the treetop," until I fell asleep.

Not only did I pay him starvation wages—but I never gave him a vacation. Once we did a television program in which the entire plot was built around Rochester pressuring me to give him a week off. When I finally did he went to visit a friend in Palm Springs. Then he happened to see an ad in the classified section in which I was advertising for a "capable, conscientious person to perform household duties." He was sure he had been fired.

Meanwhile back at my house, I was interviewing a Miss Dooley. She was fifty-two years old. She was "proud of it." She thought people who lied about their ages were ridiculous.

"Hmmmm," I said, thoughtfully.

She said she loved to cook. Her specialty was Marinated Hungarian Chili. She had recently been employed by a Mr. Forsythe in Cleveland. He was crazy about her Marinated Hungarian Chili. He had it twice a day.

I studied her references. "I don't see Mr. Forsythe's name here."

"Well," she explained, "it's because I came here directly after the funeral."

"The funeral?"

"Let me tell you—Mr. Forsythe passed away licking his lips."

I hired her anyway.

Rochester told his troubles to Don Wilson and Dennis Day. They told him they would fix me. They would scare Miss Dooley so much that she wouldn't work for me and Rochester would get his old job back. Dennis Day put on a tight-fitting dress and a flowered hat. Dennis did a very good swish—even though he's a happily married heterosexual tenor with nine lovely children. Dennis pretended to be Denise, a French maid who had formerly worked for me. She came to the house when I was out and told Miss Dooley she had returned to get her back wages and find a misplaced earring, which had fallen off when she was fending off my advances. Not only was I a victim of powerful sex drives, but I was a heavy drinker.

"Monsieur Benny, he ees, how you say?—a lush, and when he becomes drunken, he becomes veree passionate and he chases anysing zat is young."

"But I'm fifty-two," said Miss Dooley.

"To Monsieur Benny—zat is young. Madame, I am advising to you to leave here at once or else your virtue is in great dahnger!"

Just then Don Wilson entered. He was also in drag. He said he was Hilda Swenson. She had formerly worked for me, too, and had been molested when I got drunk and could not control my insatiable lust.

When I got home, Miss Dooley was so worked up about my libido that when I made a friendly gesture and just touched her arm—she gave me a karate chop that flipped me over on the floor.

Finally, however, I cleared up the whole thing and told Rochester and Dennis and Wilson that I had not fired Rochester. I planned to engage Miss Dooley only as housekeeper and assistant to Rochester. I would divide up the household chores.

"There's only one thing, Rochester," I said,

"you and Miss Dooley will have to flip a coin to see which one of you rubs me with baby oil . . ."

Until 1943, Rochester conformed to many of the traits of the stock Negro stereotype. He was addicted to what used to be called African Dominoes—or craps. He wielded a razor. He drank gin. He chased women—and caught them.

Once, he explained why he had lost his money in yet another crap game. "Boss, I walked into my lodge meeting with the best of intentions, but suddenly, ivory reared its ugly head."

Another time, his alibi was: "Well, I walked into this lodge meeting and the brothers greeted me in a circle on their knees."

During a broadcast from New York, I said that Rochester was not with me. "They wouldn't let him on the plane," I said, "because his dice threw the compass off."

I once announced, "I'm playing an engagement at Las Vegas next month. I'm not taking any salary, provided they'll permit me to go to the crap table with Rochester every day."

And yet even in the days when he played the most negative stereotyped minstrel character, Rochester was never a servile, supplicating Stepin Fetchit. I was as much the fall guy for Rochester as I was for Phil Harris or Mary Livingstone.

The front doorbell rang. I said, "Rochester, answer the door."

"Boss, you're nearer to it than I am," was his impudent reply.

In real life, Rochester often worried me because he was rarely on time for line readings, rehearsals and the broadcast itself. I'm a nail-biter and a pessimist by temperament and Rochester's tardy habits did not calm my nervous system. Every time I called him on the carpet for being late, he came up with a good excuse. I remember once it was because his mother-in-law died and he had to make the funeral arrangements.

Then there was the time we had a marvelous program planned in which Mr. and Mrs. Colman were the guest stars and in which Rochester played an extremely important part in the plot.

Rochester came so late to the Saturday rehearsal that he missed it. He started giving me his excuse but I refused to listen. I was so mad that I told Sam Perrin, who was now my head writer, that I must punish Rochester. "I want you to write him out of the show this week," I said.

The four writers set up a hue and cry. It would mean rewriting the entire show. There wasn't time enough. Rochester was punished enough already. He promised never to do it again. We would never get a show as good as this one if we wrote him out of it. They begged me to change my mind. I consented.

On Sunday, we began our first rehearsal at 12:30. The call was for noon. Rochester was not there at noon and he was not there at 12:30 and he had not telephoned to explain. At his home, Rochester's butler (he had his own butler) explained that the master had left for the NBC studio long ago. At 12:45 we began rehearsing *without* Rochester. His character didn't make his entrance until about ten minutes after the show's opening. I hoped he would arrive in the nick of time. He did not arrive.

Well, I lost my temper completely. I blew my stack. I stomped over to the control room. I opened the heavy door. I threw a look of withering scorn on my four writers, who were now huddled in a frightened heap. "Well, I have you four idiots to thank for this!" Then I departed and slammed the door shut violently.

However, the door was so heavy that its closing was controlled by an air-pressure valve which released the air slowly. Not only could I not exit on a vicious door slam—but the door closed so slowly that it let out a long razz noise like a Bronx cheer. Even the door was against me.

But I cracked up just the same. And then the writers felt it was safe to laugh. And we all laughed. And Rochester finally showed up, accompanied by two policemen in uniform.

It seems he had been driving along the Hollywood Freeway and right in front of him a five-car smashup had taken place. He had been trapped for over an hour until the traffic started moving. Knowing that I would not believe this obviously trumped-up story, Rochester had persuaded these two Los Angeles policemen to come to the studio and testify that once again Rochester had a legitimate alibi for being so late.

I once did a sketch on the show in which Rochester was my sparring partner. I was in training for a boxing match with Fred Allen when our "feud" had just begun. In one bit, I said, "Oh, I'm in great shape, Rochester, punch me, punch me hard. Come on."

"I don't wanna punch you, boss," he said.

"Oh, come on, you'll never be able to lay a glove on me."

"Well, okay, boss."

There was the sound of an arm swishing through the air. The crack of a gloved fist meeting a glass jaw. The thunk of a body hitting the floor.

"Boss, boss," Rochester cried, "git up, git up."

I rose.

So did the South.

Thousands of indignant persons below the Mason-Dixon Line wrote in to complain that permitting my Afro-American butler to punch me in the face was an attack on the white race and the dignity of the South. Until a certain contest I'll tell you about soon, this incident brought the heaviest mail we ever received on the program. You've got to realize that most of my life I've been a political innocent. It never occurred to me there was anything offensive in this humorous little episode. I was amazed at this revelation of people's strong feelings on the subject of race. To me, I was just doing a comedy show. Would it have been funny if *I* had knocked out Rochester?

I suppose if I did the above scene today, Rochester would get complaints from militant black nationalists who would criticize him for only punching me in the jaw, when he also should have kicked me, whipped me, stomped on me and then blown out my brains.

Today the world has changed so much and I have changed so much and black men and women have achieved dignity and standing in American life, that I would never have any character who was as broad and racially delineated along negative lines as was the old Rochester. But remember, you who look back with perhaps contempt or patronizing pity on the old radio programs, that like most entertainers of that period I was brought up in another time and another place. I developed and learned my trade in vaudeville. In the golden days of vaudeville, there were blackface comics and there were black comics—like Bert Williams. There were also Swedish comics, Jewish comics, Dutch comics, Italian comics and Scotch comics.

Bad as you may think this kind of humor was, I think it was a way that America heated up the national groups and the ethnic groups in a melting pot and made one people of us—or tried to do so. Everybody loved ethnic humor during vaudeville and often the people who were being ridiculed most enjoyed the kind of ethnic humor aimed at their own group. During World War II, attitudes changed. Hitler's ideology of Aryan supremacy put all ethnic humor in a bad light. It became bad taste to have Jewish jokes, Italian jokes and Negro jokes.

But let me tell you this—I never felt and I do not feel today that Rochester and Mr. Kitzel were socially harmful. You don't hate a race when you're laughing with it. You couldn't hate Rochester. You loved Kitzel. You loved Rochester.

And let me say something else. I didn't hire Rochester because I was fighting for equal rights. I hired him because he was good. He was the best man for the part of my butler and he got better and better and funnier and funnier as the years went by.

When the black man's fight for equal rights and fair play became an issue after the war, I would no longer allow Rochester to say or do anything that an audience would consider degrading to the dignity of a modern Afro-American.

So Rochester had to stop eating watermelon and drinking gin on radio and television after 1945.

Rochester was not the only black man who was on the program. Once we did the middle commercial using the four Ink Spots. They were a fine quartet. They were riding high with the country's number one record: "If I Didn't Care."

I am sure that those among you who are over thirty-nine will remember this haunting song and especially its beautiful treatment by the Ink Spots. The idea of the lyric is that a girl doesn't believe her man really cares for her and he tells her how much he really does. On the second chorus the Ink Spots did an arrangement in which their tenor sang the words and the very deep basso did a talking counterpoint.

For our middle commercial, the Ink Spots first sang a chorus of it as they usually did. Then I asked them to sing another chorus but "this time the way I wrote it for you." So now the high tenor sang about how much he cared for his girl and the bass croaked, "If I didn't care what kind of a cigarette you smoked, I'd say smoke any brand. But I do care, baby, so if you are gonna smoke cigarettes, smoke Luckies."

He was telling her about this in an aroused voice, as if he were slowly taking off her clothes in a bedroom: "Because Lucky Strike is so round, so firm, so fully packed, so free and easy on the draw and I'm telling you, baby, LS/MFT is all you gotta know."

About two years later, I participated in a benefit show, and at the afternoon rehearsal I noticed the Mills Brothers, one of the greatest and most famous of all the great black close-harmony quartets. Now I had forgotten that it was the Ink Spots who made the Lucky Strike commercial. I thought it was the Mills Brothers. But I had never met them before.

The Mills Brothers had just finished rehearsing their medley. They were hovering around the microphone. I was very anxious to show them that I remembered them. So I sauntered over. I became very cozy with them. I was so nice and sweet and full of brotherhood that it was sickening. I gave them a big smile. "Hello, fellers," I said.

"Hello, Mr. Benny," they said simultaneously in four-part harmony.

"How about that show we did together?" I said, brimming with cheer. "That was certainly a fine commercial you fellers did."

Now they are beginning to wonder if I am out of my mind or if I am perhaps making some mistake, but they are just smiling and not saying anything.

But I couldn't just leave it alone. I had to go further. I sang "If I Didn't Care"—the verse and one chorus. I even imitated all four voices as best I could, including the tenor's beautiful high romantic solo.

Yes sir, I would prove to them that I loved them—that prejudice would be the last thing to enter my heart or mind. Here before them stood a white man who believed in equality—so not only did I do a chorus of "If I Didn't Care," I even sang the basso's recitative telling how much he cared about what cigarette his girl smoked.

The faces of the four Mills Brothers had frozen into a disdainful smile before I finished the verse. On the chorus, their smiles changed into looks of pity. And when I did the release in the bass range, they began to look at one another. Finally, one of them said, "Mr. Benny, we never did any commercials with you. We think you have us mixed up with the Ink Spots."

I think I blushed from head to foot. I turned and walked away. That night I pleaded illness to

169

get out of the benefit performance so I would not have to face the Mills Brothers.

Later at a dinner party I told this tale of my most embarrassing moment, and Broadway director Josh Logan said, "Jack, do you realize that not only did you make a mistake of confusing two quartets—but in your eagerness to be so nice and unprejudiced, what you were practically saying to them was that you couldn't tell the difference between one colored quartet and another colored quartet?"

Once again I had become my radio character.

CHAPTER 9

Did you know that the fictional Jack Benny, my character on radio and television, was a bachelor? I'm surprised at how many people who followed our program didn't see that one of the poignant things about this character was that he couldn't really get a girl to care for him. The fictional Mary Livingstone never was my girlfriend. She was a kind of heckler-secretary. She always had a sarcastic edge that colored our relationship. And I never went out with glamorous girls. If a star like Marilyn Monroe was a guest on our show, I didn't get involved with her romantically. I didn't dare make a pass at a beautiful woman. Oh, I made *believe* I was a Don Juan. But I had stupid affairs with telephone operators and waitresses and even these never amounted to much. There's a kind of bittersweet side to the sex game and if you can play it somewhere between broad farce on the one hand and tragedy on the other, you get a fine irony which reflects a true-to-life situation. On December 31, 1961, we did a New Year's Eve television show which, I think, captured this Chaplinesque blending of pathos and laughter. The show opened with my cast planning the fun they would have that night. We were all invited to a big party at Don Wilson's house. Then I walked out of my dressing room and knocked them for a loop.

I was wearing top hat, tails, white tie. I twirled a cane. I looked dapper and sophisticated. I told my cast I wouldn't be able to go to Don's party because I had a heavy date with Gloria, who, I hinted, was a sophisticated *femme fatale*. Wilson asked me to bring her to his party. I didn't want to hurt his feelings, but I implied Gloria wasn't the sort of woman who would get a charge out of one of these prosaic at-home parties. They all tried to convince me to come.

I told them what I planned. Cocktails for two at an intimate, dimly lighted place near the beach. Dinner at a gourmet's rendezvous. Later, dancing and supper at a smart nightclub.

"I hope you fellows have as much fun as I'm going to have," I said, rather condescendingly.

A studio usher said there was a phone call for me from a young lady. I swaggered away, looking at them smugly, even exiting on a Fred Astaire kick of the heels . . .

The phone call was bad news. Gloria broke our

date. She said she couldn't help it. I told her it was New Year's Eve and I had already made reservations. She was sorry, but she just couldn't make it.

Crestfallen, I tried to get reinvited to Don Wilson's party but they wouldn't let me explain and they said they understood that I was a big star and, naturally, I would be bored.

They went away singing and blowing horns.

I was left utterly alone.

It was about ten o'clock. I walked down streets crowded with merrymakers and drunken revelers. Strangers threw confetti at me and blew horns in my ears. I dragged myself along, going home. One of the horns became a trumpet and wailed a few bars of the Whiffenpoof Song and you could see I felt like a poor little lamb that had lost its way. A couple passed me. The woman said I looked like Jack Benny. The man said it couldn't be, because "a big star like that wouldn't be alone on New Year's Eve."

I was the saddest man in the world.

Passing a small restaurant, a cheap neighborhood café with a counter and some tables, I went in for a bowl of hot soup. The Greek proprietor welcomed me profusely, since I was dressed to the teeth. He wanted to seat me at a window table so I would bring in more high-class customers but I placed myself at the counter. A waitress came for my order. I ordered soup. She asked me if I didn't want a sandwich.

"No."

"Not even toast?"

"No."

"Not even some crackers for the soup?"

"Just bring me the soup," I said glumly.

She did. Then she said, "Gee, Jack, I'm sorry about tonight."

Now you realized she had been my glamorous date for the evening. This washed-out blowzy plain Jane of a girl, sweaty, tired, unromantic, was Gloria.

I lost my appetite for the soup. She tried to explain that the girl who promised to work the midnight shift for her couldn't come. She said she was so terribly sorry. Couldn't I forgive her? Or, better still, could I wait until 3:00 A.M. when she was free?

"Three o'clock, huh?" I said, sulking. "Isn't that just fine and dandy. I'll give your phone number to my milkman."

I stalked away indignantly.

A second later I was back.

Gloria thought I had changed my mind. I hadn't. Sheepishly, I said I'd forgotten my cane. I picked it up from the counter. I wasn't swaggering now. I was leaning on the cane like a crutch.

At home I found Rochester in a tuxedo getting ready to go out to a New Year's Eve party. He took pity on me when he realized I was going to be alone. He didn't go out.

So we celebrated New Year's Eve—just the two of us. We opened a bottle of champagne. We put on funny hats. We blew horns. At midnight we drank a toast and sang "Auld Lang Syne" . . .

Thanks to my wonderful wife, the real-life Jack Benny was never lonely on New Year's Eve. When we lived in the big house on North Roxbury, Mary gave wonderful parties, especially on New Year's Eve. Mary has a knack of giving good parties. She's a wonderful hostess. The food is superb. She would never let us cater a dinner for less than fifty people. She planned the menus herself and our cook prepared the meals. We have had Mrs. King for thirty years. When we gave a large dinner or supper party we naturally hired extra servants to assist her. Mary selected the wines.

Above all, she had an intuitive sense of which people were compatible with other people. And she emanated such a feeling of love and hospitality that everybody felt good in our home. Her New Year's Eve parties got to be such a tradition in Hollywood that some people wouldn't even accept a New Year's Eve invitation until they found out if Mary was giving one. She sent out the invitations a month in advance and then she phoned every person to be sure they were coming.

Among those we invited one year were Honey and Don Ameche. Don said they would love to come, but they were having a small gathering at their house, so they couldn't come for the whole party. However, they'd love to come for a quick drink and some greetings and salutations. Mary said that would be fine. Of the other seventy cou-

174

ples we had asked, only one other couple said they couldn't stay for the whole party. That was Clark Gable and his wife, Carole Lombard. Clark told Mary he and Carole would love to drop in for a few minutes to say hello, but they had been invited to many parties and had decided, this year, to go party-hopping. Mary said she understood and to come as early or as late as they wanted.

It was a party to remember. On the back lawn we had set up a striped circus tent. Inside the tables were laid for the midnight supper. There were convenient bars inside and outside the house and uniformed waiters were serving champagne. Among the earliest couples to arrive were the Ameches and the Gables. I mingled with the crowd as did Mary and we chatted now with this group and now with that group and then there was supper and more champagne. And there was a dance orchestra and some of us danced in the glow of the colored lanterns. The Gables and the Ameches seemed to be enjoying themselves. They stayed on and on and on. They toasted the New Year with us at midnight. They joined us at supper. They danced. They sang songs and danced some more.

Around 1:00 A.M. some of the guests began leaving.

Around two, I got sleepy. I didn't say anything to anybody about this, as I didn't want to break up the festivities. I quietly sneaked up to bed and fell asleep with the distant sound of laughter and singing still in my ears . . .

175

Then, suddenly, I woke up. I looked at my watch. It was almost 9:00 A.M. I seemed to be hearing distant sounds of laughter from downstairs. I put on a robe and went down.

The party was still in progress, although only four revelers lingered on. They sat on the floor sipping champagne. They were telling stories and laughing their heads off. The four people were Honey and Don Ameche and Carole Lombard and Clark Gable. They had never left. Mary couldn't have been happier. It was the best New Year's Eve party I've ever been to. All six of us went into the dining room and had popovers and scrambled eggs and bacon and the most delicious coffee you ever drank. Even after we finished breakfast our last remaining guests didn't want to leave. They had had such fun that they weren't in the least sleepy.

It was a real good party.

During the early 1940's, I began selling Lucky Strikes instead of Jell-O. The American Tobacco Company made me a handsome offer which General Foods did not match. Usually in network broadcasting the sponsor "owned" the time, but NBC had given me Sunday from 7:00 to 7:30 P.M. forever, or as long as I wanted it. General Foods was not a good sport about this. With the cooperation of CBS they decided to knock me out of the leadership. They put together a spectacular variety show and they hired Kate Smith to be the star. Miss Smith was then a very big star in radio.

William S. Paley, the president of CBS, was an extremely competitive president. He wanted his network to beat NBC. He had tried to knock me out once before, back around 1935, when he pitted Eddie Cantor against me on Sunday in a spectacular variety show. It wasn't so much that CBS or General Foods was vindictive but, as my father once said about race horses, they are only human, I guess. Besides this, surveys had proved that when a program was the number one program, then the shows before it and after it were also popular because folks kept the dial tuned to the same station, sometimes for the whole evening. Kate Smith put on a good show—but the fans still loved me best.

My new sponsor felt that if I saw how the product was manufactured, I would put more sincerity into my work. I was taken to a factory in North Carolina and shown how Lucky Strikes are made. It was fascinating to see the process, involving countless machines, by which tobacco leaves become packages of twenty cigarettes, sealed with cellophane, pasted with tax stamps and zapped into cartons. But even after their careful demonstration I couldn't understand how from these little white tubes they could afford to pay me $55,000 a week. I couldn't understand how the machines did it.

I confess that to me all machines are a mystery. Airplanes are a mystery. Piston airplanes *and* jet airplanes. A radio is a mystery. A little tape recorder into which you talk and on pieces of Scotch tape your voice is recorded is a mystery to me. A television set, an automobile is a mystery to me. I've been broadcasting over the radio for close to forty years and I still do not understand how I can be in a studio and talk into a microphone and then, a thousand miles away, a person can switch on a little box and turn a knob to a certain number and out of the speaker will emanate my voice.

Once I complained of my ignorance of how radio works to George S. Kaufman.

He said, "You think you got problems? Listen —I don't even understand the hammer!"

Once a faucet in our kitchen needed a new washer and we had to call a plumber and he gave us a bill for ten dollars, just to install a new washer. I complained to Freddie De Cordova, the director of my television program. I said it was ridiculous that an intelligent human being like myself, and one who was fairly successful and even considered shrewd, was unable to install a new washer in a leaky faucet. It wasn't only that I resented paying a plumber the ten dollars, but I felt like such an idiot.

And De Cordova said, "Jack, if you think that's something—when a light bulb goes out in my bedroom, I think about moving to a new apartment."

Once at the Hillcrest Country Club, several of us were discussing flying and I remarked, "I don't care how safe they claim an airplane is, I say that anytime you go up there in a little metal thing, you're taking your life in your hands."

Irving Brecher, a movie writer, agreed. "Birds don't fly that high," he said, "and it's their business."

One of the best loved characters on the show during the Lucky Strike period was Mr. Kitzel. Mr. Kitzel was played by Artie Auerbach, a New York newspaper photographer turned actor. My first radio meeting with Mr. Kitzel was at a baseball game. He was selling hot dogs. As Mr. Kitzel peddled his frankfurters in the grandstand, he sang out the following: "Get your hot dogs, get your hot dogs, vit de peeckle in de meedle and de mustard on top—just de vay you like 'em and dey're all red hot."

Mr. Kitzel's jingle about the pickle in the middle became a favorite with the public.

This jingle was contributed by writer John Tackaberry. Tackaberry was from Houston, Texas. He had originally heard it sung by a black hot dog vendor at a ballpark in Texas, who would chant, "Git yo' hot dawgs, git yo' nice hot dawgs, they's got the pickle in the middle and the mustard on top, oh, git yo' nice sweet hot dawgs, git 'em red hot!"

Don't ask me why this became so funny when we translated it into Jewish dialect—but it did.

Soon Mr. Kitzel became a permanent part of our floating cast—one of those I ran into in the strangest places. The second time I met Mr. Kitzel was also at a ballpark, but now he wasn't selling hot dogs. He was rooting for the home team.

179

"I didn't know you liked baseball so much, Mr. Kitzel," I remarked.

"Like baseball, Meestah Benneh? I'm crazy about this national pastime, what you call. In fact, I'm telling you something, Meestah Benneh, in my youngeh days, I was a professional player. I used to pitch baseball."

"I didn't know that, Mr. Kitzel."

"Once I even had a no-heet game."

"What was the score?"

"Twenty-six to zero. We lost."

"How could you? I thought you pitched a no-hitter."

"I did—but hoo hoo HOO—deed I walk them!"

Kitzel often visited New York. He was a devotee of the stage and always caught the latest shows. While Christopher Fry's *The Lady's Not for Burning* was running, I asked Mr. Kitzel what shows he had liked on his last sojourn in Gotham and he replied, "Among the Broadway productions which I hinjoyed was *Guys and Dolls, Oklahoma!* and *The Lady's Not for Bernstein*."

I once saw Mr. Kitzel at Union Station in Los Angeles. I asked him where he was going.

"Gung? Who's gung? I'm vaiting. A train I'm meeting, Meesteh Benneh. I'm vaiting for mine son to come home from college."

"And what college does he attend?"

"Southern Methodist, Meesteh Benneh."

The joke got a yock from the studio audience as the incongruity of any son of Mr. Kitzel going to Southern Methodist University was apparent to one and all.

The following week we received—believe it or not—several letters from Jewish students at Southern Methodist University. To my surprise, I learned not only that there were several hundred Jewish students at SMU, but also two Jewish fraternities and one of these fraternities wrote in to inquire if Mr. Kitzel's son would like to pledge Zeta Beta Tau and what was his first name and how was Kitzel spelled exactly and where could they get in touch with Mr. Kitzel's offspring!

Among our mainstays was the brassiest, most worldly character, played by Phil Harris. He was loud-talking, illiterate, rude, alcoholic, arrogant, boastful, preening himself on the clever ripostes he uttered and never hesitating to compliment himself openly on his *bon mots*, which he thought superior to my dreary quips. He didn't even pretend to be polite. At least Rochester called me Mr. Benny.

To Harris, I was known as Jackson and Mary was Livvy.

And yet with all the coarseness, there was a quality of sophistication, of worldliness about the Phil Harris character that made him different not only from every other character on our program —but from every other character on radio. He was completely immoral. The character was so written and so played that you knew Phil Harris was probably the finest fornicator of all time.

When he made his first speech, which was usually a simple, "Hiya, Jackson," he somehow got across the idea that he had come to the studio right after having experienced a most satisfying orgasm.

Harris radiated vitality, *joie de vivre*, immorality and a sheer gusto in animal pleasures that made him unique among all the characters in radio. Phil Harris in his personal life was not like our imaginary Phil Harris, though the character grew out of the mannerisms of his natural style, because by nature Phil is a happy-go-lucky, self-confident guy with a zest for experience and plenty of self-esteem.

Also, his voice went with the character, with the braggadocio and, so to say, the cocksureness. He was believable. Radio characters became so believable—think of those SMU students believing in a real Mr. Kitzel with a real son who attended SMU—because you heard only their voices and you created your own images of what they looked like and what sort of personalities they were. I believe that all the characters I created were basically true to life or they would not have lasted so long.

Everybody knows at least one person who is in some way like Phil Harris. You could never dismay Harris.

"What did the doctors do about your headaches?" I once inquired.

"Plenty, Jackson," he said. "First, they gave me a complete physical. Then they gave me all the allergy tests. Then they checked my reflexes. Finally they psychoanalyzed me."

"And did they find out why you have headaches?"

"Yeah, Jackson, my band plays too loud!"

You could insult the musicianship of his band and criticize the unshaven, badly dressed and filthy appearance of his musicians—but it didn't bother Harris. He was imperturbable.

Once Ronald Colman asked Mrs. Colman while they were dining, "Benita, have you ever happened to notice Phil Harris's musicians?"

"Please, Ronnie," she said, "not while I'm eating."

This crack got one of the loudest and longest laughs from our studio audience and yet it wasn't the cleverness of the joke that did it. We had prepared our audience for this moment by a barrage of wisecracks over a period of ten years, wisecracks that described these slovenly musicians. As soon as Benita Hume spoke her line, the audience called up in their minds' eyes the image of a crowd of unshaven, badly dressed, unshowered, stinking, drunken saxophone players and trumpeters.

In radio we used to have what I once coined a good phrase for, namely, "picture jokes." This was the best picture joke we ever did. Now in television where you see everything, you have sight gags, but you don't have picture jokes.

Today, when Dean Martin is playing a happy drunken hedonist who stumbles over his lines and boasts of his love of bourbon whiskey on television, when the movies are shedding all the old-fashioned moral standards, the old Phil Harris radio character may strike you as genteel. But when we began featuring him, starting in the late 1930's, we shocked a lot of people. In fact, as I've said, there simply was no other character like Phil Harris in all of radio. He was wild. He lived for pleasure. He did not believe in sin. His philosophy was summed up beautifully once when I was in bed with chills and a fever. Harris had the ideal medicine for me—a rum flip.

"They're really great, Jackson. You see, the egg in it gives you strength . . . and the sugar gives you energy."

"What does the rum do, Phil?"

"It gives you ideas about what to do with the strength and energy."

Another time I was abed with a sprained ankle. Phil Harris paid a call. He brought flowers—not for me, but for my nurse, whom he attempted to seduce. Then he caught sight of a bottle of alcohol. He seized it and chortled, "Come on, everybody, let's get the party started."

"PUT DOWN THAT BOTTLE, PHIL," I cried. "THAT'S TO RUB ON MY BACK."

"Huh?"

"Can't you read what it says on the label? For External Use Only."

"Yeah? What's that supposed to mean, Jackson?"

"It means you're supposed to rub it into your skin."

"Man, that sure sounds like a slow way of gettin' high . . . but maybe I can make it by New Year's Eve if I rub it in now . . . well, I gotta run along, Jackson. I'm goin' down to the poolroom and rehearse my show."

"You rehearse your show in a poolroom?"

"Sure, that way I can always pick up my cue . . . HA, HA, HA."

"Please, Phil, I'm not a well man."

"Oh, Harris," Phil told himself, "you may not be the best-looking—but you sure are the smartest—'pick up my cue . . .' "

"On second thought, Phil, don't rub it in, drink it."

And you could picture Phil tilting the rubbing alcohol bottle to his mouth and swigging it—and being none the worse.

Letting character develop out of voice quality worked not only with Rochester and Phil Harris, but also with Dennis Day. He was the "dumb kid" who drove me out of my mind and then every now and then would pull off something so shrewd that it made me even madder.

Another character I was constantly meeting was Nelson. He was always called Nelson. His real name is Nelson—Frank Nelson. He was always against me. He might be a floorwalker in a department store, a doctor treating me, a barber shaving me, a real estate agent, a ticket salesman.

He hated me. He was always vicious to me—for no specific reason. I felt it.

Don't we all get this paranoid feeling sometimes that a total stranger—a bus driver, a salesclerk—hates us for no rational reason. That was the Frank Nelson character—the anonymous person in some public position who frustrates us.

Another character who had this insane touch of the irrelevant was Mr. Billingsley. He had no first name. He was on the show from 1938 to 1942. He was invented by Ed Beloin and Beloin loved him so much that he asked to play him. He did a good characterization. Mr. Billingsley boarded in my home. He was generally drunk or hung over. He was quite mad—but harmless. He paid his rent on time. He spoke in a faraway voice. We usually exchanged non sequiturs as he came in or left the house.

"Goodbye, Mr. Billingsley," I'd say.

"Well I wouldn't have thought it either," would be his reply.

Once he came downstairs and said, "Good morning, Mr. Benny."

"Good morning, Mr. Billingsley, I see you're wearing a turban."

"This is not a turban, Mr. Benny. It is a bed-sheet. I slept like a top last night . . . goodbye [hic] Mr. [hic] Benny."

We had another random lunatic who did butt-ins. He was a completely bald man. He was nameless. But you knew his voice. He also lived in my house for a few years. He would knock on the door. You heard the door creak open.

"Mr. Benny?"

"Yes?"

"May I borrow your comb and brush?"

He took them and went away.

This was the only shtick he did. Nobody ever wanted to know why a completely baldheaded man required a comb and brush.

It was a good "picture joke."

Then there was The Tout. The Tout was played by a raspy-voiced young actor, Sheldon Leonard. Mr. Leonard matured into a fine television writer and producer. He is the man responsible for the currently popular series, *I Spy*.

Every three or four weeks I would be approached by The Tout. At first I met him only at the Santa Anita racetrack and his character began as a gravel-voiced adviser who made me change my mind about the horse I wanted to bet on.

Gradually, The Tout widened his field of operations.

I was in a fruit market, buying apples.

"Bud, bud," he whispered, accosting me. "Hey, bud, whatcha doin'?"

"Buying apples."

"Nnn-nnh," he said, discouraging me.

"What do you mean, nnh-nnnh?"

"Take the oranges, bud."

"Why should I take oranges, when I want apples?"

"Because apples aren't in form today."

Standing in a hotel lobby by the bank of elevators, I heard him asking, "Hey, bud, where yuh goin'?"

"I'm taking the elevator."

"Which one?"

"Number three."

"Nnnh-nnh—take four. Three is scratched, two isn't running good today and one is slow."

Everybody used his natural voice on the show—except one person. This person was a short plump little person with a wispy mustache and big sad black eyes and a fantastic range of voices. They used to call Lon Chaney "the man of a thousand faces." Mel Blanc is the man of a thousand voices. He can play dialects—every kind—authentically. He can also play animals and birds. He is the voice of Bugs Bunny, Porky Pig and Woody Woodpecker (just to mention a few) in the cartoons. He plays my parrot. We first met when I needed someone to play Carmichael, the bear that guarded my safe in the basement. I needed to show that there really was a bear down there. Mel came to audition for me in 1939 and I said, "How can I get this polar bear to growl?" Mel said, "I could growl," and he made a terrifying sound. It was wonderful.

Mel plays my French violin teacher, Professor LeBlanc. I play my violin exercises for him—dah da dah da dah dah dah da. So terrible. Mel says, "Now Monsieur Bennee, turn zee violin upside down and play zee same ting."

"But it's just the back of the violin," I say.

"Zat's exactly what I had in mind," says M. LeBlanc.

He plays the Mexican character named Sy. Among Sy's activities is leading a small Mexican band. Sy had a limited English vocabulary which was shown for all time when he appeared on a television special I did in 1966. He came on with his little band which was billed as the Tijuana Strings. I told the audience that Herb Alpert and the Tijuana Brass were unable to appear because of the exorbitant salary they demanded, but instead I had been able to hire another fine Latin American ensemble: the Tijuana Strings.

Out shuffled eight of the most dilapidated musicians you ever saw. They were scruffier than the Phil Harris musicians. They were lugging guitars, violins, violas, and the leader was on double bass. The leader, Mel Blanc, was costumed in a tattered serape. He spoke for the Tijuana Strings.

"You are the Tijuana Strings?" I asked.

"Sí."

"I take it you people are all from Tijuana?"

"Sí."

"Am I right in assuming you are their leader?"

"Sí."

"What is your name?"

"Sy."

"You realize, of course, that the name of your group is awfully close to the Tijuana Brass. Didn't they ever object to your name?"

"Sí."

"Well what did they do?"

"Sue."

"Sue?"

"Sí."

Mel Blanc's finest hour as a vocal impersonator was not as a parrot or a violin teacher or a Mexican, but—I almost hate to write this as I do not think you will believe it—it was as my Maxwell automobile!

Yes, the old Maxwell with the dubious starter, the asthmatic engine, the rattling bolts and wheezing valves and shaking chassis and trembling fenders. It was from out of Mel's marvelous throat that all these wheezes and rattles and coughing emanated. Out there in radioland our listeners got the picture joke of this old jalopy falling apart and so we never told the true story that the Maxwell noises were produced by the human larynx.

Like every successful running gag, the Maxwell happened accidentally. Originally the sounds the Maxwell made came from a recording. One day during the show the turntable came unplugged at the last minute. Just as the Maxwell's ignition was supposed to sputter, Mel saved the day by emitting his famous string of explosive "p-tuis" into the microphone. From then on he was Maxwell.

In 1939 Paramount Pictures decided to hold the world premiere of *Man About Town* in Waukegan. They made a tie-in with the Waukegan Chamber of Commerce and Mayor Mancel Talcott. June 21 to June 25 were declared Waukegan Celebrity

Days. My co-star, Dorothy Lamour, was coming to Waukegan with me for the premiere. I was also bringing members of the cast. Mary was coming and also Don Wilson, Rochester, Phil Harris, and Andy Devine. Devine was a regular on the show for years. A huge, hulking, loose-jointed gentleman with the face of a primitive animal, he had a shrill high-pitched voice—so ridiculous for someone of his size that he was funny.

All three Waukegan theaters were playing *Man About Town*. Paramount was flying in hundreds of radio and movie critics for the event. Flags would fly, banners wave, banquets would be given and there would be a big parade down Genesee Street.

We planned our next Sunday radio program on the Santa Fe *Super Chief*, traveling east. We made the premise of the show my returning to Waukegan for a world premiere. We already had an outline and rough draft of the three spots.

In the opening spot, I am being given the keys to the city by Mayor Talcott. He makes a speech. His speech reveals that he has me confused with Fred Allen. I didn't like the idea and neither did Hilliard Marks, my producer. Hilliard, who was my brother-in-law, had become the producer two years before. He was not only a hardworking co-ordinator of those thousand and one little details that go into the making of a smooth-running broadcast operation, but he had a keen sense of comedy values and instinctively knew what would and would not play in terms of my comedic values.

It was Hickey (this was Joanie's name for Hillie when she was tiny—and it became everybody's name for him) Marks who suggested we open the show with the parade down Waukegan's main drag.

"I like that," I said.

The writers were present at the conference in my hotel suite. They agreed with me—but not just because I said I liked it. My writers were never yes men. When I had a script conference with the writers, I considered myself just one of them and that's how I wanted them to consider me—just one of the writers. But if they ever got out of line . . .

They never did . . .

"Why don't you drive some old beat-up car in the parade, Jack?" Bill Morrow suggested. "You're too stingy to spend money on a new car."

"How about," Ed Beloin said, spitballing it, as we say in the business, "how about, Jack, you drive an old Model T Ford—in fact, one of the first models Henry Ford ever put out?"

"I like that," I said, puffing a cigar.

"Wait a minute," Morrow said, getting excited. "How about in honor of the parade and being Waukegan's favorite son and all that shit, Jack *trades in* the old Model T for a new car?"

"It wouldn't be in character, fellas," I said.

"Well," Marks suggested, "maybe if Jack trades in the Model T for a new one—not a 1939 car, but say, a 1912 or 1915 car."

"That's an idea," Beloin said.

192

"I *love* it," Morrow said.

"I'll buy it," I said. "What kind of a car do you think I should trade it in for?"

Cars came flying thick and fast.

"A Stanley-Steamer?"

"Nah—too obvious."

"Hey—how about the Baker Electric?"

"It's an old ladies' car."

"A Stutz Bearcat?"

"Wouldn't fit Jack's character."

"A Locomobile?"

"Doesn't sound right."

"Fellers, listen," I said, as something deep in my memory stirred and came to light and I remembered Jimmy Melton, one of the early vocalists on the show, and his interest in antique automobiles, "I would like to suggest a car that not only had a sports model, but a touring sedan. It was called the Maxwell."

There was silence in the room.

"What was that again?" Morrow asked.

"The Maxwell."

"Well," said Morrow.

"Well, well," said Beloin. "Was there really such a car?"

"Oh, yeah," I said with assurance, "and they used to have trouble with the engine when they went over twenty-five miles an hour. There was some kind of a ping or maybe a pong in the motor."

"There really was a Maxwell made," Marks said.

193

"The idea of having a car with a name like a person—Maxwell—well, that strikes me as funny."

"The Reo," Marks said dreamily, "was named for the initials of Ransom E. Olds, who also built the first Oldsmobile." Hickey knows the most interesting facts.

"Yeah," Morrow said, "we can open with a scene where you're arguing with a used-car dealer and he takes your Model T Ford in trade for a 1912 Maxwell."

In the real Waukegan parade, I was driven in an open Packard touring car.

In the make-believe radio parade on Sunday, June 25, 1939—which we broadcast from the stage of the Genesee Theatre—I rode in an old Maxwell, driven by Rochester. Something about the picture of a miser driving a 1912 Maxwell amused the audience, and the Maxwell became a part of our mythology.

"You know that picture of my Maxwell that hangs in the den, Rochester? That's the first car I ever owned."

"Boss," said Rochester, "that's the first car *anybody* ever owned."

Rochester hated cleaning and polishing the Maxwell. He was ashamed of its dilapidated condition and its slowness. Even on a good day, the Maxwell couldn't do better than twenty miles an hour.

"Boss," he once asked me, "why don't you trade in the old car for a newer model?"

"What for?" I said. "This car takes us where we want to go."

"I know—but look how much older we are when we get there!"

As another example of the credibility of radio, you'd be amazed at how many people believe that I actually drive an old Maxwell around Beverly Hills. I have even received cash offers for my car—some going as high as two or three thousand dollars. Several years ago, while I was touring New England, a reporter writing a feature story asked me in all seriousness, "Mr. Benny, about how long have you owned this Maxwell and how many miles a year do you average on it?"

I didn't know what to say. If I told him I drove either a Rolls-Royce or a Cadillac, I would make him look stupid. It was like telling a kid there's no Santa Claus. "You'll have to ask Rochester about that," I said.

Since Rochester was racing some horses in Mexico, it wasn't likely we would be able to get hold of him for the story.

The only time I ever really drove a Maxwell is when I played Harrah's in Lake Tahoe. Bill Harrah is an antique car collector and he's got hundreds of them. Usually when a star plays one of his clubs in Reno or Vegas or Tahoe, Harrah puts a brand-new Rolls at his or her disposal. But in my case, he thought it would be good publicity if I was seen driving around town in a Maxwell. The car was a dark blue four-door job with a running board and a top that could be folded

195

down. It was a touring car, a 1923 Model B in fine condition. It handled smoothly, steered beautifully and I could do over sixty miles an hour in it over open highways. The motor sounded very smooth.

Harrah's—Daddy forgot to mention that when he played there, although he didn't drive a Rolls, he bought one. He first played Harrah's Club in Lake Tahoe in 1959, then returned yearly for the following five. Bill Harrah was quite a character. He owned two gigantic gambling casinos, that one and the other in Reno. His antique car collection was at that time the second largest in the world. He also owned the Rolls-Royce and Ferrari dealerships in Reno. (Of course Daddy got a good deal!) He also raced hydroplanes. He also owned four houses at the lake, three for VIP guests, the other for his own use. It was so enormous you could seat a hundred people in the dining room, and had its own generating plant, kind of like the *QE2*. He also owned another home of equal size in Reno.

But here's the other side: he was a tall and thin man with rimless glasses and a severe, expressionless demeanor. He looked and behaved not at all like a casino owner, more like a small-town high school principal. He was soft-spoken, painfully shy and, above all, a prude. There would be no blue material at a Harrah's Club; no off-color jokes. Of course he adored my father. They became very good friends.

I remember those Tahoe engagements fondly. Every year the family arrived en masse for a two-week stay. My two young children, Maria and Michael, who in 1961 were four and six, adored it because by now they knew their grandfather was someone special. They went to his dinner show almost every night, and I loved watching them squirm with anticipation toward the end of the show when they knew he was about to introduce them. Just as I had done years ago when I saw Danny Kaye's show, they popped right up and waved to the audience and I could hardly get them to sit down again. During the day, when he wasn't playing golf, they followed him everywhere, feeling important, reveling in being Jack Benny's grandchildren.

As for the Maxwell, like Daddy, it amazes me that people think we actually owned one. My parents drove a variety of cars over the years, but Daddy never thought much about what make they were. Although he enjoyed the perks and privileges that accompanied his fame, he never asked for them. He never made a point of his stardom. He never said, "This is Jack Benny. I want two seats down front." Being down front wasn't a big deal to him.

He didn't know that if you live in Beverly Hills you're supposed to drive a Mercedes or a BMW or Rolls. A car was a car. As long as it took him to his office or on one of his road trips and was reasonably comfortable he was happy. My mother was the one who saw to it that he drove something befitting his stardom. I remember after the war they drove his and her Cadillac convertibles (a new one every two years). Mom's was always blue, Dad's a variety of colors—until they bought the navy blue Rolls-Royce. Six or seven years later it was replaced by a white one, also from Harrah's, and finally his last car, a black Mercedes coupe.

CHAPTER 10

It seems strange to me, looking backwards, that about a quarter of a century ago the biggest question on the minds of forty million Americans was whether Jack Benny or Fred Allen would win a boxing match for the benefit of Army War Relief. It was a real fight—for three rounds. It was part of a gigantic entertainment program and rally at Madison Square Garden. It seems so long ago and I don't just mean long ago in years, but also in spirit. It was a time when Americans were emotionally involved with their radio personalities. Television has never made this kind of direct emotional impact on us.

The prizefighting match was the climax of the famous Benny-Allen feud. It started in 1936. It was a battle of wits and gags. We fought with vituperation, wisecracks, insults, innuendo and the most outrageous slaps at each other's so-called physical deficiencies. In fact, Fred Allen got so used to making fun of me that even when he wrote a letter to a friend, instead of writing the usual news and personal opinions, he fell into the feud. Fred and I made several movies together, the best one being *Love Thy Neighbor*. Writing to Groucho Marx, Fred stated:

i made a picture with jack benny. i had all of my hair, teeth, bones and blood. jack had a hairpiece that looked like a basset hound's rump, he was wearing hilliard marks' teeth, his bones were rented from a chiropractor and his blood was borrowed from a hemophiliac who started bleeding suddenly and had forgotten to bring his pail with him. when the picture came out, jack looked like a westmore dream. i looked like some fag caught in a revolving door at the sloane house.

Forty million listeners were caught up in our feud and followed it with bated breath, week by week. And I don't know how many millions thought we really hated each other's guts. Of course, Allen and I never hated each other. The feud was as phony as my stinginess, my Maxwell and Mr. Kitzel having a son at Southern Methodist University. Allen admired me. In his autobiography, *Much Ado About Me*, he wrote that I did not have an enemy in the world and that I was "the best liked actor in show business. He is the only comedian I know who dies laughing at all of the other comedians. He is my favorite comedian and I hope to be his friend until he is forty. That will be forever."

And I admired Allen—for his generous nature as a person and for his sharp and cutting wit as a comedian. His marriage to Portland Hoffa, a soft-spoken and lovely lady, was one of the great romances of show business. In vaudeville, Fred Allen's was one of the smartest acts of its time. He was always miles ahead of most other performers. He was a genuine satirist. When we were together we had wonderful evenings sitting around and drinking coffee and reminiscing about our misadventures in vaudeville and remembering some of the weird acts of that period. But when you got him off vaudeville, Allen became somebody else, a bitter and frustrated and unhappy man.

I couldn't understand him. He couldn't understand me. I couldn't figure out why he was so unhappy about life. He thought life was some sort of a miserable trap. Here was a man who was happily married to a fine woman and who had achieved success in radio and who was able to say what he wanted to say to millions of listeners and who commanded the respect of great humorists like James Thurber and Robert Benchley. Here was an educated and intelligent man who had read many books and who seemed to understand what the world was all about. What was wrong? I didn't know what he wanted or expected out of life and why he was so basically disgruntled about living. He was a religious, God-fearing man and he lived a good, honest, clean life. I couldn't understand him.

He thought I was as odd as I thought he was. He thought there was something so silly about my feeling good all the time when I took a morning walk and inhaled the fresh air, or relished a cold glass of spring water or enjoyed a good story told by one of my friends, especially, for example, Fred himself.

Allen fired the opening shot in our feud. In 1936 a ten-year-old child prodigy violinist, Stewart Canin, guested on Allen's radio show. Canin performed Dvorak's *The Bee*. This is a fast brief solo piece that was constantly confused by the radio critics and radio reporters with Rimsky-Korsakov's *Flight of the Bumble Bee*. Among those who so confused it was Fred Allen himself, who, I found out when I read his memoirs, was under the impression Canin had played *The Flight of the Bumble Bee*. Of the two insects, Dvorak's is much the harder. But that is neither here nor there.

Canin played *The Bee* as if it were a horny drone in hot pursuit of the Queen Bee. I know. I was listening to the program. Imagine my surprise when Allen congratulated the youthful violinist and then added that there was an old man named Jack Benny who thought he could play the fiddle.

"After hearing you play, Stewart," Allen said, "I think Jack should hang his head in shame. He should take the horsehairs out of his bow and return them to the tail of the horse. Benny is the only violinist who makes you feel the strings would sound better back on the cat's intestine."

(I now play *The Bee* in concert. I didn't get the hang of it until 1966. The piece lasts only one minute—but it took me thirty years to master it!)

Well, I wouldn't take this lying down and on my next broadcast, I sneered at Stewart Canin as a rank amateur and I described Fred Allen as a broken-down juggler who was tone deaf as a result of being hit in the head by some falling Indian clubs he'd failed to catch during his many years as a failure and small-time vaudeville act.

I said that I, for one, could play *The Bee* and anytime a true music lover requested this number I would be happy to oblige.

So on his next program, Allen said, "Mr. Benny, I am a music lover. I challenge you to play *The Bee*."

Now we went at each other hot and heavy. For a few weeks, we hurled insults at each other spontaneously. The argument went over so big with listeners that we decided to hold a summit meeting with my two writers and Allen's five writers and plan the strategy of our feud. It was all cold and calculated and the sky was the limit. Or rather, the mud was the limit. Some of our repartee was on a very disgusting level. Fred Allen made fun of my poor, aging, tired blood, my so-called baldness, my stinginess, my lack of talent, my debt to Mary Livingstone and Rochester and, most of all, my terrible fiddling.

Well, it wasn't in my radio character to attack

other people and my humor came out of *my* being the butt of everybody else's jokes. I was at a disadvantage. I couldn't be as nasty as he could be. Mostly I made remarks about the bags under Fred Allen's eyes and about his tired blood.

He pulled one of his most caustic jibes when Waukegan declared a Jack Benny Week and I returned in triumph to the scene of my childhood failures. That was when they named the new junior high school after me and even had a parade in my honor. The mayor planted a tree in the park. He named it the Benny Tree. Three months later the tree died.

"How," Allen asked on his program, "can they expect the tree to live in Waukegan—when the sap is in Hollywood?"

When I toured army camps and navy bases during the war, many places greeted me with the following banner strung outside the main entrance: WELCOME, FRED ALLEN.

Our prizefight, by the way, when we finally pulled it off, and did go through with it, was declared a draw. I do not think that either Fred Allen or myself had the strength or the technical skill to knock out a bee, even a common ordinary worker bee.

Fred Allen played a small but important part in one of my most successful masochistic stunts. About 1944 or 1945 my writers and I were sitting around and kicking ideas to each other and Sam Perrin came up with a premise in which I become a songwriter. We carried this running gag on for

203

several weeks while I am trying to write a torch song to a girl I'm in love with. Finally I finish the words and music of a ditty entitled, "When You Say I'll Beg Your Pardon, Then I'll Come Back to You."

A year later we were having trouble finding a strong idea that would hold up for a sequence of several shows. Perrin, who had been a musician before he went into comedy writing, naturally thought along musical lines and he said, "Jack, maybe we could do something with all these amateurs who write songs. There are millions of them. We could say you're looking for a new theme song and have a real contest and get judges who know music . . ."

"Like Oscar Levant, maybe," said Milt Josefsberg.

"Or Oscar Hammerstein," added Tackaberry.

"You could play the winner on the fiddle, Jack," Perrin said. "We could stretch this into a running gag for six or eight weeks."

"It's got possibilities," I said, puffing a cigar.

George Balzer, then the youngest member of the writing team, sat silently.

"Phil Harris could sing it," Josefsberg said.

"Dennis Day could sing his version of it," Tackaberry threw in.

"Or maybe we block out a melody line," Perrin said, "and ask people to send in lyrics for thirty-two bars."

"Why only thirty-two bars?" Josefsberg asked.

"Is that the number of bars where Phil Harris likes to drink?"

Balzer seemed to be in a trance.

"That's what all popular songs are written in, Milt," Tackaberry said, "thirty-two bars." He knew about popular songs. He had been Horace Heidt's gag writer before joining our team.

Then we all got very still. We had run out of steam.

Suddenly Balzer snapped out of his trance. "I got an idea," he said. "You know how on these commercials they're always asking people to write a letter and say why they like some toothpaste or baking powder or whatever in twenty-five words or less, or my favorite soap is Zilch's because . . . and they get a prize. Why don't we have a contest where people write in letters in twenty-five words or less, 'Why I Hate Jack Benny.' And we give prizes to the best letters."

Nobody said a word. The writers were studying my face. I didn't laugh.

I stood up and crossed to the window. I stared outside onto the sweeping expanse of green lawn. The sprinklers were going. I knew if we went through with this idea it would be the most extreme limit to which I had ever carried the masochism bit. Did I really want to publicly humiliate myself just for laughs? Public relations advisers—and my sponsor employed one of the highest-powered firms of this kind—were always telling entertainers to project a positive image of themselves to the

205

public. Here I would be going all out to dramatize what a schmuck I was . . .

The hell with public relations and images, I thought. I turned and faced the writers. "I like it," I said. "We'll do it. But I want another word instead of *hate*. Let's get another sentence for the contest."

It took us almost two hours to find the right phrase. It would be the "I Can't Stand Jack Benny Because . . ." contest and instead of twenty-five words we would allow the contestants fifty words. There would be $10,000 worth of prizes in Victory Bonds. First prize was $2,500, second was $1,500, third was $1,000 and then there were fifty prizes of $100 each.

Out of this farfetched idea came six of the most charming shows we ever did. We announced the contest on November 25, 1945, and in the following six weeks we received 277,000 letters.

We expected that at the most there would be twenty thousand letters. When the mail started flooding in to NBC we had to hire a staff of twelve women to sort out the mail and choose the most promising letters. They eliminated all but a hundred letters. These hundred were then submitted to the judges, who were Goodman Ace and Peter Lorre. They selected the best fifty-three letters and these were submitted to the final judge, who was—who else?—Fred Allen. He chose the final winners. The grand prize winner was Carroll P. Craig Sr. of Pacific Palisades, California. Mr. Craig's entry was as follows:

He fills the air with boasts and brags
And obsolete obnoxious gags.
The way he plays his violin
Is music's most obnoxious sin.
His cowardice alone, indeed,
Is matched by his obnoxious greed.
In all the things that he portrays
He shows up my own obnoxious ways.

Fred Allen gave the winners' names and then added, "The fifty winners of the $100 bonds will be notified by telegram and the bonds sent via registered mail. By the way, if Mr. Benny should deliver any of these telegrams personally, please tip him generously . . . he has been through a terrible ordeal . . . I AM HAPPY TO SAY."

At the beginning of the 1946–47 season, I experimented with a new kind of comedy commercial on the air. I employed a close harmony foursome, the Sportsmen Quartet, to chant the LS/MFT sales message in the form of a popular song parody. After they sang the commercial in fast tempo, I got angry at them. I told Don Wilson I never wanted them back. They were terrible. Don defended them. Phil Harris, Rochester and Dennis Day thought they were grand. Mary Livingstone loved them. The following week the Sportsmen Quartet returned and again they sang the first chorus of a current hit number straight and then did two choruses of parody in which they sold cigarettes. Again I blew my stack and tried to get them to stop singing. They went right on like a locomotive rushing along a track. Week after week I kept trying to fire the quartet and week after week I was frustrated. Finally, we did a sequence in which I pulled off a piece of timing of which I've always been quite proud.

I was screaming about the Sportsmen. I cried that I was the head man on my program. I was sick and tired of being pushed around by Vincent Riggio, president of the American Tobacco Company, our sponsor. I fired the quartet—right there on the air. I told them to pack up their arrangements and get out, GET OUT—I never wanted to hear their rotten voices again.

The phone rang. Mary told me it was Mr. Riggio calling.

Storming, I shouted this was fine, just fine, I was glad he was calling and I was certainly going to tell Mr. Riggio that I didn't want any rotten insubordinate singers on my program and the quartet was fired and would stay fired. Or else.

Now please remember that during the next speech, the radio audience heard only my voice and my end of the conversation.

"Hello, Vince," I said, brimming with self-confidence. ". . . uh . . . uh . . . Vincent? . . . oh, Mr. Riggio, what can I do for you, Mr. Riggio? . . . You've been listening to the show? . . . Wasn't it great? . . . Oh . . . I shouldn't have what? . . . What? . . . But I had to fire them . . . The quartet is the worst gr . . . Oh . . . uh, you don't think so? . . . Well, Mr. Riggio, sir, everybody is entitled to his opinion. That's why they put rubber mats around cuspidors . . . What? . . . I guess you're right; it didn't get a laugh here either. But about that quartet, Mr. Riggio, I definitely feel that . . . I know, but . . . But, Mr. Riggio . . . I know, but . . . Yes, but . . . You might be right, but . . . but . . . but . . . but . . . but . . . but . . . but . . . but . . ."

As I recall, the last sequence of "buts" ran almost 120 seconds and I slowed down the rhythm so there were longer and longer pauses between each "but." On the ninth "but" I took a fourteen-second pause. With all due immodesty, I can say that I played these "buts" as neatly as a fly fisherman working a fighting trout. My timing was so inspired that the listeners at home, although they heard only one "but" after another "but" could visualize what the president of the American Tobacco Company was telling me.

It has many times been written that I am a master of timing. I would agree to some extent. I am a master of *my* kind of timing. Critics are sometimes more conscious of my timing because I have a slowly paced delivery. Bob Hope, on the other hand, has a fast, Gatling gun style. Hope is as much a master of timing as I am. But it's *his* timing.

I'll tell you what timing is. Timing is not so much knowing when to speak, but when to pause. Timing is pauses. The closest to the kind of timing a comedian has to learn to master is the timing of hitting a golf ball, where your swing has to be perfect, otherwise you will hook or slice the ball or—if you're a real duffer like George Burns— even miss that ball altogether.

The next season, though the Sportsmen Quartet was still on the program, I began trying out other vocal groups. I was going to *prove* to Mr. Riggio I could find a better quartet. On one show, the quartet consisted of Bing Crosby, Dick Haymes, Andy Russell and our own Dennis Day. Now to appreciate the next story you have to realize that in those days there was no such thing as taping shows in advance and editing out fluffs and pro- fanities. You did your broadcasts live and what was said in the studio, spontaneously and other- wise, went out over the four winds.

During the quartet spot, Crosby had to sing a note that was much higher than his normal bari- tone range. Instead of the usual sweet Crosby sound, he sang a hideous squeal. This upset him and when his voice cracked on the high note, he forgot about the quartet and snarled into the mi- crophone, "Who in the hell picked this key— Dennis Day?"

I have to explain two more things. In 1947 you did not say words like "hell," "damn," "syphi- lis," "bastard" or "pregnant" on the air. Sec- ondly, in several recent pictures, most notably in the Academy Award winner, *Going My Way*, Crosby had been playing priests. In those sweet innocent old days, all performers, network exec- utives and sponsors walked in fear and trembling of a vague indefinable monster known as "public opinion."

As soon as Crosby said the magic word "hell," all heck broke loose on every member station of the NBC network and all the switchboards began lighting up and buzzing as thousands of irate listeners telephoned to register their shock at "Father" Crosby's blasphemy.

After the show ended, an NBC vice president was waiting for me in the dressing room. He was shaking his head. He was fretting and fussing and fuming. He was sure one of my writers had purposely written in this line for Crosby and had given it to him just before the show so it had not been on the mimeographed script and the NBC censors had not been able to censor it. He did not believe me when I told him it was one of those little improvised sayings that a person utters in the heat of a tense broadcast.

He blamed me for the whole business. "You did an awful thing," he said. "An awful thing. What an awful thing you did. You'll have to apologize, Jack, for the awful thing you did. Your writers will have to issue some sort of a statement justifying themselves for the awful thing they did. Your producer, Hilliard Marks, will have to apologize for the awful thing. Lucky Strikes will have to apologize. NBC will have to apologize. Bing Crosby will have to apologize."

I waited and waited while he, like my imaginary Mr. Riggio, finished blowing off every molecule

211

of steam. He was full of steam. Finally, he was out of breath.

"You listen to me," I said. "Nobody is going to apologize."

He started to scream again.

I raised my hand to silence him. "The only thing that is going to happen is that in his next movie, Crosby will wear his collar frontwards, that's all."

He didn't think I was very funny.

The Sportsmen Quartet is a good example of a running gag. So were the almost fifty appearances of the Ronald Colmans. We never planned for them to be a running gag. We had scheduled them as guest stars for one show. This was after I had casually mentioned on the air, just as a quick gag, that they were my next-door neighbors. They actually lived about a block away. But the world came to believe they lived next door.

Once I was backing my car out of the driveway on North Roxbury just as a group of sightseers in a sightseeing tour bus had poured out. They were all looking at my house and I heard a woman telling her husband, "Now that's where Jack Benny lives, and over there in that big house is where the Colmans live, you know—Ronald Colman and Benita Hume—that is, Mrs. Colman— that's where they live, right next door to Mr. Benny and he's always running over to borrow sugar and flour and my, it's such a long walk, I never imagined it was this long of a walk, did you?"

I could not resist putting my head out the car window, which was fortunately open or I would have gotten a headful of broken glass. I called out, "Madam, I happen to be Jack Benny and I have to tell you that the Colmans do not actually live in *that* house—though they do live close by."

I'll never forget the woman's jaw dropping. If I hadn't driven away very fast, the lower part of her jaw might have become permanently disconnected from the upper.

Now, you may well ask, if the Colmans were *not* my next-door neighbors, why did I invent this geographical proximity?

I had a very good reason. I wanted certain sound effects, that's why. I wanted the sound of footsteps going to their house, coming away from their house—footsteps, that's why. I loved the sound of footsteps and I varied the rhythm of footsteps and the tone of footsteps and the volume of sound on footsteps. Sound effects were an important part of the language of radio communication. If you could find an interesting combination of sound effects, you often suggested a funny picture joke.

Many comedians, like Hope, open their programs with a monologue. I also did monologues —but in a different way. You might hear my footsteps, clicking along a sidewalk, making a transition from one scene to the next, and you'd hear me talking to myself, thinking out loud. Once, you heard the sound of my footsteps as I went into a store to shop for my very first television set, and my monologue went: "While I'm in there

213

looking over television sets, I think I'll buy some new records for the phonograph . . . I'm getting sick and tired of 'Cohen on the Telephone.' "

You people under thirty-nine will not get the point of this joke and I only bring it up for reasons of personal vanity. The day after this joke aired, composer Cole Porter telephoned me—from New York yet—to say, "This is the funniest joke I have ever heard."

My interior monologues were often spoken as I was returning home. Always the *click-clack-click* of shoes against pavement. And voice over *click-clack-click*: "Gee, the neighborhood sure looks nice . . . I love those weeping willows on Claudette Colbert's front lawn . . . I don't know why the Ronald Colmans don't buy new drapes for their windows. Honestly—with all the money they make, they still have the same old drapes . . . And, gosh, how nice W. C. Fields's swimming pool looks. What a clever idea, having those marbles in the bottom—no, they're not marbles, they're olives . . ."

The original idea for the Colmans came after a broadcast in November 1945. It was our custom that as soon as one show ended, I met with my writers and producer and we began planning the next Sunday's show. We worked from week to week. I casually remarked, "Fellers, wouldn't it be funny if I went over to the Colmans' for a party and I wasn't supposed to be there in the first place?"

But we didn't get a script I liked until two weeks

214

later and it took me another week to overcome Ronald Colman's reluctance to go on my show, as he was sure he would not be able to play comedy. The Colmans made their debut as comedians on December 9, 1945.

We opened with a spot in which I was reading the mail, most of which consisted of entries in the "I Can't Stand Jack Benny" contest. Mary was reading some of the letters and needling me and Phil Harris was also needling away. Then Rochester reminded me it was time to get dressed for the formal dinner to which I had been invited by the Colmans. Mary refused to believe they invited me. I showed her the invitation. Phil Harris wondered why they mailed an invitation, since they lived next door, and I said it was a formal party so you sent out invitations by mail. I had found the invitation on the back porch. I complained to Rochester about dropping letters when he took the mail out of the box.

"Dear Jack," the invitation read, "glad to know you are safely back in America. Benita and I would love to have you for cocktails and dinner Sunday evening. Will expect you around eight. Ronald Colman."

It seemed odd to her, Mary said, that they talked about me being "safely back in America" when I hadn't been out of America, and I told her not to bother me with such petty details. I put on my tails, white tie and top hat.

Then the scene cut to the Colman house and they were discussing the guest they were expect-

215

ing, a man named Jack, but not me—an old English friend, Jack Wellington. Should they dress for dinner? No, says Ronald, Wellington is an old friend and it will be an informal evening, just the three of them. He was in an old pair of slacks and turtleneck sweater and Benita had on an everyday housedress. Then Wellington arrived, straight from the tennis courts in dirty white pants and sneakers.

The butler entered. He announced that I was outside. He presented my card. Colman read it: "Jack Benny, star of stage, screen and radio. Will sing 'Oh Promise Me' at weddings. Has own tuxedo. Will travel."

They figure it is a mistake but being good sports, the Colmans just set another place for dinner. I joined them for cocktails. We clinked glasses. I clinked a little hard and there was the sound of broken glass. Benita remarked the glass was 150 years old.

"I'm glad I didn't break any of your new stuff," I said. "Oh, you're not dressed yet. Am I early? Why don't I just sit here and read a magazine while you three go up and dress?"

Well, to sum up the whole evening, I was a terrible bore, saying the most inane things and the pathetic part of it was I didn't realize I was such a crashing bore. Finally, I had to go home. I said good night to Wellington, to Benita, to Ronald.

SOUND: FOOTSTEPS . . . DOOR OPENS . . .

"Well, good night, Ronnie, old boy . . . I had a swell time."

SOUND: DOOR SLAMS FAST.

"I'm not *out* yet," I moaned, and you knew how much they wanted to get rid of me.

"Oh, oh, pardon me," Colman said.

SOUND: DOOR OPENS.

"Well, good night, Ronnie."

"Good night, Jack."

"Good night."

"Good night."

SOUND: DOOR SLAMS. FOOTSTEPS DOWN THREE STEPS AND ALONG SIDEWALK.

Jack hums "Love in Bloom." "Gee, they're such nice people, the Colmans, Ronnie and Benita . . . 'Can it be the breeze that fills the trees . . .' "

So many sound cues—slams of doors and opening of doors and creaking of doors and footsteps here and footsteps there. How much we got out of footsteps and door slams in those golden days of radio! How important they were in conveying a mood or setting a scene so the listeners created the pictures in their own minds. When I think of the hours I've spent worrying about the placement of a footstep or a slamming door . . .

You see, in radio's golden age we, and by we I mean all of us who were playing comedy: Hope and Wynn and Cantor and Fred Allen and Edgar Bergen (how can you ever do a ventriloquist act

217

on radio? People wondered until Bergen showed us how)—all of us, we invented a new technique of communicating comedy situations. We learned how to orchestrate voices, sound effects, pauses, silences, shrill voices, growls, eerie voices—and we strived to build moments and scenes just for the *ear*. We found out that if you have the ear, the outline and the colors, a picture was painted in the mind's eye. It was fabulous what the human imagination was able to project to itself.

Now you could pick up one of our scripts and read it and read the sound cues and the dialogue and maybe it would not be very funny. Well, let me tell you something. We didn't write to be read the way S. J. Perelman or Robert Benchley or James Thurber wrote. Nor did we write action in the sense in which playwrights wrote their scenes. Playwrights don't write words—they write actions. We wrote and we acted to be heard. We wrote pictures, made out of various sounds and voices.

To bring out this point, let me tell you something that happened around 1947. At that time, John Crosby, a new radio critic, was writing a fine column about radio three times a week in the late lamented *New York Herald Tribune*. Mr. Crosby was one of my greatest admirers. He always had nice things to say in print, but one Monday he went even beyond his usual flattery. He said that on the previous show I had excelled even myself. That show, he wrote, was simply a comic masterpiece, with brilliant writing and gleaming execution, inspired timing, magnificent conceptions. It was, all in all, the finest radio comedy program he had ever heard. And I, well, I was just about one of the swellest human beings in broadcasting with infinite talent.

I wrote Mr. Crosby a note of appreciation.

He replied to my note and said he was still so enthralled by that program that he would be grateful if I sent him a copy of the script since he wished to keep it as a memento. I had a professional typist from the outside type up a special edition of this script on fine heavy-duty rag paper, using special script type, and then I had this bound in calfskin and the binding stamped in gold with Mr. Crosby's name and the date of this historic broadcast. Then I airmailed it to him. The airmail charges alone amounted to three dollars and fifteen cents and I hate to tell you what the typing and the binding and the gold stamping cost.

All I will tell you is that this was the last time I ever sent one of my scripts to a radio critic. I wouldn't even send one of them an ordinary tattered mimeographed copy by *regular* mail. They can beg me all they want, but I never would. Because, two weeks later there appeared another John Crosby column, in which he started by taking back the rave he had previously written about that historical masterpiece of Jack Benny radio comedy.

"I have the script before me now," he said. "I have read it twice. It is turgid, flat, pointless, senseless, humorless, gutless, boring and belabored. What I mistook for good writing was a plethora of sound effects and what I mistook for good acting was Benny putting in a *hmmmmm* or a *welllll* every now and then." And to hammer home his point, he reproduced a page of the script.

And he was right. On paper there were not too many excruciatingly funny jokes. But there were two humorous door slams and a hilarious sequence of footsteps.

And my fine feathered critic could not ever come to realize how difficult it is to find the right place to put in a *hmmmmm* or a *welllll* and give it just the right inflection and volume and, yes, interpretive reading.

Oh, it's much easier to make an impact by yelling, "Oh, my God, he's bleeding to death," or "Come into my arms and let me look into your eyes and let us forget the whole world and think only of our love," or even, "Alas, poor Yorick, I knew him well"—than just to say, "Hmmmmm" and hit the audience so hard they laugh, or to say just the word "but"—that plain simple conjunction, "but"—and say it nine times in a row and make your laughs build and build and build.

CHAPTER 11

Many people, including myself, are very surprised that I'm well known in show business circles as being a good audience for other comedians. In fact, I would rather enjoy watching another comedian than perform myself. I don't know why this is. Entertainers are supposed to be self-centered, egotistical people; exhibitionists, who always want to be on, who love to have the center of the stage. Not me. Let someone else be at the center of the stage. Let me be in the audience laughing at *their* jokes.

Danny Kaye, for instance, will tell you that I am the most "sensational" audience for another comedian. He says I'm a dream audience. He says I don't just laugh with my mouth—but my whole body. He likes to tell about the time, way back in 1940, when he was a young and unknown japester, fresh from the Jewish hotels in the Catskill Mountains, and he was playing his first show in his first Broadway nightclub, La Martinique. From his first number on, he noticed a well-dressed, suntanned gentleman sitting at a ringside table. This man was howling with laughter, gasping, squealing, screaming. As Danny went on with his routine, I lost control of myself and started pounding the table. Eventually I fell on the floor—literally—and pounded it like a laughing hyena. Kaye never had such a reaction from anybody in his life and I guess he wasn't sure if I was some lunatic or if he was really so funny, so he turned to the bandleader and whispered, "Who's that?"

"That's Jack Benny," the maestro answered.

"Benny?" repeated Kaye. "And he's laughing at me?"

Well, I've been laughing at him ever since—

and loving it and not being jealous or competitive about it. I guess I'm a connoisseur of comedy. I appreciate a comic style or a comic personality the way other people appreciate fine paintings or rare wines. George Burns claims that because I am such an appreciative audience I have everybody in the business working for me for nothing and that Groucho Marx or Burns or George Jessel or Danny Kaye would rather put on a free show for me at home than play in a theater and get paid.

Of course Daddy laughed at George Burns the most. As George told me, "I hounded and harassed your father ever since we became friends. I played the most outrageous practical jokes on him. People who didn't know about us thought I was sadistic. I wasn't. Jack loved me to play jokes on him. He would have been hurt if I didn't do these terrible things. He would have thought I hated him.

"It all began on the day after we first met when he phoned and said, 'Let's have dinner at Leone's.' Leone's was a speakeasy then and Jack thought it had the best food in town. While we were talking on the phone, we got disconnected. That night when I met him for dinner, that's when I found out I was the world's greatest comedian. He fell down, he hit the floor, he screamed and laughed. I said, 'What are you laughing at?'

"He said, 'You're the funniest man in the

world. You hung up on me in the middle of a phone conversation.'

"After that I always hung up on him. I wanted him to go on thinking I was the world's greatest comedian."

The best movie I ever made, *To Be or Not to Be* (which I'll tell you more about later), was such a hit with audiences and critics that Warner Brothers signed me to a contract and the first movie they asked me to make for them was *George Washington Slept Here*, by George Kaufman and Moss Hart. It was a Broadway hit of the 1940–41 season and it brings to mind another comedian I appreciated highly: Percy Kilbride.

Jack Warner assigned the production of the picture to Jerry Wald, a young screenwriter who had never produced a picture before. Wald sent me the original play to read. It was about a naive man, a nature lover who buys an old decrepit house in Bucks County, Pennsylvania, because he loves antiques and American history. He is married to a hard-boiled woman who loves life in the city and hates this whole idea. The play is about their funny quarrels and all the trouble the husband has fixing up the house—which has no indoor toilet and, in fact, no water at all, as the well has run dry. In the stage version the wife, who was played by Jean Dixon, had all the comedy lines and her husband, a kind of sweet, meek little fellow, played by Ernest Truex, had all the straight lines.

I wanted to see the play before I made a decision. I flew to New York and saw the show and discovered that in it was one of the most beautifully drawn comic portraits I have ever seen. This character's name was Mr. Kimber, a handyman and would-be contractor who is supposed to help the husband modernize the house with local labor and, in addition, advise him on tree-spraying, fertilization and other agricultural esoterica. Mr. Kimber was played by an actor with an absolutely deadpan face, nasal voice and rasping delivery. I went out of my mind when I saw him. Percy Kilbride was unknown in Hollywood then. I thought Kilbride stole the show from the married couple who were supposed to be the leading characters. I thought Kilbride's was one of the wildest performances I had ever seen and I laughed every time he opened his mouth. I laughed even *before* I heard his lines.

Even so, I had another problem. Of the two leads, the woman had all the laughs. When I returned and met with Jerry Wald I asked if he was expecting me to play a straight part. They had already cast Ann Sheridan to play my wife.

"There's nothing to it," Wald said. "I'll show you how easy it is. We will take the lines that the wife speaks in the play and give them to you. And we'll give the man's lines to Ann Sheridan. She'll be the one who buys the run-down house in Bucks County and you'll be the man who hates nature and loves life in Manhattan. You'll see, Jack, it will work. Take my word for it."

He was right. The writers who were adapting the play only had to make a handful of minor changes. Otherwise Jean Dixon's speeches were intact but spoken by me, and Miss Sheridan had all Mr. Truex's speeches. It shows you what creative screenwriting can accomplish in adapting a Broadway play to the cinema.

On the day I signed the contract to make this picture, I asked Jack Warner to bring Percy Kilbride out to California. I told him that Kilbride played Mr. Kimber to perfection and he should also play the part in the movie. Warner told me that he had many fine character actors under contract, who were on a weekly salary and could play parts like this in their sleep.

"This will never work," I said. "This is a special kind of character. Percy Kilbride is unique. I'm telling you—he makes the play. Without him it would fall apart. I'm telling you this guy is great. You've got to hire him. He'll become a great comic movie actor. Mark my words, Jack, he'll be great in the movies."

Warner looked at me quizzically. "If what you say is true, Percy Kilbride will steal the picture."

"He sure will," I said.

"But, Jack," he said, "I don't understand. You and Ann Sheridan are the stars—why would you be willing to have this Percy Kilbride steal the movie?" He shook his head. "You're sure he'll steal the picture?"

"You're goddamn right he will," I said. "Somebody better steal it because, believe me, as it stands it is not a very strong vehicle. Without Kilbride, you've got nothing."

"I won't do it, Jack," he said.

"At least go to New York and see him in it."

"I haven't got time."

"So bring him out here and give him a screen test."

"It's a waste of money," he said.

I was getting mad. I knew I was right and he was wrong. "All right," I said, "you bring him out here. You do a test with him. If you don't agree with me, I'll pay all the expenses and I mean *all*—transportation, living expenses for Kilbride, cost of cameraman, director, film, makeup man —the works."

Warner was still shaking his head. "I never heard of such a thing," he said. "You want me to test a man who will steal the picture from you? You'll pay all the expenses? All right, I give in. I'll test him. I'll pay all the expenses. But on one condition."

"Name it," I said.

"You've got to do the test with Kilbride."

I was only too happy to agree. So we planned a fifteen-minute screen test, just him and me, doing a scene in Act I. Now you've got to realize that in this scene I hate Kilbride. My wife has dragged me into this ridiculous situation by secretly buying a hovel in the Pennsylvania countryside and now it's going to cost me a small fortune to get the place in shape. Kilbride is the man coming to me all the time about new disasters I have to shell out money for. I hate this man because he has a new bill for me every time I turn around. The only trouble was that I couldn't even look at Kilbride without breaking up. The minute he read a line, I went into convulsions.

We did the test with an assistant director, a cameraman and Miss Sheridan's stand-in reading her lines. We started with some dialogue showing that I'm furious to find out there's no water on this property my wife has bought so a well must be dug. At first I managed to keep a straight face. Even when Kilbride told me we need a cesspool, I had control of myself. We planned to finish the test with a scene from the first act. I was wrangling with my wife about our troubles when Kilbride entered and said he had good news: "We've drilled down four hundred and twenty feet and what do you think? We just struck mud."

I was supposed to glare at my wife and say, "Gee, that's just dandy. Those hot nights in August, when I say to our maid, 'Oh, Katie, make us a big pitcher of iced mud . . .' "

But I couldn't get the lines out. I was doubled over with laughter. After an hour we got it on film with the next lines about the gravel we needed and the lime for the lawn. Then he went into the speech about spraying the elm trees for elm blight, the oaks for the oak borers and the willow trees for caterpillars, measuring worms and I don't know what. I'm supposed to get madder and madder at my wife, especially when she agrees to spray every tree on the property. I had a funny line in which I shout, "Well, who runs through the woods and sprays all those wild trees in the forest, Mr. Kimber? *They* seem to be doing all right."

But I was choking up. I couldn't look at Kilbride's hatchet face. He didn't even crack a smile. The assistant director was blowing his top. He shot and reshot and then we reshot again.

When Mr. Kimber told us that we needed several truckloads of manure and it now cost $45 a load I was supposed to comment to my wife, "When manure costs more than a sirloin steak, darling, it kind of makes you stop and think." Except I couldn't comment. I just plainly and completely *plotzed*. I couldn't go on.

The screen test was a fiasco.

So then they brought in Ann Sheridan to make the test and they got *my* stand-in to read the lines. But *her* stand-in told Ann about the effect Kilbride had on me, so now she couldn't look at Kilbride with a straight face herself. Then they brought William Keighley, who was directing the film, to make the tests, either with me or with Ann or with both of us, but it was a lost cause. Finally Keighley decided to take Kilbride without a test.

But when at last we began to make the movie, I was in trouble all over again. Every time I had a scene with Kilbride, I broke up. We had to do twenty, thirty, forty takes on account of this. We were running weeks behind schedule and the costs of the movie were mounting. Finally Wald and

Keighley laid down the law. They threatened to throw me out of the picture if I didn't stop laughing at Kilbride. I stopped. I stopped by not sleeping the night before we did scenes with him and I came on the set so exhausted that I simply didn't have the strength to laugh at him.

At the sneak preview Percy Kilbride stole the show and began a long career in movies. He made the Ma and Pa Kettle series for Universal with Marjorie Main as Ma Kettle. He was a strange little man—Kilbride. What he played in movies was the person he was in life. He lived all alone. He had no friends. He wanted just so much salary for his work. He wouldn't take more and he wouldn't take less. He was a self-reliant, independent New Englander. I thought of making him a permanent part of our radio cast of characters and he was on the show several times. But radio made him nervous and he never came through the way, for instance, Parker Fennelly, another nasal-voiced New England character actor, did for Fred Allen.

Ernst Lubitsch directed me in the best picture I ever made, *To Be or Not to Be*. We made this picture, an anti-fascist satire, in 1941. I was thrilled to be working in this brilliant movie and being directed by such a great man. One day during shooting I asked him, "Ernst, tell me something—since I am a comedian, not an actor, why did you want me for this picture?"

He slapped his portly stomach and laughed.

"Jack," he said, "I tell you. In the first place, you are known as an entertainer and not as an actor. Consequently, if in this film you give a fine dramatic performance—I, Lubitsch, will get all the credit.

"That, Jack, is number one. Now I tell you number two. You think you are a comedian. You are not a comedian. You are not even a clown. You are fooling the public for thirty years. You are fooling even yourself. A clown—he is a performer what is doing funny things. A comedian —he is a performer what is saying funny things. But you, Jack, you are an actor, you are an actor playing the part of a comedian and this you are doing very well. But do not worry, I keep your secret to myself."

Carole Lombard played opposite me. The story was about a Polish Shakespearean ham actor in Warsaw during the Nazi occupation. I played this actor. I was in the Polish underground fighting the Nazis, but to provide a cover for my clandestine activities I pretended to be a Nazi collaborator.

While I was shooting the film, my father was living in Florida, where he had retired. He liked to stay at simple, unpretentious inns, patronized by elderly Orthodox Jews like himself. He took "dips" in the ocean and played pinochle with his friends. And he listened to the radio. Everybody he met had to listen to my show and be crazy about me or Papa would have a fight with them. Every Monday like clockwork he wrote me a letter in broken English. The closing sentence was always the same: "No matter who I meet they always know about my son, Jack Benny."

He carried around stacks of my pictures, which he handed out to strangers. Everyone in his hotel, Sundays at seven, had to sit in the lobby and hear the show. Once in his Monday letter, he said, "I met a man never heard of you. He never heard your programs. Could you believe such a thing? But don't feel bad, son. He was just an old Jew."

During his last years, Papa needed a full-time nurse, but even so, he went for strolls and his favorite pastime was going to my movies. He saw every one of them at least six times. I always felt sorry for the nurse.

To Be or Not to Be came to Miami Beach. In the first scene in the movie I wore a Nazi uniform and was seated in my office in the theater. Another actor entered and my right hand shot up in the Nazi salute. "Heil Hitler," I said.

My father watched the movie for about one minute and when he saw this scene he grabbed the nurse's arm and stomped out of the theater. The nurse couldn't believe that for once she didn't have to sit through another Jack Benny picture. I imagine she was the happiest nurse in all of Florida.

For two weeks I didn't receive the regular weekly letter. I wrote him. He didn't answer. I telephoned. He was never "in." Finally, one evening he answered the phone instead of the nurse when I called.

"Hello, Dad," I said.

No answer at the other end.

"This is Jack—your son."

"You're no son of mine! I got nothing to discuss with you."

"What did I do?"

"You gave the salute to Hitler is what you did."

"Did you stay for the whole picture?"

"I should stay for such a picture? I was never so ashamed in my life. I don't tell people anymore I'm the father of Jack Benny."

"But that was only the beginning of the picture. If you had waited you would see that I'm *against* the Nazis. I'm fighting them. Please go back and see it all the way through."

So he did. And how he loved that movie now. By his own actual count, Papa saw *To Be or Not to Be* forty-six times. Imagine.

In 1945 I toured Germany with a unit that included Larry Adler, who played the harmonica; Martha Tilton, who sang; and Ingrid Bergman, who spoke dramatic monologues. We traveled to Cologne and Munich and Wurzberg and Wiesbaden—wherever our soldiers were garrisoned. We saw terrible destruction everywhere, especially in the cities, where almost all the buildings were razed and the remaining civilian population lived in basements amid the rubble. Thinking of how much the Allied armies had suffered, how much the enemy had suffered and how six million Jews had been wiped out for no sane reason, I was in a kind of shock a lot of the time. Putting my feelings into words seemed to weaken the impact of the sights and sounds and smell of death in the air and the dust that lay like a pall over these great cities. Like so many American Jews, I had the special pang of knowing that but for the grace of God and my father's emigration, I could have been one of the victims of Dachau or Buchenwald or Auschwitz.

I was never in much of a mood to go out and tell jokes, but that was what I had been sent to Europe to do and, God knows, nobody needed laughter in those dark hours more than the men in Patton's armored battalions, the navigators, pilots and bombardiers or the weary foot soldiers who had fought for freedom.

We brought them laughter. We were a link with their families, their homes and the lives they had to leave. They didn't look at me as a celebrity. I was an old acquaintance, even a friend, an eccentric uncle maybe, who came to their homes every Sunday evening. I realized I was part of the memories of growing up in America, of everybody who had been ten years old or more in 1932.

Wherever the troupe went, I was hailed with shouts:

"Give my regards to Mary Livingstone!"

"Hey—where's Rochester?"

"How's Fred Allen?"

"Did you bring the Maxwell?"

"Is Mary with you?"

After the war, Ingrid Bergman played in Maxwell Anderson's play, *Joan of Lorraine*. The night we saw the play, Mary and I went backstage afterward and sat visiting with Miss Bergman in her dressing room. I asked her if she liked acting in a stage play. This was her first experience in the theater.

"Jack," she said, "I tell you it is nice to come out the stage door where the fans are waiting. They are very nice about wanting my autograph and saying sweet things, but the nicest thing is that not one person is asking about Rochester or Mary Livingstone or Fred Allen."

One evening after we had played for our troops in Stuttgart, we all got into a jeep to be driven back to our quarters. It was a warm night with a full moon. As we rattled along, an American M.P. stationed at an intersection yelled to our driver, "Halt!"

Our driver slowed up but kept going and the M.P. pulled out his revolver and fired at us. Several bullets came uncomfortably close to killing me. The driver, pale as a ghost, jammed on the brakes. The M.P. examined our papers and then signaled us to continue. Just as we began to move, a very large and majestic black cat stepped off the curb into the path of our jeep and slowly crossed the street, walking right in front of us. I looked at the black cat and said, *"Now* he tells us."

I was forty-seven when the war began. I was too old for the armed services. I served in the only branch of the service for which I was eligible—

Rochester and the Maxwell—with Frank Sinatra.
Courtesy Mark Wanamaker Collection

A family portrait in our Library, circa 1947.
Joan Benny Family Collection

Mother and Daddy with George and Gracie, mid-30's.
(Mom before she had her nose bobbed.)
Joan Benny Family Collection

On the Air for Lucky Strike cigarettes. From left: Dad, Phil Harris, Frank Nelson, Mom, Dennis Day.
Courtesy Department of Special Collections, University Research Library, UCLA

At a Friar's Roast
Top row, left to right: Danny Kaye, Pat O'Brien, Bob Hope, Al Jolson; hidden behind: George Burns and Eddie Cantor; bottom row, left to right: Daddy, George Jessel, Louis B. Mayer.

Courtesy Mark Wanamaker Collection

The last picture ever taken of Daddy (about six weeks
before his death).

Joan Benny Family Collection

the United Service Organization. I guess I'm prouder of this service than of all the other successes in my career. Leo Rosten, writing in *Look* magazine, was once kind enough to say, "No other trouper, with the exception of Robert Hope, was as generous of his time or profligate of his energy."

Hope was number one in our show business ranks—and he's still flying to every outpost in the world to entertain our men in uniform. No actor during the war traveled so far to so many places and lifted the spirits of so many servicemen as my ski-nosed old friend. But Hope represented the mightiest effort show business ever made to serve our country. He was one of thousands of comedians, dance acts, ventriloquists, animal acts, jugglers, magicians, chorus girls, concert musicians like Yehudi Menuhin, singers like Jan Peerce and noted stage actors like Maurice Evans, who gave his famous G.I. version of Hamlet.

By 1942 there were theaters in every large camp and naval base, with hundreds of U.S.O. units hitting the road. You played circuits similar to those of vaudeville. I began playing camp shows in 1942 and toured all over the country, usually playing the camps from Monday through Thursday, working with my writers in camp, and then flying back to Hollywood for two days' rehearsal and the show.

It was so much like the days when Salisbury & Kubelsky worked the Western Vaudeville Circuit. There were the same one-night stands, split weeks, packing and unpacking, rushing for a bus or train or plane, grabbing a few hours of sleep whenever you could and plastering on that smile. The audiences were different though—they were the most enthusiastic any performer ever could have.

I loved it—even though I was thirty years older and had the responsibility of a network broadcast every week. I had to find special jokes and stories that would reflect the attitudes and experiences of servicemen. Having been in the navy myself, I knew that the basis of all military humor is griping—about the food, K.P. duty, weekend passes and the brass. Jokes had to fit the military. One of the jokes the enlisted men loved was, "I saw a colonel dancing with a girl and he was holding her so tight, his shoulder eagles were hatching her earrings."

During the war we did a show in which Washington asks me to contribute the Maxwell to the scrap metal drive. I hated to part with it, but I was finally persuaded of its importance to the war drive. Then I fell asleep. I was restless. I had a dream about my Maxwell. I dreamed that it became a B-29. You hear the ear-splitting roar of bomber after bomber, winging across the Pacific Ocean. The roar becomes louder and louder. Suddenly there is a discordant grinding, a clunking of bolts, a wheezing and a groaning . . .

I didn't have to explain what *that* bomber had formerly been.

At one of the first army camps a medical officer

asked me to go through the hospital wards. He said that many performers were squeamish and he would understand if I refused, but he said these men could sure use a morale boost—I didn't have to put on a regular show, but just kind of walk through, tell a few stories and try to cheer up the sick men.

I did it. The response was so warm. I saw how wonderful it was for the patients. Even if my material wasn't great, even if they only saw me. They were so lonely and it was good to just know that somebody cared about them. From then on, wherever we toured, I would request permission either to put on an impromptu show in a large room at a hospital or stroll through the wards and talk to as many convalescents and invalids as I could.

I'll never forget one harrowing experience. Ed Sullivan put on shows for the patients at a large army hospital on Staten Island and one evening he took me along with him and some other actors. I brought my fiddle. There was a raised platform at one end of a recreation room that was crowded with men. Some had been wheeled in on their beds, others were in wheelchairs and many others—almost all healthy—were sitting or standing around. But they were a tense audience. I don't know why—but they were. Some had suffered nervous breakdowns during combat and seemed to be so wretched that nothing could make them laugh.

After I did a monologue of about fifty minutes, I picked up the fiddle and began to tune it. I'd been making jokes about my rotten playing for so long that I liked to finish my routine with a medley of tunes. This always got a thundering ovation because people were surprised I even knew how to play six notes on the violin, let alone the great catchy ragtime versions I did of "Fascinating Rhythm," "Puttin' on the Ritz" and "Sweet Georgia Brown." I usually opened with a few bars of "Love in Bloom."

On this occasion I went into the chorus of "Love in Bloom." Just as I got to the part about "can it be the breeze," one poor emaciated man in a wheelchair who had not smiled once during my monologue suddenly began shaking violently. Spit ran down his mouth and he fell out of the wheelchair to the floor in an epileptic fit. Two nurses ran to him, picked him up and wheeled him out.

I knew I had to say something to break the tension in that room. "Well," I ventured, "here's a guy who got sick only when I started to play the fiddle. Let me tell you fellows—this happens frequently when I play the violin to people who *aren't* in the hospital."

Everybody laughed. The tension was broken. Even the men who had been watching with grim faces during the monologue broke up and roared with laughter. The psychiatrist on the ward told me that that one joke was the equivalent of six months of psychotherapy. Well, I hope so.

In July 1943 I made my first overseas tour for the U.S.O. It began with a briefing at the Pentagon. My troupe consisted of Larry Adler, the singer Wini Shaw and the British actress Anna Lee. We picked up a piano accompanist, Jack Snyder, at Ascension Island. We started out in an old army transport plane in Miami, flew to Puerto Rico for the first show, hopped to British Guiana, then Belém in Brazil and then to Ascension. There we were given the use of a C-54 transport plane that would be ours for the rest of the trip. We named it "Five Jerks to Cairo," had the title painted on the plane and off we flew to Accra in West Africa.

Two, three, four shows a day. It was a rough schedule. Back in the plane. On to the next base, to the Sudan, Khartoum, Eritrea, Aden and Nigeria, flying in violent rainstorms, burning heat, through sandstorms and on to Cairo where I got my first mail from home. From Cairo we flew to Benghazi over the shifting sands of the desert where Montgomery had chased Rommel from El Alamein. Below us, partly covered by the sands, lay the skeletons of battered Nazi tanks.

At Benghazi I broke a bottle of champagne across a new B-17 Flying Fortress, christened BUCKSHEESH BENNY RIDES AGAIN. ("Bucksheesh" is Arabic for a tip.) They put this title on the plane in full color and then on one of its bombs they painted TO ADOLF HITLER— WITH LOVE IN BOOM . . .

From Benghazi to Tripoli, from Tripoli back to Cairo and now playing outdoor shows to audiences of as many as seven thousand. Then to Ismailia where I found a small kosher Jewish restaurant that served the best gefilte fish I ever tasted, and back to Cairo and then to Tel Aviv in what was then British Palestine, and on to Jerusalem, the Persian Gulf and the town of Abadan in Iran. We were the first American entertainers to come to this area. It was summer and the heat in the shade was 140 degrees. One afternoon in the sun it went up to 187 degrees. Our plane had to circle Abadan for an hour because of a sandstorm and finally had to land in Basra, fifty miles away.

Abadan had then become the second largest center of oil refining in the world and we were producing gasoline for our planes as well as British and Soviet planes. I am not exaggerating when I say that Abadan is the hottest place in the world. Between 1:00 P.M. and 4:00 the sun is so killing that all work in the refinery has to stop. Our men were doing a marvelous job in Abadan. Those who had guard duty had to stand watch even during those murderously hot afternoons.

At Abadan I had an unsettling run-in with racial prejudice. I had gone into a canteen to get a sandwich and a ginger ale. There was no air-conditioning in the place. A ceiling fan was lethargically stirring up the hot air. I got my food and sat down. A sergeant sat down beside me and said, "Hi, Mistuh Benny. Ah'm comin' to see your show t'night. You all got Rochester with you?"

"No," I said.

"Well, I sho am disappointed. You cain't have

240

much of a show without that Rochester. He's just about the funniest damn coon in the world."

I didn't think it was my place to get into a discussion with him about his racist language, so I merely said, "Well, I hope we'll put on a nice show even without Rochester." I was there to bring our men a little time out for laughter—they sure needed any relief at all with the monotony and the unbearable heat.

But this fool wasn't satisfied. "Seems to me, Mistuh Benny, without Rochester, you ain't got no show."

"You really love Rochester, don't you?" I said.

"Love him? Why, sir, ah tell you ah'd walk ten miles to see that Rochester."

"You love him that much, huh? Well, let me ask you something. Would you walk into this canteen and sit down with him and eat with him at the same table?"

His expression got nasty. "Well, sir, ah come from a part of the country where we don't sit down with nigras."

"I thought so, young man, and that's why I didn't bring Rochester on this trip. I didn't want him to be embarrassed and humiliated by ignorant folks like you. You say you love Rochester. You'll walk ten miles to see him perform. But you won't sit down at the same table and drink a glass of Coca-Cola with him. You make me sick."

I walked out of that canteen.

From Abadan to Teheran to Ahwaz to Alexandria

to Tripoli to Tunis to Catania in Sicily, to Lentini and Palermo, where I caught a cold. It got serious and they sent me to the 59th Evacuation Hospital where I was in a ward with five soldiers, three with malaria and two with yellow jaundice. After shows in Algiers and Marrakech, it was on to Prestwick in Scotland and Iceland for more shows and then back to New York. We arrived on September 28, having flown 32,000 miles and given 168 performances in ten weeks.

The following summer I went on an even more strenuous tour, island-hopping the South Pacific: Hawaii, New Guinea, Australia, the Solomon Islands, the Marianas, the Gilberts, Kwajalein—wherever there was an outpost of marines, an airbase, an army barracks, a hospital—in a town or on a small atoll, to bring a time out of war. This trip we flew some seventy thousand miles, back and forth. In Nadzab, New Guinea, Dr. Charles Mayo, one of the Mayo brothers, was in charge of a large naval hospital. He introduced himself to me at a show in Port Moresby and asked me and the company to go through the wards. Carole Landis was especially sympathetic with the patients. She had a way of sitting on the edge of a patient's bed and holding his hand and just getting into a friendly conversation. You soon forgot she was Carole Landis, the Sex Symbol, the Hollywood Star, the sweater girl, because she was a real human being and had a warm heart that spilled over with kindness. I guess it finally spilled over and drowned her because she committed suicide some years later after an unhappy love affair with a movie actor who was not able to marry her.

Dr. Mayo and I became great friends in New Guinea. I loved his way of telling stories and his earthy sense of humor. When we parted, Dr. Mayo said, "Jack, when this war is over and we get back home, we have to keep up our friendship."

"We certainly must, Chuck," I said.

Ten years went by after the war and we never once talked to each other. Then a friend of mine was going to the Mayo Clinic for a checkup and I called Dr. Mayo to ask him to look in on my friend while he was going through the tests. "Chuck?" I said. "This is Jack Benny."

"Why, Jack, how nice to hear from you," he said in his amiable voice. "And it's about time, too. Again, let me thank you for what you did for our men in the hospital."

I told him about my friend and we chatted.

"Let's get together real soon," he said and we hung up.

Now *eight* more years passed and we still had not gotten together or even talked and then I decided to go to the Mayo Clinic for a checkup myself. I decided to call Dr. Mayo. I called at night and rang his home.

"Hello," said the familiar voice.

"Oh, hello, Chuck, this is Jack Benny."

"*Again?*" he snapped, giving it the sigh and the weary tone of a pediatrician who's been getting calls every fifteen minutes from the anxious mother of a first baby.

In 1946 during our tour of occupied Germany I wanted to get to see Berlin, which was then out of bounds to U.S.O. entertainers. I did some shows in Munich and had a visit with General Patton, who told me he'd call General Eisenhower—perhaps when we played Frankfurt and Wiesbaden I could get permission from Eisenhower to go to Berlin.

Patton arranged an appointment for me and when I got to Ike's office his secretary warned me that only ten minutes were allotted to me. Larry Adler accompanied me and the two of us walked into the great man's office filled with awe. In two minutes his smile and friendliness made us feel at home. I introduced him to Adler, saying, "This young man has been traveling with our troupe. He plays the harmonica like Heifetz plays the violin. His name is Larry Adler."

Adler said hello and sat down quietly, saying nothing.

Instead of ten minutes, I spent almost an hour with General Eisenhower, telling him stories and jokes. I didn't realize it then but I'd really been doing a U.S.O. camp show for a soldier who very much needed some laughter. It's true I put on the show for just one soldier, instead of thousands, but that one soldier was carrying the burdens of millions of American soldiers on his shoulders.

Seven years passed and now Ike was President.

In 1952 I went to Washington to attend the Inaugural Ball. We only had time to exchange a few brief sentences, but just before we separated he said, "Say—how's that nice harmonica player of yours—Larry Adler, wasn't it?"

"With all the things on your mind, Mr. President," I said, "how did you remember that?"

And he smiled.

Now, many more years passed and Ike was visiting Palm Springs. One morning I heard he was playing golf at Tamarisk and I went over to renew our acquaintance and study his technique. I caught up with him at the fourth tee. He was getting ready to drive when I walked over and said, "Hello, General."

He smiled and said, "Hello, Jack."

We talked a few moments and then he hefted his club and began getting into a swing. Just before he hit the ball, he stopped short, looked over at me, his eyes twinkling and said, "Remember the time we met in Frankfurt?"

"I sure do," I said, "and tell me, what was the name of the harmonica player who was with me?"

"Mr. Adler," he said, quick as a flash, smiling like a kid who has gotten 100 in an algebra exam!

CHAPTER 12

Compared to Daddy's, my memories of the war are blurred. Hazily, I remember a time of high excitement. Although I can't recall Pearl Harbor and President Roosevelt's famous speech, by the time the war was in full swing I was old enough to understand and even take part in the war effort. I remember Daddy leaving for his trips overseas, the letters he sent me (I wish I had kept them), and the thrill of meeting his train when he arrived home. And my parents talking of battles with exotic names in remote places: Guadalcanal, Kwajalein, Iwo Jima. And the air raid drills at school. Once in a while an air raid siren would wail—just for practice. And the barrage balloons anchored up and down the California coastline. And the patriotic fervor—walking to school because of gas rationing, collecting tinfoil from my mother's Parliament cigarette packages, singing those rousing songs: "From the halls of Montezuma to the shores of Tripoli," "Anchors aweigh, my boys," "Off we go, into the wild blue yonder." And on the way to Palm Springs driving by March Field where we could watch the fighters and bombers taking off and landing. The men looked so handsome in their uniforms.

My parents of course participated full-time: entertaining and selling war bonds. While Dad was away overseas, Mom served as a member of the V.A.C.'s, a volunteer group of celebrity women who hostessed at the local armed forces facilities.

My real contributions to the war effort, other than wadding up the tinfoil, were gardening, collecting eggs and knitting. Originally, the large courtyard at the back of our driveway contained a badminton court, but during the war it was dug

246

up, fenced in and became my victory garden. I was given my own hoe and rake and with the help of Bill, the gardener, I made neat little trenches and planted vegetable seeds. I only recall the radishes and carrots, because they grew the fastest and to my impatient self were the most rewarding. I tended my garden daily—watering and watching its progress. I couldn't wait to get home from school to see if something had grown. I remember my victory garden fondly because I've never been able to grow a thing since.

Behind the pool house, next to the gentlemen's changing room, we set up an area for Rhode Island Red chickens. We must have had forty or fifty of them, each in a separate cage in two rows, one on top of the other. It was my job to collect the eggs.

But my favorite and most idiotic contribution was knitting. Once a week in the afternoons my little friends and I gathered with our nannies at each other's homes for tea and knitting. We were taught how to make simple squares that could be sewn together to make blankets for "our men in uniform." We knitted—only knitted, none of us was clever enough to purl. Someone else did the assembling. Can you imagine this spoiled group of six- to ten-year-old Hollywood brats with nannies in attendance to pick up all the dropped stitches, sitting by the pool or in the living room of one of our grand homes, or in some cases, estates, making stupid, ugly little squares? Then being served tea from a Georgian tea service and pastries on a silver salver covered with a lace doily by the butler and waitress? As they say, "Only in Hollywood!" I still feel sorry for the men who received those pathetic misshapen blankets.

The group at those knitting affairs included the daughters of Loretta Young (Judy), Joan Bennett (Melinda), Robert Montgomery (Elizabeth), Gary Cooper (Maria), Jack Warner (Barbara), Darryl Zanuck (Susan), Jules Stein of MCA (Jean and Susan), the granddaughter of L. B. Mayer (Barbara Goetz), the sons of Edward G. Robinson (Manny—or Eddie Jr.), Ray Milland (Danny), Barbara Stanwyck (Skip), Andy Devine (Tad) and of course, Sandra and Ronnie Burns. Yes, the boys knitted squares, too.

Bens left to become a part of the war effort when I was about six. She joined the Army and Navy Y in San Pedro and was then sent to the Hawaiian Islands for five years. Her successor was the remarkable, indefatigable spinster from the midlands of England, the very British Miss Julia Vallance. Since I was now really too old for a nanny, she started life with the Bennys as my governess, continued as housekeeper and general factotum, and stayed until her retirement some thirty years later at age seventy. I called her V. She was wonderful—a Mary Poppins type who wouldn't have surprised me one little bit had she come to us from the sky holding her umbrella. She insisted on good manners at all times and, though reasonably strict, had a sense of fairness, fun and, above all, humor. It's thanks to her that

I have reasonably good posture today and have never had back problems. She used to tell me that she grew up in a family where if she slouched at the dinner table, her father put a rod behind her back. I never met him but I was always afraid of that father.

It's also thanks to her I have some semblance of sanity. She was the most down-to-earth person I've ever known. She was the epitome of "sensible." She acted as a go-between with my mom and me. If she thought my mother was being too strict or unreasonable, she eased the situation. If I got on my high horse she threw me off. She listened patiently to my problems, encouraged me in all my endeavors, and took great pride in my small accomplishments. Above all, she was my best friend and confidante.

My best contemporary friend was Sandy Burns. Although we see very little of each other today because she lives in San Diego and I spend most of my time in New York, my friendship with Sandy goes back practically to day one, and there's a bond between us that will last our lifetimes. We were three months apart in age (she's the younger) and we were adopted within two months of each other. Sandy came from the Cradle in Chicago, I from The Free Synagogue in New York. The Burnses and the Bennys moved to California during the same year. We were wheeled in our prams together, played in the sandbox together and later got into trouble together.

We learned to use our blonde hair, blue eyes

249

and angelic faces to the best advangage, always protesting our innocence, and most of the time it worked—but then came Ronnie, Sandy's brother. Ronnie was a year younger, out-angeled us, and was the apple of his parents' eyes. He was a quick study. He soon discovered he could do anything he damn well pleased, blame it on us and get away with it. I remember once when he rang the burglar alarm. Three squad cars with sirens blaring arrived at the same time as George and Gracie were returning home from dinner. Sandy and I told them the truth, "Ronnie did it." Ronnie said, "They did it." Guess who got punished?

On Saturday nights Sandy and I frequently stayed over at each other's houses. Sunday mornings Sandy had to go to nine o'clock mass at our local Catholic church, the Church of the Good Shepherd, so naturally I went with her. (Gracie, as you probably know, was an Irish Catholic.) Mother didn't care—she was still sleeping; Daddy didn't care—he was playing golf. I used to claim I was Jewish six days a week and Catholic on Sundays; Sandy said she was Catholic six days a week and Jewish like her father on Fridays because she hated fish.

Back to the subject of religion—as I said before, it wasn't a big deal in my family. First of all Daddy wasn't a "Jewish comic," he wasn't even a comic in the true sense, rather a comedian who was Jewish. He rarely if ever did Jewish humor or told Jewish jokes. Although he came from a religious home, once he left he never really practiced his religion again. I used to jokingly say his religion was show business. It didn't matter what church you went to or what color your skin happened to be, as long as you were doing well! Being Jewish was simply not an issue. On the other hand, Daddy felt strongly about the fact that there were Gentile country clubs where no Jews were allowed membership, and hotels and restaurants where blacks were unwelcome. Not that he actively campaigned against anti-Semitism or discrimination—that wasn't in his nature. He just didn't understand it. It made no sense to him.

Being a member of the Jewish country club, Hillcrest, suited him better anyway. The food was—and still is—sensational, better than any other club, and besides, all his best friends were there: Burns, Jessel, Cantor, Jolson, Groucho, Berle, Danny Kaye. We were also members of the Wilshire Boulevard Temple but never attended services, nor did we observe the holidays except for every year on Yom Kippur when Daddy would remember his father and say, "I really should go to temple today for my father." I don't think he ever did. (I went to my first seder when I was in my late twenties.)

When I was about seven I must have expressed some curiosity about being Jewish—or was I Catholic, too?—because Mother and Daddy all of a sudden decided that I should go to Sunday temple school. So instead of church with Sandy I went to temple with Deedee. It was short-lived. Three weeks in a row we were caught reading comic books behind our study books and warned not to do it again. On the fourth week we were kicked out. I guess my parents thought it was enough—my just being inside the temple—because they couldn't have cared less. I went back to church with Sandy.

I have often been asked, "What was Gracie like?" That's a tough question for me because just like separating "Jack Benny" from Daddy, she was "Gracie Allen" publicly, but in my personal relationship with her she was "Sandy's mom." She was "Watch out, your mother's coming!" My outstanding memory of her is the picture of her scolding Sandy. Gracie didn't even reach five feet and Sandy, by the time she was a teenager, must have been five feet ten. She towered over both her parents. Seeing Gracie looking up at her daughter and shaking her fist was a riot.

The Burnses lived about half a mile away on North Maple Drive in a house similar to ours. Actually theirs had been built first by the same architect, ours was a copy on a slightly larger scale. They lived a bit more simply; fewer servants, less formal entertaining. But I think Gracie was more secure than my mother and had less need to show off their success. They spent more time with family—they had a much bigger one—and close friends and entertained more simply. They were certainly a major part of the Hollywood scene and went to the Hollywood parties and had a few of their own, but all in all they lived a quieter life.

In the front of both houses narrow beds of flowers (ours were pansies) and a low white brick wall separated the sidewalk from the lawn. A red brick path led to the front door and was bordered by two hedges with tall rose bushes and seasonal flowers in between, and next to the house itself, all the way across, were more flowers and bushes. A large expanse of lawn made up the rest of the garden. The front yards of our houses were almost identical. The driveways, as you faced the house, were on the left, each with one white brick post at the sidewalk edge. Each of our posts stood about three feet high by two feet square. Actually they were square only some of the time—when they had been recently repaired.

At our house every morning the butler brought Daddy's car to the side door, but sometimes Daddy left early and went to the garage to get it himself. Although there was plenty of space to turn around in the courtyard, he didn't always bother to use it and backed the car all the way out to the front. Now, our driveway was wide and fairly straight and really not difficult to maneuver, at least not for Mother or later for me, but Daddy was a poor driver at best with his mind usually elsewhere. He didn't hit the post every time—just about once a month.

A few years later, at great expense, the post was moved about twelve inches over, away from the driveway. My mother thought that would solve the problem and save on repair bills. Wrong! If the post had been placed on the next block, he still would have found a way to hit it.

The Burnses' white brick post stood in exactly the same place in relation to their house, but their driveway was narrower and curvier. George hit theirs even more often than Daddy hit ours. Sometimes they hit each other's!

Our driveway was the starting point for many of Daddy's vacations. One character who, though mentioned frequently, never actually appeared on the show was Frank Remley, the heavy-drinking guitar player in Phil Harris's band. Not only was Frank real, he did indeed play guitar in the band and he even drank a little. He laughed louder than anyone else—when I listen to tapes of Dad's radio shows, I can still hear Frank's laughter clearly. He was also one of Dad's closest cronies. (Laughing a lot was a requisite for friendship with Dad.)

Next to the violin and golf, driving was my father's favorite pastime, and just like the violin and golf he wasn't very good at it—his mind was usually elsewhere. But he loved it anyway, and he was blessed. He never had a serious accident. Whenever he had a few days to spare, off he'd go with one of his pals. Some men like to hunt or fish or sail—Daddy liked to drive leisurely with frequent stops to sightsee, play golf and go to movies. Over the years he must have taken hundreds of trips in addition to those he took to entertain the troops—to the Southwest, north to Seattle or Canada, and even across the country. I remember sometimes when we had to go to New York, he'd say, "Mary, you and Joanie take the train, I'll drive."

"Rem" was one of his favorite driving companions. Gloria Stewart, Jimmy's wife, recently recalled: "I met the Bennys before I married Jimmy. That was when I was married to Ned McLean, and I met them at some Hollywood party or other and knew them quite well. As a matter of fact, once Jack was going to drive to Las Vegas and Ned was at the ranch in Colorado Springs and I said I was going there and Jack said, 'Oh, drive with us and then we'll drop you off in Denver.' I said, 'Fine.' So Frank Remley, your father and I started out. Frank would start off driving. Jack got in the car and said, 'Good morning, Frank.' Frank would start to laugh so hard that we'd be going about four miles an hour. Now Jack didn't do any driving on this trip, so then I'd say, 'Well, okay, now it's my shift,' and I'd drive and I'd pass all these cars and then Frank would get behind the wheel again and Jack would say something, Frank would start to laugh and then all the cars I'd passed would pass us. So I did most of the driving to get to Denver. We were hysterical. If your father said, 'Frank,' he'd fall right down. Your father had a way of saying 'Frank.' He was a nifty guy."

Mel Blanc told me a story that made Daddy fall down laughing: "Your dad and I had a favorite expression that we used with each other all the time. I had just got a Rolls-Royce and I wanted to give it my personal license plate. So I went to the License Bureau and I said, 'I want one with KMIT on it.' The guy asked, 'Are you on a radio station—because it can't be an advertisement.' I said no. So he said, 'Well what does KMIT stand for? It can't be anything dirty, you know.' 'Oh,' I said, 'It's not dirty—KMIT—Know Me In Truth.' He said, 'Okay, that's very nice.' Actually, it means Kir Mir Im Tuchas, which is Yiddish for Kiss My Ass. Your dad loved it."

Mel Blanc was the only cast member with whom Dad had a close personal relationship. The reason is simple: Dad liked people who made him laugh. Dennis and Don and Roch were not funny in person. (Phil was funny but he and his wife, Alice Faye, had a whole other set of friends.) Mel made him laugh. And it was a man-to-man thing. Mom and Estelle Blanc, although they liked each other, were not what I would call "girlfriends," nor did the Bennys and the Blancs see each other socially. But Mel and Daddy adored each other. They had constant running gags. And of course I was crazy about Mel because he was always willing and ready to do Bugs or Tweetie Pie or Sylvester and I pestered him constantly.

The Blancs had a summer home at Big Bear Lake, and I remember one July when I was fourteen Daddy and I and a girlfriend of mine went to visit them. Not only did Mel do all my favorite voices but in the evenings he would make up funny songs ("Do you wanna, do you wanna, do you wanna see, see, see Tee-a-juana . . .") and play the guitar. The highlight of the trip was an attempt to teach my father to water-ski. It was a hilarious failure. He wasn't what I would call a natural athlete, and after about ten awkward tries he gave up and refused to try again.

Another of Daddy's favorite things, somewhere between the violin and golf and driving, was baseball. Until the mid 1950's, Los Angeles didn't have major-league ball. We were in the Pacific Coast League, and our local teams were the Hollywood Stars and the Los Angeles Angels. Daddy was an avid Stars fan. (Of course when he went to New York he attended the real ballgames. He was a Giants fan—and a Yankees fan.) Gilmore Stadium, home to the Stars, stood on the site of what is now CBS Television City, where coincidentally Daddy did many years of telecasts. Everyone had a box there: the Burnses, the LeMaires (Deedee's parents), Jessel, Danny Kaye, most of the Marx Brothers, etc., etc. When the Stars played their home games he went with his pals almost every night. On weekends he took me. George took Sandy and Ronnie, Rufus LeMaire took Deedee and her brother. Those evenings were like huge parties, all our friends were there. I loved going to the games. Of course I loved it —it was something else I could share with my father. I learned the players' numbers, the ERAs and RBIs, all the statistics. I wanted Daddy to be proud of me—or was I just showing off?

Many years later the Brooklyn Dodgers moved to Los Angeles and my father switched allegiance. They played in the Coliseum while their new stadium was under construction, and it was there that Daddy and I watched them win the World Series against Chicago in 1959. Then in 1965 they did it again, this time against Minnesota at Dodger Stadium. Those were the most memorable and thrilling ballgames I've ever seen. Daddy and I were invited to sit in Dodger owner Walter O'Malley's box for the whole series, and there was one day when we were literally holding on to each other by the seventh inning as we anxiously watched pitcher Sandy Koufax going for a perfect game. By the ninth inning we weren't even breathing. He did it! I know there are many football and basketball fans out there, but don't tell me baseball isn't exciting!

Our dining room, like the Burnses', was simply a larger version of the breakfast room, and the center of major family occasions. The Bennys and Burnses dined at each other's homes frequently. Those evenings were hilarious, not only because George was funny and sometimes outrageous, but for another, somewhat bizarre reason—we all ate like vacuum cleaners. This eating style, which we children copied, probably stemmed from all those years in vaudeville, doing six or more shows a day, rushing to catch a train and having to grab a bite in between. Mother was the exception. She had not been in vaudeville and consequently ate like a normal human being.

These were the unspoken rules. You began eating as soon as you were served, no waiting for the hostess. For Daddy and George the soup had to be boiling hot, still bubbling, or it was sent back. You were expected to eat as fast as you could. Pity the poor butler who had to keep up with the seven (six, not counting Mother) of us. It looked like an old silent film with the action on fast forward. By the time he served meat and potatoes to the fourth person, the first one had finished and wanted the next course. And so it went. How amazing that both families kept their butlers as long as they did. We should have bought them roller skates.

George, or Natty to his close friends and family (his real name is Nathan Birnbaum), as you might assume, was always a riot, whether at a party or just with the family. Everyone loved him. Me too. I loved his wit and I loved to listen to him tell vaudeville stories about all the crazy acts like Singer's Midgets and Fink's Mules. I loved the practical jokes he constantly played on my father, and I loved their relationship. George could make Daddy laugh by hardly doing anything at all.

Ronald Reagan remembers a time when George did one of his numbers on Daddy. "It was at a dinner party at our house. Three or four of us, including George, were standing together talking and Jack joined us. He spoke of a new comedian he had seen in the east at some club. He was most enthusiastic and called the new comedian one of the funniest performers he'd ever seen. George interrupted him: 'Jack,' he said, 'you think he's great because you're a sucker audience. We probably wouldn't think he was funny at all.' Jack remonstrated, but George wouldn't be stopped.

259

He said that he was going to do something with his cigar that he'd lighted and none of us would think it was funny, but Jack would fall right to the floor laughing. Then, he took his cigar and flicked ashes on Jack's lapel and Jack ended up on his knees, beating the floor as he laughed."

George was always great fun. But far more than just fun. I think one of the greatest privileges of my privileged life was growing up with George Burns.

CHAPTER 13

Daddy had a charmingly trusting, childlike quality that, though endearing, had its negative side. Because he was an honest man, he assumed everyone else was, too—not so much through stupidity or naivete, but because he had more important things on his mind—next Sunday's show, for example—than worrying about whether or not someone was telling him the truth. He did have a tendency to be mentally lazy about people in whom he had little interest. It was easier to take them at face value. Discrimination was not one of his many virtues! He was fortunate that it only got him into serious trouble once.

Back before the war Daddy and Mother met a man by the name of Albert N. Chaperau at a dinner party in Beverly Hills. According to Daddy, he looked a little like George Sanders, dressed conservatively in expensive Peal shoes and Sulka shirts and represented himself as a diplomat who had been born in France, but was a Nicaraguan citizen. He told everyone he was a consular attaché for Nicaragua. He was on intimate terms with some of the finest people in the movie colony, including George and Gracie. He fascinated everyone—he knew the vintage years of the good wines, was an authority on women's clothes, antique furniture and fine jewelry. He was a popular bachelor who moved in the best circles.

As it turned out, he was a professional criminal with a record, although his diplomatic credentials were genuine enough. There were rumors that he was mixed up in various international gold and narcotics smuggling capers. One of his methods was to buy jewels from the many then increasingly desperate people in Europe—somehow forgetting to transfer title—and smuggle them into New York where he sold them under the table, untaxed and undeclared. Chaperau's charm and lifestyle enabled him to cultivate relatively unsophisticated celebrities like Daddy as a cover for his criminal activities. It's also possible that he thought he could sucker him into a trap by letting him unwittingly participate in a crime—and then blackmail him.

In the summer of 1938 Mother and Daddy made a grand tour of Europe, ending on the Riviera in September. And who should turn up in Cannes but their old acquaintance, Albert Chaperau. He was delighted to see them again and insisted on taking them to little cafés and restaurants that were unspoiled by tourists. Because he was fluent in French and its history, he was a wonderful guide. When Mother expressed interest in shopping for jewelry, which of course she did all the time, he knew of a splendid bijouterie where the proprietor was an old friend and would give them a "break." Daddy ended up buying Mother two gold clips studded with small diamonds and a gold bracelet, also set with diamonds. He paid less than $1,000 for them.

A week or so later when Chaperau was going back to the States, leaving my parents in Europe, he asked if he could do them a small favor in return for all their hospitality. Because he had certain diplomatic rights as a commercial attaché, he said he could legally bring jewelry into the States without going through customs and paying import duty. Daddy certainly didn't need the few hundred dollars he'd save by not declaring the three pieces of jewelry. But Chaperau was carrying on about his feelings being hurt, and to be a nice guy Daddy gave him Mother's jewelry to take home.

The following winter the Treasury Department discovered that Chaperau was an international thief with "connections" to both the Burnses and the Bennys, among many others. Fifteen of his society friends were subpoenaed. The T-men told Daddy if he pleaded guilty and testified against Chaperau he would merely be fined and receive a suspended sentence. At first Daddy refused to do this, feeling strongly that he was *not* guilty. But legal mills grind slowly and by the time Daddy's trial came up Chaperau had been tried, convicted and sentenced to five years in prison.

I think I'll let Daddy finish the story:

The executives at NBC, General Foods and the advertising agency were in a state of hysteria as the scandal erupted on the front pages of every newspaper. Would the ratings go down? Would my popularity be ruined forever? The fact that my life might be wrecked was beside the point. They kept talking about "public relations" and "strategy" for handling the press and what kind of statements I should make. To these people I was a pawn in a gigantic chess game of competition for ratings and the sales of boxes of powdered gelatin. The main problem was how would this influence the sales curve of Jell-O?

I didn't want to plead guilty. I had been having meetings and conferences with network brass and sponsor representatives and they kept me in a state of nervous tension so I couldn't think straight. My show was the number one rated show in radio. At that moment I was probably the single most popular radio star in the country. They finally decided to take a chance and continue sponsoring me—or "risk their necks," as they put it—and let me go on the air every Sunday.

The only reference I made to the case on my

show was in a scene in which Rochester and I are hiking in the desert near Palm Springs. There's a sound effect of rattling.

"Look out," Rochester warned, "there's a rattlesnake."

"Listen, rattlesnake," said I, "would you please leave me alone? I'm in enough trouble as it is."

The rattlesnake stopped rattling.

It was in April 1939 that I returned to New York to stand trial, determined to fight the case. William J. (Wild Bill) Donovan was retained as associate counsel. Donovan was a vigorous, aggressive attorney and a World War I hero who would distinguish himself in World War II as the director of the O.S.S. I was surprised when Donovan, known for being a fighter, advised me to plead guilty. "There are times, Mr. Benny," I remember Donovan saying, "when an honest man gets into trouble without meaning to and then the bravest thing is to take your punishment even if the world—even if the whole world—thinks you're admitting you're bad by doing this. As long as you know in your soul that you are right—that is all that matters. And I'll make a guess—in the long run, you'll find that the American people will not only forgive—they will forget."

So I pleaded guilty. I was fined $10,000 and given a six-month suspended sentence. George was fined $15,000 and given a year and a day's suspended sentence.

I went back to the Coast. Every Sunday when

I left the studio, crowds of men and women and kids were outside. They still wanted my autograph and seemed to be so friendly to me. Though the true story of my "diamond smuggling" had not been printed, and despite all the scandalous things that were printed, as well as all the gossip, they seemed to believe in me and still love me.

But what would the ratings show? Would my listeners across the nation stop listening to me?

The day before I was indicted, my Crossley rating was 37.4. Three months after I pleaded guilty and had been fined and humiliated, my next Crossley rating showed a leap to 40.1.

I am very proud of such a vote of confidence from the American public.

Daddy's run-in with Chaperau did have an effect on me—though indirectly. I had to be *good:* well behaved, polite, mannerly, discreet, courteous, respectful and *above all*—don't get into trouble. I remember those lectures well! The reason given was that anything I did would reflect on my father. The newspaper headline wouldn't read, JOAN BENNY . . . , it would read, JACK BENNY'S DAUGHTER . . .

I tried to follow the rules. I was usually, though not always, well behaved; I was extremely polite and courteous. But I had a problem with the "above all," the troublemaking part. I was a born rebel—still am—a mischief maker and occasional practical joker. Fortunately I was clever enough not to get caught—at least not very often.

Those rules were very simply what they were —rules. The reason given satisfied me at the time. I didn't know then that there was a reason behind the reason.

As children we all accept our parents as they are, more or less without question. My parents seemed to me just like other parents. No, Mom didn't do housework or laundry or make breakfast for me or drive me to school and Daddy didn't mow the lawn or change light bulbs or help me with my homework, but I didn't know as a child that there were parents who did those things. Daddy went to work like other fathers. Mom had lunch with her girlfriends and went shopping and played golf just like many other mothers. When they came home they discussed the day's events, and at dinner they discussed, no, not what was happening in glamorous Tinsel Town—they compared their golf games, hole by hole. Dinner conversation, along with Tuesday's liver and Friday's fish, was not a thrill. They always did this and they always would.

It never occurs to us that anything can change. I was lucky—nothing ever did for me. But it could have. I didn't know about such things as sponsors or networks. I didn't know about contracts and how they came up for renewal every year. Dad's was a family show, families gathered together to hear it and later to watch. During the decades of radio and early television the shows had to be squeaky clean, and the actors on them above reproach. A cast member would be summarily fired for any hint of scandal. If the scandal involved the star, especially one whose name was the show, the whole show would be out the window, down the drain, kaput! It was many years later, as an adult, that I finally understood the vital importance of those words, "You have to be good!"

Although my upbringing was very strict as far as manners and discipline were concerned, in other ways I was terribly spoiled. I got away with a lot because my mother slept late and never knew what went on in the mornings, and although Daddy was up, he was less than concerned about whether or not I did chores. I didn't have to make my bed (except for a brief time when Miss V insisted)—a maid did that. I never had to do dishes—the cook did that. I was told to pick up my clothes, but I quickly learned how to get around that. I discovered at an early age that if I left them on the floor or on a chair long enough, they would eventually disappear, only to reappear sometime later, cleaned, pressed and neatly hung in my closet. Magic!

I have a friend who to this day teases me about my childhood. If I ask him for a glass of water he says, "Would you like it in a Steuben glass on a silver tray with a linen doily?" Well, that's the way it was done where I grew up. Not all the time of course. My bedroom was right by the back stairway and most of the time when I wanted something from the kitchen I flew downstairs and got it for myself—tap water in a kitchen glass or ice cream in a kitchen bowl. I really never asked to be waited on. I certainly never called down and asked for something to be sent up. I wasn't that spoiled! The only time the silver tray and doily appeared was when my mother called the kitchen on the intercom to order something. When asked if I'd like something, too, like a coke or a sandwich, it was brought with all the fancy trimmings. Daddy, like me, did his own fetching.

I was taught impeccable manners. Dinners were served formally, even when my parents didn't join us. The table was set with linen place mats and napkins, Wedgwood service plates, assorted dinner plates depending on the formality and menu of the evening, Steuben crystal and Tiffany sterling. I learned at an early age which utensil to use (we had every known shape and size), how to place them apart on your plate when you weren't finished, together when you were and even how to set a proper table myself. When we were seated the butler placed the first course, salad or soup, on top of the service plates. When we had finished it was all removed and replaced by dinner plates. He passed the main course around on a silver serving dish (or dishes), each of us helping ourselves. After that came the fingerbowls, each with a small porcelain flower in it, and then dessert. The fingerbowl was a ritual—it was placed on top of a linen doily on top of the dessert plate. You held the doily with your left hand, the bowl with your right and lifting the two together, placed them at the upper left-hand corner of the place setting. Then dessert could be served on the now bare dessert plate.

The fingerbowl ritual led to some wonderfully funny and embarrassing moments for my teenage friends unfamiliar with formal service. More than once, an unobservant guest either didn't remove the bowl at all or worse—removed the bowl but forgot the doily. What do you do when the butler appears at your side with a bowl of ice cream, you take a helping, you're holding the large spoons filled with ice cream, both hands poised in the air? Can you plunk it on top of a doily? You look at the other guests (you should have done that earlier) and notice that everyone else has removed his doily. I remember many a red face.

I was taught to be polite, never to talk back or sass, and at all times to have respect for my elders. "You stand up when an adult, including your mother, enters the room. You curtsy to practically everyone. You are to be seen and not heard. You speak only when spoken to." The first two rules were easy, the second two impossible. I had a big mouth! I spoke whenever there was a pause in a conversation, at the slightest opening or opportunity.

That definitive line between child and adult was daunting to say the least, intimidating at best. As an adult I found it difficult to erase. The role of the perfect child was so deeply ingrained that I had trouble later changing attitudes, becoming an equal, treating people I had known as my parents' friends as mine, as contemporaries. Some of their friends were quite young, more my age than theirs, yet they remained people to be figuratively curtsied to. Even when I was married—when my husband and I were involved in business and social occasions, frequently with those same friends—I would find myself, instead of acting like a woman and wife, reverting to Jack and Mary's little girl. Normally, I'm rather gregarious, sometimes funny, occasionally even witty, but all of a sudden I was a child again and, worst of all, I was boring. I could see it happening—like standing outside myself and watching my behavior (and hating myself for it)—but I couldn't seem to help it. By now I have changed, but it took many years and much anguish.

There was one thing about my upbringing I truly hated and resented: my parents' attitude toward my health. I was treated like a hothouse orchid. I don't know why they acted as they did—perhaps it was Dad's hypochondria, or the fact that I was adopted, or that they were both natural worriers, or their best friends were doing it. I don't know. I was actually very strong and hardy and, except for the usual measles and whooping cough and a winter cold or two, extremely healthy. But you couldn't tell it from Mother and Dad's actions. If I coughed I was sent to bed and the doctor called. I was supposed to be allergic to everything. I couldn't even have a comfortable pillow because I was allergic to down. I couldn't eat certain foods because I was allergic. Worst of all, I was allergic to animals. I remember being given a puppy, a cocker spaniel, when I was about three. Just when I had grown to love it, it was given away. I must have sneezed. There were two more: an Irish setter and a dachshund. Same story.

Of course I really wasn't allergic to anything—never have been. Perhaps "my-child-is-allergic" was the in thing back then, like the cod liver oil I had to swallow every morning. That kind of hysteria over my health remained with me and certainly had an effect on the way I raised my children. They grew up quite happily, doctors being called or visited only for emergencies. Colds and minor illnesses took care of themselves.

One day when my mother came to visit me and her grandchildren, my elder son, Michael, then about three, was playing with our new puppy. He made a ghastly faux pas—he sneezed! Mother said, "I think, Joanie, you should give the dog away. Michael's allergic." Not wanting an argument I muttered something noncommittal. Mother left. The dog stayed.

From kindergarten through eighth grade I attended El Rodeo, our local public school. I did homework, played skip rope and jacks after school, was a fairly decent kickball and volleyball player, made some friends and a few enemies. After lunch my girlfriends and I traded playing cards—a popular hobby of the 1940's. I was a teacher's pet, more I suspect because I was a good

271

and cooperative student than because of Dad's celebrity status. I also got into a fair share of trouble—talking in class, passing notes and playing hooky. My parents came to school functions: pageants, Christmas programs, parents' days, graduations, and never even seemed disappointed when in the annual school play I usually portrayed one of the rabbits or a tree. Being Jack Benny's daughter didn't help me there. My lack of acting ability was recognized early on.

My twelfth year was memorable.

I learned about sex:

I knew absolutely nothing about it and was very curious. I had tried asking my mother, but she just changed the subject. (You understand, this was in the 1940's.) Miss Vallance was only slightly more helpful. She kept repeating the same thing, "When you're married a little act of love takes place." But she would never tell me just what that little act was and of course she only succeeded in making me more curious than ever. I tried my friends. They were as ignorant as I and equally inquisitive. "If you find out anything, let me know." We talked and pondered and pondered and talked and got nowhere. And then I met Marcia.

Marcia was new in town and had recently joined my class in school. She was cute and funny and terrific in sports and we became instant friends. We started going to each other's houses after school to play. This particular day we were at my house, and after a few games of handball decided to get some refreshments. While sitting on the fenders of Mom's new Cadillac, drinking our Cokes and talking, I discovered that Marcia had two older brothers, both in college, and she *knew!* Although Marcia had all the right information, I found it difficult to believe. A little later when Deedee's older sister, Gloria, was getting married, Deedee swiped her marriage manual. She brought it to school, we took it to the girls' room and there, locked in one of the stalls, we avidly learned all there was to know about the technical aspects of love. Hallelujah!

I had my first lesson in the tribulations of love:

I was in the eighth grade and my steady boyfriend dumped me for a younger woman. She was in the seventh grade.

I ran away from home:

I had been spotted by our English teacher, Mrs. Moore, handing a note to a friend across the aisle. Not a very serious transgression, it only warranted a warning. But the following day, not being one to learn from my mistakes, I tried it again. Caught red-handed! Off to Mr. Wiley, the principal, who told me to come back after school when a note concerning my execrable behavior would be given me to take home to be signed by one of my parents and returned to him the next day.

What to do? I figured this was a serious enough offense for Mother to tell Daddy, and of course I couldn't let that happen. I couldn't show her the note. After much thought I came up with a plan —I would forge her signature. I found an old signed report card, smeared black ink on the back, practiced tracing on a blank sheet of paper until I had it just right, no wobbles, no hesitations, then I did the deed. The next morning I returned the note with its perfectly forged signature to school. How clever, how brilliant, how smug I was! I thought I'd gotten away with my crime, but during my very first class I was told to see Mr. Wiley at lunchtime. "I've been caught," I thought, and shook with fear all morning long. But no, as it turned out I had no reason to worry. Mr. Wiley just wanted to know how my mother had taken it. "Were you punished?" he asked.

"Yes," I replied.

"How?" he continued. Now I had to think fast.

"Well," I said, "Mother told me I couldn't go to the class Halloween party."

"I see," he said. "You may go to lunch." I breathed a sigh of relief and smiled through the rest of the school day.

What I didn't know was that I had outsmarted myself. After I left his office, Mr. Wiley called my mother to say that he thought the punishment a bit excessive.

"After all, Joan is a good student, and writing notes in class is not really a very serious infraction." Needless to say, my mother didn't know what he was talking about. He told her!

At 3:10, still smiling, knowing nothing of the

phone conversation, I was picked up by Miss Vallance. "Your mother wants to see you when you get home," she said.

"Oh, why?" I asked.

"The principal called her," was the reply.

I froze. I panicked. I had received a bad behavior note; I had lied to Mother by omission; I had lied to Mr. Wiley; and worst of all, I was guilty of forgery. I figured I would go to prison, or at the very least reform school!

When I arrived home Mom was out, and I was told to go to my room to await her return, when I would be dealt with. That was too much for me. I simply couldn't face it, so I packed a bag with pajamas and toothbrush and underwear, sneaked down the back stairs and left. The problem was where to go. Not to a friend's house—I would be found too easily. What were the alternatives? I started walking south toward Wilshire Boulevard, mulling it over, when all of a sudden I thought of the perfect place, Miss Vallance's house. She rented a little guest cottage at the back of a driveway behind another house on the eastern edge of Beverly Hills, about a mile and a half away. She used it on her days off and when she wasn't there it was peaceful, hidden and very private. Perfect.

By the time I arrived it was dark. Fortunately it was a warm night because I didn't have a key, and although I was by now a hardened criminal, I had not learned the fine art of picking a lock. So I sat on her outdoor rocking chair and rocked and hummed and looked at the stars, trying to identify the constellations and thinking not at all of what might happen next. I was quite comfortable for a while, but after an hour or so I discovered I was hungry. I went up the driveway to the back door of the big house. The lights were on and I could see the couple who lived there sitting in the living room. The door was unlocked. Very quietly I opened it, crept in, took an apple from their fridge and returned to my chair to eat it. But still not having learned to leave well enough alone, I went back for seconds and just as in school I was caught again! The man and his wife called my parents. And then the fun began.

Three minutes later a black and white Beverly Hills police car arrived. Two policemen got out and wordlessly escorted me into the back seat. Off we went—the only things lacking were handcuffs and siren. I was little to begin with, but I think I shrank three inches during that ride. At home there were four other police cars, two in front and two in the driveway, and all the floodlights were on. *It was awful!*

My escorts left me at the front door. I walked in and there were my parents and, of course, as in all emergencies, the Burnses. Mother was prostrate on the sofa—she had fainted and Gracie was holding a cloth to her forehead. Daddy was pacing the floor and wouldn't look at me. At first no one said a word. I shrank a little more. Finally, my father stopped, glowered at me, and practically frothing at the mouth said, "How could you frighten us like this? We thought you had been kidnapped. How could you do this to us? Haven't we always loved you? What have we ever done that you could treat us like this? Look at your mother. She's been sick with worry."

I don't remember what else he said, but I was sent upstairs to bed. At least a week passed before Daddy spoke to me again. No hugs, no kisses, no attention, no words, no nothing. That was the worst punishment of all.

CHAPTER 14

As far back as I can remember we had a home in Palm Springs. The first few were rented, then along about 1950 my parents bought the first of the two houses they would own.

A great deal of my teenage life centered around Palm Springs. My parents and I spent almost every holiday there, except in summer, and almost every weekend. They loved the desert air and the golf; I loved everything except the golf. My earliest memories are of a small desert town, sparsely populated, sleepy, always sunny and warm, with a strong feeling of the culture of the Indians who owned the land. There were very few hotels back then. I remember only the grand El Mirador, the Lone Palm with its eponymous tree and a bland white building called the Colonial House.

Our first house that I remember was named Shrangri-La, and stood just up the block from the Colonial House. Tyrone Power with his wife, Annabella, lived next door. They were casual friends of my parents and occasionally came over for dinner. I was as impressed as any fan—I mean, he was gorgeous! I spent a good deal of time bicycling back and forth in front of his house hoping to see him.

The main drag was and still is Palm Canyon Drive. There were two movie theaters, many dress shops featuring resort clothes, a fabulous candy store called Fun in the Sun, a few restaurants (our favorite was Ruby's Dunes), an ice cream parlor and a nightclub, the Chi-Chi. The Chi-Chi was the first nightclub I was ever allowed to go to. Tony Martin was playing there, and because he was such a close family friend, my parents took me with them to see his act. It was a heady experience for a thirteen-year-old.

My mother felt very strongly about certain aspects of my growing up—about privileges and milestones. The most common answer to my question, "Why can't I? . . . go on a date, wear lipstick, see a nightclub show," was, "Because if you do this now, you'll have nothing to look forward to." Although I considered that reply quite unreasonable at the time, it is wisdom I have used in raising my own children.

Since freeways then had not been thought of, the drive to the Springs took a bit over three hours. I drove with either my parents or with Bens, later Miss Vallance, and our chauffeur, Richard. I was horribly bored on those long drives. But once there it was grand. I rode my bicycle, explored the neighborhood, went to movies, drank lots of date milk shakes until one day some years later I drank one too many and became deathly ill. To this day I cannot look at a date.

One frequent visitor was Barbara Stanwyck, who usually brought her son, Skip, with her. Skip was Frank Fay's (Barbara's first husband) and Barbara's adopted son. He used the surname Stanwyck—his first name was originally Dion, then Skip and later Tony. He was my first boyfriend and our romance began in Palm Springs. He was adorable with his freckles and sandy blond hair. He sent me my first love letter—in almost indecipherable capital letters scrawled all over the page it said with classic simplicity, "I love you." I was four and he was five. Together we picked wild flowers in an enormous field behind the El Mirador, rode our bikes (I'm not even sure they were two-wheelers yet) and explored the neighborhood. And possibly each other as well.

Later, riding and tennis became my passions. I spent every morning at the stable and every afternoon at the brand new Racquet Club. I rode a beautiful strawberry roan named Rosin. He didn't belong to me, but he might as well have. I rode him every day, mucked out his stall, curried him, even trained him. We rode out in the desert in the early mornings, galloped along the huge arroyos, and sometimes went up to Tahquitz Canyon where we followed a lovely stream that led to a waterfall. I would dismount, tie Rosin to a tree and wade in the stream. I can still taste that clear, cold, unpolluted water. I even tried my hand at roping, practicing on cactus, but I never did get the hang of it. I imagine Tahquitz Canyon still exists today, but I am sure the arroyos have long since disappeared. They are probably housing developments, shopping centers and multiplex cinemas.

During the 1940's and early 1950's my riding stable featured Friday night chuck wagons. Mother and Daddy and some of their friends frequently joined in. The dress was jeans, Western boots, a Western shirt, and heavy jacket—nights are cold in the desert. My parents bought their beautifully tailored, custom-made outfits from the local Western apparel store. I wore jeans. We would show up at the stable about five o'clock. Most of the horses were saddled and ready to go, the others hitched to the wagons. We would mount up and ride with a group of about twenty people for an hour or so out into the desert, find a place to camp and then enjoy the cookout barbecued ribs and steaks. My most vivid memory of those evenings is my parents all decked out in their fancy duds riding on top of one of the straw-strewn wagons. Neither of them knew how to ride a horse. In *Buck Benny Rides Again* I'm sure Daddy used a double.

The Racquet Club, about a mile west of the town, was for many years the in club. I started playing tennis there when I was about ten and continued until my late thirties when my parents sold their last house. By then I'd bought a house in Lake Arrowhead where I took my children, and Palm Springs became a place of the past. My parents came to the club occasionally for lunch or dinner or to watch me play but, since they were golfers, didn't hang out there. Through my horse phase, after my horse phase and well into my boy phase much of my life centered around the tennis courts, the swimming pool and bar. Tex, the bartender, made the best orange freeze I've ever tasted.

Daddy could hardly be called a tense person, but in Palm Springs he seemed even more relaxed—less focused on the show perhaps, more interested in the world around him, the world outside show business.

George Burns tells a story about Daddy and Palm Springs:

"Jack was so relaxed that he could fall asleep anywhere at any time, even in a room full of people talking and arguing. Jack and I were the owners of a ranch in Indio, California. We were partners with Leonard Firestone. How we got into the ranch business is that Jack and I were once sitting around the Tamarisk Country Club in Palm Springs.

" 'Jack,' I said, 'everybody in Palm Springs has a ranch except us. All you do is tell jokes and play the fiddle. All I do is tell jokes and sing a song. We ought to have a ranch.'

" 'Sure,' he agreed, 'let's buy a ranch right now.

281

Buck Benny will ride again. You know of any good ranches for sale around here?'

" 'No,' I said.

"Just then Firestone joined us. He knew just the ranch for us. There was a nice piece of land on the market. He had not seen it but if we would go out and inspect it he would go in with us if we liked it. It was 180 acres over in Indio, which is a few miles from Palm Springs.

"The next morning we drove out with a real estate agent who started giving us a description of the commercial possibilities of this property. By the third sentence, Jack fell into a deep and restful sleep. He didn't hear a word about the boundless wealth we would make from growing oranges, cotton and dates. We arrived at the property. We were out in the desert. All around us was sand. Sand. Sand. Sand. Not even a palm tree was visible. I poked Jack. He woke up.

" 'Jack,' I said, 'this is the ranch.'

"He looked out the window. 'Fine,' he said, 'let's buy it.'

" 'Jack, you're looking out the wrong window. It's on the other side.'

" 'Gentlemen,' the agent said, 'will you be good enough to step out so I can show you the property better.'

" 'What's the use of going out?' Jack asked. 'It's just sand.'

"But we talked him into leaving the car. We walked around on the property.

282

" 'What makes this ranch great,' said the agent, 'is that there's seven dunes on it.'

" 'Seven dunes, eh?' said Jack lethargically.

" 'We're finally making an intelligent business move,' I told Jack. 'Some buyers get five dunes, some get six dunes, but we're getting seven dunes, which is a nice way to start if you're buying a ranch.'

" 'I'd like to see one of these dunes,' Jack said.

"He drove a hard bargain.

" 'You're standing on one of them right now,' said the agent."

I believe they bought the property—it was a *date* ranch—not a ranch where you raise cattle or sheep. They also tried to raise oranges and cotton but I don't believe they made any money on it. In Palm Springs Daddy played golf *every* day, read books and magazines, even enjoyed a scotch and soda before dinner—something he rarely if ever did at home. I can't say he spent more time with me, since during the day our activities were entirely different and at night he and Mom were usually with their friends, but our relationship was easier there and seemed closer.

There was plenty of room at our house for guests. One I remember clearly was Kay Williams. I met Kay when I was about eight. She was a friend of my mother's; a young blonde starlet, down on her luck, not a penny to her name. She stayed with us for almost that entire winter season, helping around the house and playing golf with my mother. She was particularly nice to me. I mean she actually went bicycling and riding with me, and of course she was so beautiful I absolutely adored her.

After that winter season she seemed to have completely disappeared. Eight years later, to my astonishment, she reappeared in a house across the street from us in Beverly Hills. It was twice the size of ours. The poor little waif was now the rich, elegant Mrs. Adolph Spreckels (of the Spreckels Sugar fortune). Except for her outward accoutrements, she hadn't changed a bit. She was just as sweet and friendly and funny as ever—and even more beautiful.

Although her marriage to Mr. Spreckels didn't last, her life had a perfect, fairy-tale ending. Back in the Palm Springs days she had met a man and had fallen head over heels in love with him, but he was married and that was that! So, knowing she couldn't have him she gave up and married Adolph Spreckels, who had been pursuing her. After her divorce some years later, she met her true love again. She was still crazy about him. He was now single, he fell in love with her and shortly after she became Mrs. Clark Gable. Their marriage lasted blissfully until his death. A few months after he died she bore his only child, a son.

I was always encouraged to bring along a friend or two when we went to Palm Springs—usually

Sandy and/or Deedee. The Terrible Trio was riding again! At Shrangri-La, we precipitated a traumatic event. We were thirteen, and one of our favorite pastimes was strolling down Palm Canyon shopping, looking for boys and generally trying to drum up some fun! One day, a bit bored with studying the window of one of the many Indian jewelry shops, Sandy said, "Let's go in and buy turquoise friendship rings. We'll all get the same ones."

"Okay, but we don't have enough money," said I. We had about six dollars between us and the rings were five dollars each.

"Well, let's go look anyway." In we went. A saleslady pulled out tray after tray of rings. We tried them on, discussed them, hemmed and hawed and finally, much to the saleslady's disgust, left empty-handed. Or so I and the saleslady thought. But when we had walked a block farther down the street Sandy said, "Look," and pulled three rings from the pocket of her jeans.

"Wow, you *stole* them," we said, delighted and even a little awed at our friend's nerve and dexterity. We put them on and giggled all the way home.

Of course we couldn't let my mother see them. She would ask questions, knowing we had no money. So we hid them in my bedside table, certain she would never look there. I guess our giggles and guilty expressions gave us away because that evening when she came in to say good night she looked us over very carefully and said, "You're up to something. I just know you've done something you shouldn't. You look like the cats who ate the cream. What is it?"

We protested our innocence, trying to look wide-eyed and angelic (something at which we were quite adept), but she must have caught one of us glancing at the bedstand because she marched right to it, opened the drawer, and pulled out the rings.

Caught red-handed! We said we were sorry, we don't know how we could have done anything so foolish, it was just a mischievous prank, we'll never do it again, of course we'll pay for them with our allowances for the next two months. No good. No good at all!

"Here's what you *will* do—tomorrow you are coming back to the store with me. We will call the owner, and you will return the rings to him personally. Each of you is to confess that you stole them and apologize for your crime. Then you are going to apologize to the saleslady. And you are *never* to do anything like this again. Do you know what your father is going to say when I tell him? Do you know what would have happened if someone other than I had caught you? Can you picture the headlines: JACK BENNY'S DAUGHTER AND GEORGE BURNS'S DAUGHTER . . . ?" Shades of Chaperau.

My mother was apoplectic. Looking back I can hardly blame her. And the punishment was fitting. We stumbled into the store, heads down, held out the rings and mumbled our apologies.

We were utterly and abjectly humiliated and never did such a thing again.

Following our graduation from grade school, Dee-dee and Sandy and I were sent to Chadwick, a coed boarding high school situated on a knoll in the Rolling Hills section of Palos Verdes, about an hour's drive from home. Beverly High was out—the girls there wore lipstick!—and there were only two other private schools in Los Angeles: Marlborough (no Jews allowed then) and Westlake (it had Jewish quotas of which my parents disapproved). Thus Chadwick was chosen by a process of elimination.

Coed boarding schools were few and far between in 1947, and Chadwick was a peculiar place, to say the least, but it seemed quite popular with celebrity and problem children. The school had its share of both, including Christina Crawford. (She was about five years behind me, in the lower school, so I didn't know her well.)

Chadwick was run by Commander (navy, retired) and Mrs. Chadwick. Although older, he resembled Clark Gable and always had a twinkle in his eye. She was what we used to call "a pill." They were an extremely odd couple. In spite of the fact that our parents paid a fortune to send us there (I think it was $2,000 a year and this was in 1947), the Chadwicks were what you might call frugal. We students not only went to classes, study halls and did homework, we also did chores. The girls were assigned, in rotation, to cleaning halls, doing dishes, waiting on table, vacuuming the dorm and scrubbing the johns. The boys did the heavy work: with professional equipment they waxed and polished the floors, cleaned windows and, their favorite—worked at the stable or on the farm. Yes, Chadwick had a farm, complete with chickens, rabbits, sheep and possibly even a cow or two. I remember eating rabbit for dinner and having to listen to one of the boys at the table describe graphically how he had killed it.

During our first year we were allowed to go home only one weekend a month. Later, more frequently. Strangely enough, all three of us adored Chadwick. It may have been peculiar, but it was never boring. We even managed to get a good education. We made wonderful girlfriends and we each had boyfriends.

Louis Hansen was my first serious romance. It began when I was thirteen and a half, a freshman, and it lasted two years. His father was an electrician and Louis was a day student from San Pedro, on scholarship. It all began one night backstage (what would you expect from a show biz kid?) while we were rehearsing for the annual Christmas pageant. I was playing the part of Ruth—you know—"Whither thou goest . . ."—and Louis was the pageant's electrician. At the end of rehearsal he asked if he could walk me back to the girls' dorm. I had noticed him on campus earlier, and thought he was very cute so I said yes and he did and he kissed me good night and I was in love and so was he.

When my parents arrived at school two weeks later to see their daughter in her very dramatic role, I introduced them to Louis and his parents, who had come to see their son's dramatic lighting effects. Everyone was perfectly cordial, and nothing was said, no questions asked, until later when I had changed out of my costume into my normal attire for the ride home for Christmas vacation. I met them at the car. Mother took one look at me and screeched, *"What is that you're wearing?"* She was referring to Louis's letterman sweater, which hung down well below my knees and which I wore constantly (I practically slept in it), and to the enormous skull and crossbones ring that dangled on a long thick chain around my neck. I explained, "Louis gave them to me and I wear them all the time. We're getting married when we get out of school. We're in love."

Needless to say, that went over big. As usual Daddy let Mother do the talking. She ranted and raved for a while and then I guess she realized, first, she wasn't going to change my mind and, second, time would probably take care of everything—after all, I was only thirteen. She didn't have to worry too much just yet. She finally accepted my romance as part of growing up—although an electrician's son was not quite up to her standards for me. And she *hated* the sweater and the ring, practically gnashed her teeth every time she saw them. Daddy liked Louis well enough.

He simply didn't pay much attention to the situation. Certainly the sweater and the ring didn't seem to faze him.

Mom was right. She really had nothing to worry about—at least not then. We were indeed very young and although we remained as hot and heavy as ever for the next two years, Louis then graduated and left for Johns Hopkins. We just fizzled out. Absence didn't do what the cliché says it does.

One of the friends we made at Chadwick was a girl named Laura—not her real name. At least we thought she was our friend . . .

During our sophomore year one afternoon, while sitting on the lawn after lunch, chatting and minding our own business, Sandy and I were suddenly called to Commander and Mrs. Chadwick's office. Immediately! Our behavior of late had been reasonably acceptable, so we couldn't imagine what this peremptory summons was about. The Chadwicks met us at the door of the office with grim faces, and informed us that we were shortly to be picked up and driven home. Completely at a loss and somewhat startled, we asked why, and were told we would find out when we arrived at my parents' house in Beverly Hills. They would say no more. We were to remain in the outer office until the car arrived.

About thirty minutes later, the Chadwicks wordlessly escorted us out to the car and, without even a goodbye, we were driven off. The butler was driving and of course he hadn't been told the reason for our apprehension, so we had to suffer in ignorance for the entire hour's drive. We tried to guess. We racked our brains, but couldn't come up with even a clue. By the time we reached home we were terrified.

We walked in the back door and were informed that our parents were waiting for us in the living room. Had we been told they were in the library we might have relaxed a little. The library meant a little trouble, perhaps a mild punishment. But the living room meant terror; the rack or the iron maiden at the very least. And *both* parents together meant a firing squad! We slowly walked that last mile to the living room and there they were, Mom and Gracie sitting on a sofa, George and Daddy standing. George wasn't even smoking a cigar.

Daddy, being his mild-mannered self, and always rather sheepish at such confrontational moments, didn't know what to say and remained mute. George had no such problem and was the spokesman.

"How could you have done such a thing? How could you do this to us? Do you know what this means when it gets into the papers? Have we been such terrible parents? Why would you steal clothing from the May Company? Don't you have enough to wear?" Our mothers echoed these questions and added a few of their own. Daddy stood there looking grim and unhappy.

Sandy and I listened to this tirade with consternation and our mouths open. Steal clothing from the May Company? What was this about? We hadn't done it! But how to convince them of our innocence? We had no alibis, we had no proof. We were being accused of something we knew nothing about. And, to make matters worse, only two years had passed since the Palm Springs ring-stealing episode, a crime of which we *had* been guilty, and one still well remembered by our parents. (If we could do it once, we could do it again.)

After a confusion of shouting: "We didn't do it"—"We don't believe you"—"We're innocent —"You're guilty"—"We swear we didn't do it" —"Yes, you did!"—the story finally came out. The Bennys and the Burnses had been called by an executive of the May Company who told them that Sandy and I had stolen some clothing from their store on Wilshire Boulevard. We had not been arrested, because out of respect for our parents and fearing bad publicity, the store had decided it would be best to deal with the incident privately. How did they know we had stolen anything, since we had not been caught or searched or arrested? Well, it seemed they had caught a girl named Laura, a friend of ours, but a girl whose parents were not famous. She had been searched and found with the goods. When arrested and questioned, she confessed that yes she was guilty but that she had not been alone. She had been with her two best friends who had also lifted a few items. Guess who those friends were?

Laura knew of our previous ring stealing, and thought to lessen her own culpability by saying she was just one of a group. She believed she could draw us into it and make it stick. The fact is she almost did!

Now that we knew what had happened we could at least fight back, though it still wasn't easy. We didn't have an alibi. We could have been in the store that weekend. It was still her word against ours. We fought tooth and nail to be believed! Finally, after what seemed hours of battle, my mother came up with the idea that our rooms should be searched, both at home and at school. The Chadwicks were to do the honors at school; Gracie, George and Sandy went back to their house, Gracie to investigate; and Mom searched my room. When nothing was found we were at last, happily for us, and a bit reluctantly on the part of our parents, exonerated. I think that even then, after the search, they didn't totally believe us.

The story eventually had a happy ending. Sometime later our dear friend confessed that neither Sandy nor Joan had had anything to do with her theft at the May Company.

To finish off these stories of criminal confrontations and the repercussions following the ring-stealing episode, I must now fast forward to my sophomore year at Stanford. Besides my allowance at that time I was allowed to have one charge account, at a store in San Francisco called the White House, one of a chain of stores in Northern California. My parents made the stipulation that I spend no more than a given amount each month. My memory, no longer what it used to be, tells me that it was about $100. This was to include all clothing, cosmetics and sundries. Self-discipline was never one of my attributes and I frequently went over my limit, for which the punishment was a month's cancellation of charge privileges.

I was at home for Thanksgiving vacation and my parents and I were sitting in the library having tea, finger sandwiches and scones. My mother had taken up the British ritual of afternoon tea upon her recent return from a trip to London. She considered it the height of elegance and chic. When the phone rang, I hopped up to answer it and heard a woman's voice say, "Is Mr. Benny there? This is the White House calling."

Oh, Good Lord! I had recently, in a fit of extravagance, purchased a beautiful, sophisticated, low-backed black and brown taffeta cocktail dress to wear to an upcoming party. It cost $150—a fortune then—but it was irresistible. When this lady said that the White House wanted to talk to Mr. Benny, I, in my paranoia, naturally assumed that I was in trouble again. I had either gone over my limit and was being duly reported to my father, or worse, I was about to be accused of stealing again.

I hemmed and hawed and cleared my throat, and in a very tentative voice asked, "Well . . . uh . . . who is it who wants to talk to Mr. Benny?"

"The President," she replied.

Oh, God! I thought. I must really be in *terrible* trouble. Why else would the president of the store want to speak to Daddy? So I said, "Perhaps—I mean—well—is there anything I can do or answer for you?"

In a rather exasperated tone she replied, "No! Would you please put Mr. Benny on the line? President Eisenhower would like to speak with him!"

Oh—*that* White House.

My first trip to Europe came when I had just turned fourteen. We sailed in June of 1948 from New York to Southampton on the Cunard liner *Queen Elizabeth*. My parents were on their way to fulfill a two-week engagement at the London Palladium to be followed by a trip to Germany to entertain the troops. The *Queen Elizabeth* was at that time the largest ship afloat and boarding it was one of the most exciting events of my life. It was magnificent beyond description—a floating city; a royal palace.

Two of Dad's writers were on board. They supplied nonstop laughter across the ocean. Phil Harris, with his new bride, Alice Faye, was combining business with honeymooning. After throwing confetti and waving goodbyes to our friends on shore, the tugs backed us out of the pier, and we all went up on deck as we sailed out of New York harbor past the Statue of Liberty. Then Phil and Alice disappeared below to their cabin, never to be seen again until we docked five days later.

Mother and Daddy and Miss Vallance and I had a suite; two bedrooms with a living room between. Shipboard activities went on and on—games in the morning, bouillon in your deck chair at eleven, a walk around the promenade, a little reading, a little shopping, lunch, more games, tea and pastries at four, a short rest, change to evening attire, dinner in the Veranda Grill, a choice of either horse racing in the grand salon or playing the ship's pool table in the small salon, dancing and finally a late-night snack with perhaps more dancing in the Veranda Grill. Not a bad life!

The only fly in the ointment was my boyfriend, Louis. I didn't want to leave him that summer. I still wore his ring around my neck and refused to take it off except in the evening. Mom still went on about it. I wrote him long letters every day and complained frequently about missing him. I was truly a pain in the you know what.

London in 1948 was very different from what it is today. Yes, there was the changing of the guard at Buckingham Palace, Westminster Abbey, the theaters, the museums, the Houses of Parliament, but it was still a war-torn city of rubble. You would be walking down a perfectly normal-looking street of houses and all of a sudden there would be a gap of what looked like two or three empty lots, some cleaned and ready for rebuilding and some looking as though they had been bombed yesterday.

Daddy worried a lot that the English wouldn't understand or respond to his character, but his worries were unfounded. The show opened to wonderful reviews with headlines such as "The irresistible Jack Benny is a natural" and "Oh good, Mr. Benny, oh, very good."

The following is an excerpt from my favorite review:

"A young man in the row behind touched me on the shoulder and said, 'Excuse me, could you tell me who that is?' I said that it was Jack Benny. A few minutes later, while Mr. Benny was looking at his fingernails as if he had never seen them before, the same young man leaned forward and asked me when the man on the stage was going to do something. As quietly as possible, I explained that Jack Benny never did anything, which was his particular genius. 'Thank you,' whispered the young man, politely."

The engagement at the Palladium was a great success and sold out every performance. Daddy returned in 1950 and again in 1952. How many of you remember the Merry Macs? And their hit record, "Roleo Rolling Along"? Well, they opened the show. I loved them and stood in the wings night after night to see them.

Marilyn Maxwell sang and did a skit with my father as the "sexy dumb blonde," similar to the role Marilyn Monroe later played once on his TV show. She had made her reputation as one of Bob Hope's "girls," visiting our troops during the war. Max never made it big, but her name was well known, she had a nice singing voice and a fair amount of talent. She was soft-spoken and had a sweet quality about her, yet was a great character with a wildly funny sense of humor. Sexy and glamorous—yes, very—but hardly dumb. I liked her because she was one of the few of the many people who came in and out of my life who paid attention to me, gave me credit for brains, and treated me as an equal. We became good friends during that trip and she would often come to my room to chat. Sometimes in the evenings I became lady's maid, doing up her zipper or pinning her bra.

One evening, one I shall never forget, she arrived in my room wearing a robe and carrying a very sexy black dress. When I saw the dress I nearly fainted. I had seen plenty of low-cut gowns, but this was ridiculous. It had a round, scooped hardly-a-neckline—more like a bosom-line, and Max had plenty of bosom! And to put it delicately, the kind that needed a little help.

"How are you going to get into that thing?" I asked. "You can't possibly wear a bra."

"No," she said. "I'll need your help." With that, she handed me a roll of extra-wide adhesive tape and a pair of scissors. "We have to tape me." For those of you who have never tried it, it works like this: you cut two long strips and run them tightly from under the armpit across the underpart of the breast to the other side—one in one direction, one in the other. The support is fantastic. The tighter you pull, the better. Then lots of smaller strips for extra lift. It really works. Although I have never worn anything as décolleté as that, I have used it over the years for certain asymmetrical or backless dresses. Does it hurt when you take it off? Yes! But only for a minute.

I never saw her again (show business friendships can be like that) but I enjoyed knowing Max for that short time. She was a neat lady.

After the show closed, my parents left for Germany and Miss Vallance and I took the boat across the channel, then overnight on the *Blue Train* to Cannes, where we stayed for about ten days. We drove along the highest corniche to Monte Carlo and back, ate in charming bistros, went frequently to Eden Roc where I loved to dive from the cliff (I was a strong diver and pretty nervy back then), and water-skied daily. One day Miss Vallance and I drove to La Reserve for lunch. We had an absolutely exquisite meal sitting at a window table overlooking the brilliantly blue Mediterranean. After lunch as we were walking through the foyer Miss Vallance spotted Clark Gable. Although she didn't know him well, I think that she, like any normal red-blooded female, had a crush on him. She had met him when, before she came to us, she had worked for Tyrone Power. I had never met Mr. Gable.

"Oh, Joanie," she said, "go introduce yourself to him."

I was much too shy to do that—to introduce myself to anyone, for that matter. I refused. But V was determined.

"If you won't, I will," and with that she grabbed my hand and dragged me over to him.

"Mr. Gable," she said. He turned around. "This is Jack Benny's daughter, Joan."

I was so embarrassed I wanted to disappear into the woodwork. When I finally had the nerve to look up, there he was, looking straight at me with those gorgeous eyes and smiling that fabulous smile. (I later found out those beautiful white teeth were false!)

He put out his hand and said, "I'm so happy to meet you." Not a very original line, but no one ever said it the way he did at that moment. There was no doubt—he had been waiting all his life just to meet me! I shook his hand and my knees almost knocked out loud.

CHAPTER 15

Back in the 1950's, not only was smoking a normal thing to do, it was more, it was a sign of sophistication, of being grown up. Everyone did it. Mother smoked two or three packs of Parliaments a day. Daddy smoked cigars. I remember he smoked cigarettes when I was very little but somewhere along the line had given them up.

My friends and I tried very hard to be grown up by emulating our parents and their friends, starting when we were children by lighting matches, then graduating to cigarettes. By the time we were at Chadwick we were surreptitiously smoking, against the rules of course. Unfortunately I got caught, and my punishment was being "campused," having to stay at school on a week-end when everyone else had gone home. The first time this happened Mother and Daddy admonished me for breaking the rules but otherwise were pretty cool; the second incident turned into a near disaster. My timing couldn't have been worse. (Why hadn't I learned about timing from my father?) I had to remain at school the weekend after the end of the semester, June 16 and 17, the seventeenth being my sixteenth birthday—the day I was to get my first car.

I knew about the car—I had picked it out. Daddy said I could have any one of the Big Three's least expensive models: a Chevy, a Ford or a Plymouth. I didn't want any of the above, I wanted a Pontiac—desperately. It was the G.M. car one step up from a Chevy. It had an Indian head for the hood ornament and since the Indian was Stanford's emblem (the football team then was the Stanford Indians) and since I knew I was going to Stanford I thought a Pontiac was the spiffiest car I could own. Not only a Pontiac, it had to be a convertible. Not only a convertible, it had to have a special paint job—powder blue. Mother said no, but again I prevailed on Daddy, just as I did to get my red Christmas tree so long ago. Again he gave in. I could have my powder blue Pontiac. Okay, I was spoiled! But very, very lucky!

So my shiny new car with its big red bow around the door sat in the driveway waiting for me. When I finally arrived home the day after my birthday my excitement must have been catching because although I was admonished for my transgression all was forgiven. Daddy got the first ride. I drove him to Malibu for lunch, remembering those Sundays when he had taken me. I insisted on paying—to thank him for my beautiful car—and after a bit of an argument he let me. As I recall, we talked primarily about school and why I so frequently got into trouble. He didn't like that and asked me if I couldn't try to follow the rules a bit more closely. He wasn't angry, just sort of wistful. He was proud of my accomplishments, my good grades, and wished only that my conduct would match. We also talked about my being allowed to smoke. He thought I was too young, but if it was okay with Mom then it was okay with him.

Mother knew that I had been smoking on the sly for quite a while. She had been saying for at least two years, "You're too young, you're too young." Finally she'd said, "Okay, when you're sixteen you can smoke without sneaking." I knew that now she would invite me to join her for a cigarette, and my major problem was: *I didn't know how!* It was all a sham, a fake. I had only done it to try to be grown up but I had never learned how to inhale!

Mother will laugh at me, she'll make fun of me, I thought. I'll be smoking in front of her and blowing out big puffs of smoke. I can't let that happen. It would be too embarrassing. So that night I took a pack of cigarettes, settled down in my "playroom," and learned to inhale. I coughed and choked and choked and coughed and, though I was nauseous and dizzy, I got through the entire pack. The next afternoon I smoked my birthday cigarette with Mother—not a word was said—no laughing. I inhaled like a veteran! I have, I regret to say, smoked ever since.

I learned on Lucky Strikes, Daddy's sponsor, because the American Tobacco Co. sent us two cartons of Luckies and two cartons of Pall Malls every week, not only during the years of sponsorship but for at least ten years afterward. We had such an enormous store in the closet off my bedroom that it wasn't until I was in my thirties that I actually had to buy a pack of cigarettes. Being the thrifty sort, when I had gone through all the cartons of Luckies I switched to Pall Malls. I still smoke them.

Stewart Granger and his then wife, Jean Simmons, were frequent guests, and one evening at our house, I lit a cigarette. Mr. Granger, who had always been quite pleasant to me, looked at me rather sternly and said, "Why do you smoke? You're much too young. It looks disgusting!"

In addition to the car, I was given my very own "Hollywood Party." At first my parents had agreed to let me invite a few close friends for dinner and a movie. But in the planning stages, given Mother's own inimitable style, the party grew. And it grew and grew and somehow snowballed into a major event, something like their early New Year's Eve parties, only now it was "Joanie's Sweet Sixteen Birthday Dance." About eighty of my friends, some from Chadwick, some not, were invited—along with a passel of my parents' friends: the Grangers, Ray and Mal Milland, the Burnses, Dinah (Shore) and George Montgomery, Cyd (Charisse) and Tony Martin and Frank Sinatra, to name some of the brighter lights.

The patio was tented and decorated; a florist, caterer and orchestra hired and a dance floor laid. Mother and I (for the first time) did the place-carding. Mother's dressmaker, Mrs. MacKenzie, made me a strapless, tight-bodiced, full-skirted evening gown of pale blue satin and tulle. I will never forget making my entrance that evening after all the guests had arrived. I floated down our grand staircase like a princess in that gorgeous dress. The only thing missing was the tiara! It always makes me think of Bette Davis in *Jezebel*. (I have a friend who, having been at that party all those years ago, still teases me by calling me "Fairy Princess." She particularly enjoys embarrassing me by doing it in public.)

After dinner and dancing, along about midnight, we all gathered in the living room, where my parents' friends, all of whom had joined the early evening's festivities, finally got to do what they liked best—perform. Frank, Tony and Dinah sang. George Burns did a routine. But it was something else that made this particular night different.

We had houseguests at the time, two of Mother

and Daddy's oldest friends and fellow vaudevillians, Benny Fields and Blossom Seeley (Mrs.
Fields). Today very few people under sixty would
remember them, but for thirty years—from the
early 1900's until talking pictures took hold in the
1930's—they were stars. They headlined, which
means they played next to closing, at the Palace
Theatre. To play the Palace, even in the worst
slot, meant you had arrived. To be a headliner
meant you were a mega-star—akin to Bruce
Springsteen or the Beatles today. Although I had
known Blossom and Benny all my life and had
heard countless tales about how fabulous they
were, I had never seen them perform. They were
even before my time.

While everyone was gathered in the living room
listening raptly to Dinah, Mother suddenly drew
me aside and whispered, "Come up to my room.
We have a problem."

I hurriedly followed her, and when she had
closed the bedroom door she said, "I don't know
what to do. I completely forgot about Blossom
and Benny. Should we ask them to perform? It
would be rude not to, but the kids have never
even heard of them, and it would be embarrassing
if the kids don't respond. Maybe we shouldn't ask
them. But they're staying here and oh, I don't
know. You decide."

"I don't know, either. Let's get Daddy to decide."

With that I ran down the stairs and grabbed
Daddy to come join the conference. When we told

him of the dilemma he replied briefly, "What's the problem? Of course we'll ask them. We have to ask them."

I became the designated emissary, and when I said to Blossom and Benny, "Please, could you . . . ?" they were thrilled. Mother, however, was worried about how the guests would respond.

By now Frank was on. The kids loved him and applauded enthusiastically. When he finished Daddy went over to the piano and introduced Blossom and Benny, telling the kids something about them. They did some of their old act, just as they did at the Palace. Blossom sang, Benny played the piano and occasionally joined in. According to George Burns she had been a great beauty, and had begun her career as a teenager singing in the waterfront saloons of San Francisco. Baby Blossom, as she was billed, wore a big tiger's head between her legs when she performed, and would catch the silver dollars thrown to her in its mouth. Later, she dropped the tiger, graduated to vaudeville, then teamed up with and married another performer, Benny Fields. She got down on one knee before Jolson ever did and he sang with a megaphone before Rudy Vallee.

They were by now in their sixties. Blossom was short and chubby with bleached blonde hair—or was it a wig? They performed for an audience of teenagers—many of them sophisticated show biz kids who had never even heard of them. Nevertheless, they were the hit of the evening. And when Blossom closed their act with her big song, "Toddling the Todalo," the kids, including me, went wild. They wanted more and more. Blossom and Benny wowed 'em—which only goes to prove that a star is a star and talent is talent. You can't take that away. Eighty young people went home that night having learned what it meant when they heard that someone had been a headliner at the Palace.

I had learned how to drive during the Easter vacation before my birthday, taking a series of lessons from a local driving school. Getting my license was a peculiar occasion. Celebrities then received privileges that no longer exist. One of them was you didn't have to go to the local motor vehicle office and mingle with the "peasants." No, a man came to your house and it was all done privately. So, by appointment, made through Daddy's office, the day after I came home from school, the man arrived. He asked if I knew all the driving rules and regulations. "Yes," I said. "Okay, that takes care of the written test, but since this is your first license, I'll have to give you a driving test." We got into my car and he told me to drive around the block. Our block was a triangle so I made three right-hand turns, two of which I botched—the back wheels scraped the curb—and pulled up in front of our house. He signed my license and I was now a legal, if not very accomplished, driver.

Even though I had a job—selling records at the

local music store—I became the town chauffeur since I was the first of my crowd to have a car. Every day that summer when I wasn't working or doing exercises at the gym, I picked up my friends and sped (after I stopped hitting curbs) to the beach. When I drove with Mother or Dad in my Blue Bomb, I crept along at a sedate 30 mph, but without them I was usually speeding. I can remember racing with friends up the Pacific Coast Highway yelling, "Look! No hands!" How did I survive? Just the luck of the young and foolhardy, I guess. And fortunately I never once received a speeding citation. I had been warned that if I ever got a speeding ticket my car would be taken away.

One Sunday in November we were all going to Palm Springs, my parents in their car after the four o'clock radio show, and Deedee and I in my car earlier in the day. Because we were on standard time, I'd been told by my mother, in no uncertain terms, to be there before dark. I thought Mom's command quite unreasonable—after all, I had been driving for six months by then and was perfectly capable of driving at night and, furthermore, didn't like being treated as if I were a baby. So, the rebel in me took over, and quite deliberately Deedee and I left my house at 4:30, the same time my folks would be leaving from the studio.

There were no freeways then, just regular highways with many stops. Two major routes led from Beverly Hills to Palm Springs, both taking the same amount of time. You had to travel one road

308

for about an hour, then came a point where there was a large drive-in restaurant, and shortly after that a fork where you could go either of two ways. These two roads converged another hour or so later at Beaumont, with another thirty minutes remaining, again on a single road. My parents always went the same way and always drove at a slightly-faster-than-snail's-pace. My plan, which worked like a charm, was to get to the drive-in before they did and then "race them" (without their knowledge) to Palm Springs. It was a simple feat considering the difference in our speeds. We parked out of sight behind the restaurant and waited for Mom's Cadillac to creep by, gave it a five-minute head start, then left the drive-in, taking the alternate route. By the time we reached Beaumont I knew we were way ahead and could just sail on into Palm Springs.

We arrived at the house, unpacked, put on bathing suits and terry cover-ups, and when my parents walked in the door they found us sitting at the card table playing gin rummy as if we had been at it for hours. We had even filled up the scorepad with fake game numbers to make the scene perfect.

"Hi! How was the drive?"

"Oh, we've been here for hours. We've been swimming and we've had dinner and now Deedee's beating me at gin. How was the show?" I asked with an angelic, innocent look on my face.

"Fine," Daddy said. "I'm glad you got here early. You know how your mother worries!"

Then came Christmas vacation. We spent it in Palm Springs, and one day at the Racquet Club while eating lunch with some friends Vic Damone joined us. He was twenty-three years old and the new singing sensation with a couple of gold records already to his credit. He asked me for a date. I was thrilled. He was my first grown-up boyfriend and my first celebrity boyfriend.

Mother was thrilled, too. After a string of what she called "nobodies" I was finally going out with "somebody." Daddy liked him, but then what did he know? Daddy liked everyone. Vic being young and new to the business was suitably impressed, and I never did figure out whether he was enamored of me, Joan, or me, Jack Benny's daughter, or maybe just the proximity to my parents. Quite frankly, I didn't much care. I was having the time of my life. Daytimes they played golf together (just what I needed—another golfer!) while I played tennis; evenings were spent sometimes with my parents and/or other friends, sometimes alone. I remember how romantic it was—driving out into the desert late at night and sitting in Vic's car under a magnificent clear sky with him singing to me. I don't know if I was truly in love but being sung to in the moonlight went a long way. Vic, at one of his recording sessions, even made a demo of "My Sin" just for me!

CHAPTER 16

By today's standards my mother was not a career woman. The writing team of a radio show put in a fair week's work, but the cast put in minimal hours. On *The Jack Benny Show* it was about an hour for the run-through on Saturday and three or four hours for the run-through, notes and show on Sunday. So, except for camp tours in this country during the war years and the one movie she made, Mom had plenty of spare time. That one film—long and happily forgotten—was called *This Way Please*. It was made by Paramount in the late 1930's and starred Betty Grable and John Payne. Mom played an usherette.

My earliest memories of her, as I try to recapture them, are confusing. Unlike my feelings for my father, which were never less than unadulterated adoration, those for her ran the scale from one extreme to the other. She was beautiful, I thought, and glamorous, and full of fun and humor and life. Yet there was an elegance about her that bordered on haughtiness, and a striving for perfection that made her formidable and more than a little scary. On the one hand I tried very hard to be the perfect daughter I felt would gain her love and approval; on the other I was strong-willed, rebellious and frequently naughty—which captured her attention if not her approbation. Unlike my relationship with my father, which was always easygoing, casual and warm, that with my mother was a continuing struggle, a war of two temperaments.

During the summers of the early years in the Roxbury house there was a feeling of constant gaiety. The noise and laughter that wafted so enticingly up to my bedroom where I was supposed to be napping—Mom's friends splashing in the pool, playing Ping-Pong and cards, someone noodling on the spinet—all that dolce vita came from my mother. On those balmy afternoons Daddy must have been working or playing golf because in my mind's eye he isn't in the scene. When I was allowed to join such guests as Betty Grable, George Raft, Barbara Stanwyck and Robert Taylor, we played pool games, threw each other in, dove for pennies and raced underwater. Mom was wonderful, including me in all the activities. Those afternoons in the late 1930's typified the side of my mother that was full of fun and laughter—the side I admired and loved. But there was another, a less admirable and lovable side, which all too often obliterated the other.

Despite her gaiety and humor when she was with her friends, I always felt that my mother was basically an unhappy woman. When she and Daddy first moved to California he was well on his way to stardom and she wanted desperately to be a star's wife—to belong in that rarefied society. That meant competing with glamorous movie stars like Claudette Colbert, Barbara Stanwyck or Betty

312

Grable; not only for her husband's attention, but socially as well.

The two leading hostesses in Hollywood at that time (and for the next twenty-five years) were Louis B. Mayer's daughters, Edith Goetz and Irene Selznick. They were the Hollywood princesses, "to the manor born." After all, movie stars, no matter how famous, were only employees, to be hired and fired at a producer's whim. Being invited to the Jimmy Stewarts' or the Gary Coopers' wasn't exactly chopped liver, but an invitation to the Goetzes' or the Selznicks' signified total, complete acceptance. You had arrived.

Mom was neither a gorgeous movie star nor was she the daughter of a famous father. I think she never really got away from being Sadie Marks to herself (even though legally Mary Livingstone), a shopgirl from Seattle, a woman with no credentials, little sophistication or experience. It didn't occur to her that her competition, Lana Turner, Ann Sheridan, Hedy Lamarr and a host of others, came from similar backgrounds. They were no more to the manor born than she. But that didn't matter. Her insecurity knew no bounds, and was compounded by the close friendship with George and Gracie. A brilliant, experienced actress-turned-comedienne, Gracie had been performing since childhood. She didn't have to prove anything. She was totally secure. Mom had had to learn her trade as she went—and considering her lack of training became an extremely accomplished comedienne. But not in a class with Gracie. And she knew it.

The Burnses, when they moved west, quite naturally became part of the Hollywood scene, but they never cared much about it. Ironically, Mom cared a lot. She thought that if she owned a grander house, bought more expensive clothes, bigger and better jewels, threw more lavish parties, she would be "one of them." It worked. The combination of Dad's stardom and her spending resulted in her close friendship with Edie Goetz and thus her integral part in Hollywood's inner circle. (Daddy and Bill Goetz adored each other. Bill had a terrific sense of humor.) Yet she was always competing and there was always a part of her that felt she didn't really belong. Her insecurity and extravagance continued all her life.

If a psychiatrist were to ask me to say the first adjective that comes to mind when describing my mother, that word would be "hypercritical." I think she wanted me to be a beautiful child as a reflection of her, and a funny and witty one to fit in with the Hollywood image and her Hollywood friends. I was none of the above, at least not in her eyes. Although at the beginning I was too young to understand such emotions, perhaps she was vying with me for Daddy's affection. Looking back at the way he adored her, it's hard to believe. Of course this kind of jealousy would have been buried deep in her subconscious. It's still hard for me to take in on an intellectual level. Rationally speaking, she had no competition, none at all.

If that psychiatrist were to ask me to say the first adjective that comes to mind when describing myself in relation to my mother it would be "scared." Not that she ever hit me or spanked me, although once—I must have been about ten —she slapped me in the face. I had been cavorting in the pool and my hair was wet. She said, "Go comb your hair—it looks a mess." I responded instantly, "So does yours."

Her slap was well deserved for I had committed one of the two unforgivable crimes on which no leeway was permitted: sassing her. I was not even allowed to talk back—only, "Yes, Mother"—no arguments, no disagreements. Sassing was beyond the pale!

The other unbreakable rule was I had to stand up when she entered my room, and wait for permission to be seated. I never fouled up on that one and it became so deeply ingrained I continued the practice until the end of her life. I don't think I could have *not* stood up. All the other rules: respect for one's elders, impeccable table manners, being seen and not heard, being at all times polite, I followed faithfully because I was afraid not to. When Mom was angry she seemed so formidable and cold, she scared me, although I don't know what terrible thing I thought she might do to me. I don't recall any particularly harsh punishments, so I can only believe that my fear must have been that she would tell Daddy and then he wouldn't love me anymore.

Mother's room was upstairs at the front of the house. It was a large room with three windows looking out over the front lawn. Her big bed always looked neat, though she spent a lot of time in it, reading or watching television. When I was in grade school and returned home in mid-afternoon, unless I had brought a friend to play with or had a piano lesson, the very first thing I had to do was go to Mother's room for a kind of command performance. She'd be sitting up on her side of the queen-size bed, I'd go around it, give her a kiss and then settle down cross-legged on the other side. "Your hair looks terrible." "Why did you wear that ugly dress?" "When are you going to stop biting your nails?" I realize that memory plays tricks and I'm admittedly being unfair because many times we had pleasant conversations, but those phrases of nagging and criticism stand out vividly in my mind. Was she seeing her faults in me? Was she seeing my faults as hers? Was it part of the rivalry?

Deedee recalls: "Your mother scared me to death. She always criticized me—my hair was too short, my hair was too long, my skirt was the wrong color—nothing was ever right, ever! I never heard her say, 'You look nice.' "

Bens said about me as a three-year-old: "She kept her own council." I, of course, don't remember how I acted when I was that young, but I do remember that at some early stage I learned to tune out, to mentally retreat into my own private world, a world she couldn't enter. I sat through those bedside chats as though disembodied, as though she were speaking to someone else—listening only enough to reply with an appropriate, "Yes, Mother" or "No, Mother" during pauses. I thought I had succeeded in looking blank, but apparently not, because when she'd finished she would often say, "Wipe that smirk off your face."

When I could in fact retreat, I went to my room, closed the door and put a record on the gramophone. Music was not something that interested my mother, but later it would be something to share with Daddy.

I was frightened of her too because she was constantly unpredictable. I never knew what to expect. I would be praised one day and admonished the next for exactly the same thing. ("Why did you wear that dress today? You know I hate it." "But Mother, you liked it the last time I wore it. Besides, you picked it out." Oops, that was talking back.) She would promise something and then, when reminded of it, deny she had ever made the promise. I had always to be on my guard with her. I could never relax, never feel completely comfortable.

I never doubted that she loved me. All my life I heard from her friends how proud she was of me; of my brains, my prowess in school, my accomplishments, my taste. What a shame I so rarely heard those words of approval from her.

317

Shopping for clothes was Mom's favorite activity—for me as well as for herself. I remember going with her to a small store in an arcade on Beverly Drive. They specialized in a particular style of little girl's dresses—a peasant blouse with puffed short sleeves, a full gathered skirt on a wide waistband with a bow in back and attached suspenders. The blouses were white, the skirts various plaids, checks and prints. It was like a uniform—most of my friends wore them, too. By the time I was in fifth grade or so, I thought they were too babyish—I especially hated the suspenders. The other girls in my class were by now wearing regular skirts and here was I in these silly things. In seventh grade I complained so much that I was given the privilege of choosing my own dresses—with Mom's approval of course. No more sashes, ruffles or suspenders.

Mother had gorgeous clothes. I always admired her taste, and I hope I learned from her. If she had any fault at all, it was perhaps that she was too conservative. As an adult I went shopping with her frequently. She would try on a dress and say, "I love it, but could you take the pouf or the flower or the ruffle off?"

"The pouf looks wonderful, Mom. The outfit doesn't have to be absolutely plain." But the pouf came off.

She loved beautiful, expensive fabrics, perfect tailoring and simple lines. She was always well groomed and elegant. In the early days Howard

Greer made her clothes. I remember going with her to his chic salon on Rodeo Drive (before it became RODEO DRIVE) and watching him flamboyantly drape fabrics on her—swirling and swathing, just like in those fancy dress salons you see in the early movies. I thought her more glamorous than any movie star.

Before we left for London when I was fourteen, we spent a week in New York and Mom took me shopping. She wanted me to be beautifully dressed for dinners on the ship and parties in Europe. For some unfathomable reason she decided I should look sophisticated and grown-up, so along with many lovely stylish outfits, she bought me a pair of black high-heeled shoes—my first. Like most children, I couldn't wait to look grown-up and now I did. I was even allowed to wear lipstick. I wore my new shoes, new dress and lipstick for the first time the night before we sailed when Mom and Dad took me to the Stork Club—another first—for dinner. I waltzed in with my head high, proud as a peacock, as though I owned the place.

The new me lasted throughout the two-month trip: on board the ship, in London, Paris and on the Riviera, on the return crossing, the *Twentieth Century Limited* and the *Super Chief* back to California. And then, much to my surprise, Mother changed her mind—that unpredictability I mentioned. I was no longer to be an adult. The shoes, the lipstick and most of the clothes disappeared and I was "back in Kansas." It would be another two years before I was allowed to be sophisticated again.

About this time Mrs. McKenzie, the dress-maker, came to our house. She made very few things for me because she was much too expensive. The exceptions were my sweet sixteen and graduation dresses. Mom had a petite size 6 figure and by now I fit perfectly into her things. Mrs. McKenzie made most of Mom's wardrobe, some designed by the two of them, some taken from magazine photos. There was one dress I was absolutely crazy about. I tried it on many times, prancing around and preening in front of the mirror. It was a short black satin cocktail dress with a tight bodice, and the full skirt was fashioned of cut-out petals with a bright pink lining. The petals grew larger from the waist to the hem, and although the skirt seemed to be all black, the pink showed as you moved. It was fabulous! On occasion, Mother did let me wear her clothes, but this particular dress was taboo. She had not worn it yet.

Skip to New Year's Eve, 1952. I had been invited to a very special party. My parents had already left for theirs. What should I wear? Nothing in my closet would do, so maybe something of Mom's. I tried on a number of her dresses but you can guess which I chose. It wasn't that I meant to be deliberately mean or rebellious—I just *had* to wear that dress. It cried out to me, I couldn't resist. I no longer remember anything about the party, not even the name of my date, but I will never forget arriving home about two in the morning and breathing a sigh of relief! They weren't home yet. As I got out of the car I was making my plan: I could undress quickly, hang the dress back in her closet, be in my bedclothes by the time she came in and she would never know. Just as my date and I were waiting for Frank to open the side door, my parents' car pulled into the driveway. There was no escape. I was caught out again—like the proverbial rat in a trap! I had no excuse, Mom was furious (as well she might have been), went into her "after all I've done for you" diatribe and I wasn't allowed to wear any of her clothes for ages.

Irving Fein, Daddy's manager, said to me recently, "I think Mary was always a strange woman, even before she moved to Hollywood. George Burns told me a story that went back to 1932 when they lived at the Essex House—they were going out to dinner. Jack came down, but not Mary. They finally went up to the suite and there was Mary in a slip with a closetful of clothes. She didn't know which black dress to wear. She must have had fifteen black dresses. She'd only been married five years. Gracie only had one black dress.

"Once they were playing at the Capitol Theatre and some shopgirl came and delivered something. The girl was wearing a cute blouse—it was very inexpensive, but on her it looked good—a cute girl with a cute figure. Mary said, 'I love that blouse—get it for me in black, green, white, pink,

321

yellow and red.' The girl ran out and got them for her. Mary did that all the time."

We had a lot of different servants over the years, many who stayed for a long time. Mother presided over them with a kind of professional shrewdness. They all naturally adored my father, but then he wasn't the one who gave the orders. My mother was the heavy. She set the rules (Thursdays and every other Sunday off—standard practice); interviewed, hired, disciplined and fired. And she was as tough with them as she was with me.

Staffs of servants varied from the grand to grander to grandest in the homes of Hollywood during the 1930's and 1940's. We had what I would call your garden-variety staff. A European cook, an English (usually) butler, an upstairs maid who doubled as Mother's personal maid, a downstairs maid, my nanny (governess or whatever), a full-time laundress and a full-time gardener. This was pauper-like compared to a "grandest" at the Jack Warner or Harold Lloyd home. They didn't employ a staff, it was more like a small army.

Some of our help stand out in my mind, most are long forgotten. I remember a maid named Anna because she would awaken me in the early morning by banging into my room and whooshing open the curtains. (I like to wake up gently.) I pleaded with her in the politest way I knew how to let me wake up in quiet and darkness. She ignored me. I hated her and the bright blast of sunlight that assaulted my peaceful sleep.

Our cooks seemed to last the longest and were always fabulous. Mrs. King was my favorite. Because my parents entertained so much, my mother was very fussy about meals. She was experienced and knowledgeable and she knew good food. When a new cook was hired she was given specific test meals for the first three days. If she passed, chances were she stayed for many years. Although demanding, my mother never interfered in the kitchen and was not difficult to cook for because she knew exactly what she wanted.

Except for party evenings, the daily routine was unvarying. Mother slept late and her breakfast was served to her in bed on a beautiful breakfast tray, with lovely linens, Limoges china and a fresh flower in a bud vase. It was then that Bens would bring me in to see her—before I was old enough to start school. She would ask Bens what we were going to do and plan the day for us. Bens told me recently that she was often terrified because she had no conception of how to handle me. "It was touch and go. I had never taken care of children before. I was an only child. In a lot of ways, I think the fact that I was so naive was good as far as Mrs. Benny was concerned—I was easy to mold. I had no preconceived ideas about how a child should be brought up."

After breakfast, the cook came in with her pad and pencil to discuss that evening's dinner menu. If there was to be a party, it was planned long in advance. The cook then made lunch for the staff, later tea and sandwiches and pastry for Mother

323

and whoever else might join her, then the staff's dinner, then, finally, the family dinner.

Mrs. King was the best. I think she was Czech. Short and plump, of indeterminate age, she was invariably jolly. Not only were her meals delicious and her pastry delectable, there were always extras. The fridge overflowed with leftovers and snacks, the cookie jar was filled with freshly baked goodies. Daddy was a nosher. His favorite snack was chicken: baked, broiled, roasted or fried—he didn't care. He adored Mrs. King; he hugged and kissed her and told her how wonderful she was, so of course she went out of her way to please him, and saw to it that there was chicken in the fridge at all times.

In later years, when I came home at night from a date, my date and I sometimes made a beeline to the kitchen for an ice box raid. Daddy, in his robe, would often join us. I don't know if it was coincidence or whether perhaps he heard the door open, but he showed up with amazing frequency. I think he particularly enjoyed these nighttime raids. He was by nature gregarious; he loved to be with people. Although he spent many busy hours, he was alone: practicing his violin, writing speeches, working on scripts and reading. When he wasn't busy, he didn't like to be alone. He wanted company. So downstairs to the kitchen he came.

By this time he had developed a mild form of diabetes. He didn't take insulin; it was more easily controlled than that by a pill called Orinase, but he was supposed to watch his diet and Mother saw to it that he did. She was very strict with him. But Mother wasn't there! So with a childlike grin on his face he joined us and headed for the chicken, the ice cream and the cookies. Perhaps I should have stopped him. After all, I loved him and was concerned about his welfare, but he looked so pleased and contented, and it seemed to me that an occasional splurge was probably as good if not better for his mental health as it might be bad for his physical health. Happily, since he lived to be eighty, I was proved right.

Mom's social competition or her competition with me vis-à-vis my father was at least something I can understand, but when she started competing with me for my boyfriend, I found it hard to take, to say the least. You notice I use the singular. That's because it only happened once. She didn't consider any of my boyfriends worth the effort until I met Vic Damone. Normally, when she stayed home during the day she didn't bother to put on makeup. All of a sudden, now that Vic was dropping by unexpectedly, she managed always to be dressed and made up. I played tennis every day so she invited him to join her for golf. When we all went to Las Vegas she somehow arranged that they should drive there together while Daddy and I flew. She spent more time with him than I did. Vic, of course, didn't notice anything amiss —nor did Daddy—men never do!

And then there was one awful night. Vic came

to the Roxbury house to pick me up for a date. I was a few minutes late, so Mother chatted with him in the library while I put on the finishing touches. When I entered the library Mother said, "That dress looks terrible on you—it makes you look heavy. Don't you think you should wear the—"

Before she could complete the sentence I replied. "Excuse me, I'll be right back. I forgot something." I fled the room, ran to the powder room and burst into tears. I had to spend a few minutes collecting myself. I wasn't about to let her know she had upset me. After wiping my eyes and fixing my makeup, I returned as though nothing unusual had occurred, as though I hadn't even heard what she said.

"Sorry to be late, Vic. Let's go. Good night, Mother," I said coldly, as I swept out of the room.

That rivalry could be a killer.

I recently asked the playwright Leonard Gershe, author of *Butterflies Are Free* and a close family friend, why he thought Mom was so insecure. He answered, "I would guess because she had been thrown into a world that she didn't come from and I don't think she felt that she was a performer. She didn't really like performing—she liked it on radio but she hated, was terrified of television. That was it—the need to be secure could only be assuaged by self-gratification. Buying, shopping. If Claudette Colbert had something, she had to have it in every color—it was that kind of insecurity—she had to have what people she secretly admired had, and more of it."

Mel Blanc's wife, Estelle, was from Denver and her family knew my mother's family there before they moved to Seattle where Mom was born. My mother's grandfather had apparently burned down his business for the insurance money and I've told you the horse thief story—there were certainly some unsavory dealings in that family! Estelle thought maybe Mom wanted to get away from that tarnished image. Estelle also thought this was the reason she could never really be friends with Mother: "Because I had known her family back in Denver. I think Mary was afraid that I might bring up something about her family that she didn't want to know about. I always had that feeling—that I might have heard stories that she wouldn't have wanted other people to know. I'm sure about that. Mary didn't want to be reminded of her mother's past. And she didn't want to be reminded that she'd been Sadie. I was friendlier and more open with Gracie than I was with Mary. I was afraid I'd bring up something that might offend her in some way."

When I was a child and told my troubles to my Aunt Babe, she had to tread on rather thin ice. She had to be very diplomatic to agree with me when I complained about Mother and yet not criticize her too strongly. Later, when I grew up, Babe gave it to me straight and told me exactly how she felt. She didn't think much of her pretentious, social-climbing sister who treated her like a poor relation. Babe had no pretensions. She had her own circle of friends with whom she drank, played cards, went to the movies, partied and had a generally raucous good old time.

I was at Lake Arrowhead with my children when Babe died and my mother called and told me the exact time and place—noon at Forest Lawn in Burbank—of the funeral. It turned out to be something of a Keystone Kops comedy of errors for me, as well as a completely unintended occasion for me to infuriate my mother. I only kept jeans and bathing suits at the lake, so I had asked my older daughter, Maria, to meet me early at Forest Lawn with some clothes from home. I could make a quick change. Through a series of misadventures involving the lack of a road map, a freeway that had never been completed and a child who had to be delivered from the lake to his home in Pasadena, I arrived at three minutes before twelve, wet-headed and barefoot in a bathing suit and a terry cover-up. Though I made a beeline to the ladies' room my mother had spotted me, and was as outraged as I'd ever seen her. I knew that somewhere Babe must be laughing gleefully.

Mom's insecurity manifested itself in her having to be seen at the *right* restaurants, driving the *right* car, shopping in the *right* stores and wearing the *right* labels. When I was a child the birthday or Christmas gifts I gave her would usually get a thank-you and then disappear, never to be seen again. I don't remember ever having my little school accomplishments displayed. Later, when I could afford it, I tried hard to please her by buying the *right* gifts from the *right* places. I once bought her a pair of gold earrings from Neiman-Marcus. She loved them and was very appreciative. Finally, I'd made a hit! Another time I bought her a red satin evening bag. It was by Prada, an expensive line I had seen on a trip to Texas. A lot of the wealthy Houston ladies were carrying Prada bags, so when I saw one in Beverly Hills I bought it for Mom's birthday. She had never heard of Prada so she thanked me with little enthusiasm. I then proceeded to explain that Prada was *very* expensive and *very* chic and the *very* latest thing. The oil-rich ladies wouldn't be without one. "Really?" she said, perking up. The next day she called to tell me that she had been out to dinner and had taken her new bag and her friends loved it. I'd made another hit!

She had to be with the *right* people as well.

Irving Fein continued: "Jack used to go out alone—to all these big dinners—big functions— Friars dinners and charity dinners and Mary would always have a cold or something. If it was a party for Sinatra or Gregory Peck, she would go. But a Friars dinner, she thought that was beneath her."

There was a great deal of conflict between Irving and my mother. For years they tolerated each other with barely cordial dislike. Mom wanted everyone, including Daddy, to think she had been responsible for his success and that she played a major role in his career decisions. She discovered Dennis Day, true, and Dad did discuss business matters with her, but Irving, who had a well-deserved reputation as one of the best managers in the business, and who after my father's death became George Burns's manager, was the real decision maker. My father's success, certainly in his later years, was attributable in great part to Irving's professional skills. Mom was jealous. It became a tug-of-war and she was losing. It became more and more difficult for her to convince anyone that she was involved in major decisions. Daddy listened to Irving, which did not exactly endear him to my mother. She wanted more of the credit.

As Irving said, "Mary loved being a big shot. When they went to the races the second race would be over and everyone would be saying, 'Oh, Christ, I can't pick a horse.' Then Mary would reach in her pocket and say, 'I've got the winner!' Then the third race: 'I've got the winner!' She used to buy six or seven tickets for each race so she'd always have the winner. And Jack would say, 'Isn't she brilliant?' She liked to show how smart she was."

On the other hand Mom had many admirable qualities.

In 1961 Mel Blanc was in a nearly fatal automobile accident that resulted in a three-month hospital stay. Estelle Blanc said, "Mary was always very nice to me and Mel. She was a very good friend, too. The day of Mel's accident she said, 'Estelle, I live closer than you do. If you want to come and stay here and stay as long as you like, I have room for you and you don't have to go so far back and forth to the hospital.' I thought that was dear of her. You had to know Mary. A lot of people didn't and they didn't understand her—a lot of the writers' wives, we'd talk about her, but you had to know her to appreciate her. She was reserved. She didn't mean to be haughty, she was just a reserved person. You had the feeling she was keeping herself within herself."

Claudette Colbert told me, "Your mother had a wonderful sense of humor about herself. Most people who'd had facial surgery kept it a big secret. But your mother came right out about it—which in those days nobody did. I remember once she sneezed and she took her handkerchief and then started to laugh. I said, 'What's the matter?' And she said, 'Well you know I have to remember that my nose is up here!'

"I discovered one thing about her when she came to Barbados. This was shortly after your father died. She had been there only one day. There were some nasty steps to the beach. She tripped on cement and coral mixed. She cut her leg from here to there—it was bleeding and everything and I thought, 'Well, there goes the whole visit.' So I went up and I got the alcohol and bandaged it up. She was *such* a good sport. There was never a peep out of her, she did everything that we did except go in swimming. We took long walks, we were very active and it was as if nothing had happened. We kept saying, 'How do you feel?' And she'd say, 'I feel fine.' "

Janet De Cordova, Fred's wife, remembered, "I'd only just met Mary, and she invited me to a party as a solo woman—which was really great, to be a single woman in this town and to be invited alone. That's the way she was. We became very good friends. I remember one marvelous thing about Mary—her generosity. One night I was at her house and I had a tortoiseshell cigarette case that I was very proud of, and Mary said, 'I can't stand it. I've got a case for you.' And she went upstairs and brought down a beautiful little gold case with diamonds and gave it to me.

"We had such great times in Palm Springs. I remember when your parents bought the house that had belonged to Tom May, the founder of the May Company. Mary was thrilled. It was her ultimate dream—years ago she had sold stockings in his store and now she *owned* his house. We always had a great time in Palm Springs. Mary and I would sit up until three in the morning playing cards. And Jack would come out of his bedroom every once in a while and moon us—and go back to bed."

Lennie Gershe recalls, "Mary could be very funny—one time a friend was going to Africa and she gave him two pith helmets with a note that read, 'One for the jungle and one to pith in.'

"Mary always had the best food and the prettiest

china. Of course the Hollywood hostesses all tried to outdo each other, to have the most beautiful table. Mary's was as good as anybody's. She did it very well, even after Jack was gone. Her favorite thing was to give a barbecue which she did every September and the food was done by Chasen's and indeed there were ribs, but I remember that somebody called and asked how to dress. Mary said, 'Let me put it this way. I don't own a pair of jeans.' Mary would dress to the nines. Her parties were always star-studded. She and Jack moved in a group of top-drawer celebrities. And there was nobody more top-drawer than the Jack Bennys. The 'crème' would always be at the Bennys' . . . the parties ranged in size from a small group of twelve to big ones where they would put up tents for sixty to a hundred. Mary always had a pianist—not all of the hostesses did. Whatever Mary did she was big about it—maybe she got it from Jack or maybe he got it from her or maybe that's what attracted them to each other. She too in her way was extremely generous. She could also be petty about some things but that was part of her neurosis. She was very careful about who surrounded Jack. She had an eye for what was good—what was right for him. He had fierce loyalties that she felt sometimes were misplaced. She protected him socially, surrounded him with the people she felt were best—she wasn't wrong—and he appreciated it."

Rex Kennamer, her doctor and friend, saw it all: "Your mother was always very good to me—

I mean, she was very demanding, I made a lot of house calls that weren't necessary and things like that, but it never bothered me. I always took that in stride. I always took that as part of her. I liked your mother and, God knows, your dad treated her like a queen. I can remember going to the house up on Roxbury and everybody tippy-toeing around because Mary was still asleep. That was life in the big house. Making useless house calls never bothered me—it was okay. I used to go up there and sit and talk to her. She liked to talk about everything from what she was reading to the crossword puzzle she was working on. And you know, she used me a lot. Frequently when she didn't want to go to a party I had to pronounce that Mary had a cold. I think people knew I was lying. Mary was a little sad. I think Mary tended to be reclusive. I don't think she thoroughly enjoyed who she was or got as much fun out of life as I thought she should have. I think her reclusive tendency became more pronounced with time. She seemed to withdraw more and more into her bedroom. That just evoked sympathy from me, that she just didn't get more out of life. It didn't anger me or anything like that. It wasn't to such a degree that it was really pathological. It's just you felt she wasn't enjoying things to the fullest. And I think your father did.

"When she did go out I think she had a pretty good time. But I think she was one of those people who found it easier to stay home.

"Mary used to go to the hospital for checkups.

She sent her own sheets and her own china down to the hospital. Once we got all ready for her, we got the room all fixed up, her sheets on the bed, and she changed her mind and didn't come! I don't think she knew how much trouble that was for us to get that room ready—but it was all right. That went with the territory."

The saddest thing about my mom was the reclusiveness Rex spoke of. I remember those afternoons at the pool: the fun and laughter. Then it changed—gradually, I suppose. I wasn't aware of the change. I was busy with my own activities, then later I was away at boarding school. I didn't notice as the years passed that fewer days were spent with friends, that there was less gaiety, that she spent more and more time at home alone. All of a sudden one day I woke up and realized what was happening—she was spending almost every day at home, not getting dressed, not putting on makeup or combing her hair. She sat in Daddy's room all day watching television, having her lunch sent up on a tray. She was hardly going out at all. No more golf, no more lunches with a girlfriend. The hairdresser and manicurist came to the house. She rarely went shopping. She had clothes sent to the house, picked what she wanted, and sent the rest back. Except for Dad's birthday and Christmas presents, the other gifts for the family, including mine, were bought by Miss Vallance. I remember one Christmas being very angry with her over that because she had promised to go herself to buy her grandchildren's gifts. And then she lied to me; told me she had done it. I knew better. The owner of our local toy store let it slip that Miss Vallance had been there. So when my children opened their presents that Christmas Eve and went over to give their grandmother a kiss and say thank you I said, "Go give Miss V a kiss and thank you, too. It was Miss V who did the shopping and picked them out." Maybe it was a nasty thing to do, but I just had to let my mother know that she couldn't always get away with her lies. She glared—but didn't say a word.

She also lied to Daddy frequently. I remember being in the sitting room with her in the late afternoon. Daddy would arrive home and ask about her day. She would tell him she had been out to lunch and shopping. I don't know whether or not he believed her, but then he had no reason not to.

However, there were exceptions. She still went with Dad to Las Vegas, Palm Springs, Lake Tahoe, sometimes to New York, and had a wonderful time. She still entertained lavishly, if less often. She could be as funny, as happy and as fun-loving as ever. I remember wonderful times spent with her during my adult years. She did occasionally go out to buy clothes. She did occasionally go shopping with me. But more and more she canceled social engagements at the last minute, and, gradually, more and more she became a recluse.

Today the phrase "women need their own identity" has become a cliché, yet in my mother's case, a relevant one. Yes, she was Mary Livingstone, a personality in her own right, but in her mind it wasn't enough—she was not important or famous enough. Since she did so little television, when radio died the name Mary Livingstone died with it. She had always referred to herself as Mrs. Jack Benny, but from the mid 1950's on, being Mrs. Jack Benny became the center of her life.

She would call a restaurant for a reservation, "Hello, this is Mrs. Jack Benny. I want the best table," or a store, "Hello, this is Mrs. Jack Benny. Send me . . ." or when we went shopping together to my embarrassment (I tried hiding in corners), "I'm Mrs. Jack Benny. Show me your best . . ." She used it, traded on it, reveled in it. It seemed to be all she had, her be-all and end-all. In her mind she had no identity of her own. None.

As a child I was an extension of her identity—and perhaps that's why she was so critical of me, why she took my misbehavior so personally. After I grew up, being Mrs. Jack Benny worked for her for many years. The table was waiting, the stores delivered, people jumped to do her bidding—until the end of 1974 when Jack Benny died. Gradually over the next few years that magical name lost its magic. Hollywood is not a place of "what have you done for me lately?," but of "what can you do for me tomorrow?" and Jack Benny couldn't do a blessed thing for anybody tomorrow. "Hello, this is Mrs. Jack Benny," more and more often received a response of, "So . . . ?" Mom couldn't deal with it. She had no resources to fall back on.

Also, after Dad died, the invitations to social events and parties decreased. Her bad habits—canceling a sit-down dinner at the last minute, ignoring the niceties of a thank-you note or phone call—caught up with her. That, along with the fact she was now an extra woman, effectively took her off the invitation lists. Hostesses who had previously put up with her because they adored her husband no longer had to pretend she was welcome.

On her trips to Barbados she pulled herself together and had a good time—mainly because of Claudette Colbert, who remained a loyal and close friend—but on other travels she was miserable. She went with me to New York twice, and both times she got sick on the second day and stayed in her hotel room the rest of the trip. Psychosomatic, I'm sure. When she had been in the city with Daddy, they were out every night, invited everywhere by everybody. She couldn't admit that now there were no invitations, so instead she became ill. When she returned home she could say how unhappy she'd been in New York that she couldn't do all the wonderful things and go to all the wonderful places because she'd come down with the flu.

A current medical term, "clinical depression," is perhaps applicable. Less was known about it before her death; today it might be an appropriate diagnosis. I've read articles about it, and many symptoms jibe with hers, but I'm not qualified to judge. I just don't know. I only know that she had been on a downhill path long before my father died, but afterward her insecurities took over her life.

During the last year of her life I worried about her and tried everything to get her to see Dr. Kennamer's associate, Gary Sugarman, as Rex was semiretired. She had fainting spells, more than were normal for her, she had fallen and cut her forehead while walking around in the middle of the night, she occasionally became disoriented. She wouldn't go to see him. She refused. After the falling incident I called Gary to come see her, but when he arrived at the house, at first she wouldn't see him. He called me, I rushed over (I could get there in three minutes) and personally escorted him into her room. She was angry but I insisted and she finally gave in. Gary told her he wanted her to come to his office for tests. She reluctantly agreed, and they made an appointment for the following week. She never kept it.

One afternoon a few weeks later she had made an appointment for a manicure. It was quite an afternoon. Jessica, the owner of a manicure salon in Los Angeles (where they give the best manicures in the world!), was to come do Mom's nails. Nancy Reagan, who wanted the privacy of a home, was coming to get her manicure at the same time. I stopped in briefly just to check on my mother. Having no idea of these arrangements I was rather surprised to find the courtyard filled with black cars and Secret Servicemen. They almost wouldn't let me in. The sitting room was quite a scene: Jessica was putting polish on Nancy's nails and Mother was lying on the sofa looking wan and tired, but very, very happy with all the attention and activity—to say nothing of having the First Lady there. During the middle of that night she quietly passed away. The doctor said it was a heart attack, but I have always felt she just gradually faded out of life.

Did I love my mother? Like many daughters, my feelings ran the gamut. I was frequently angry, sometimes furious with her, sometimes I disliked her. I often thought she was unfair and there were times I resented her—hardly an unusual relationship between mother and daughter. Over all, yes, I loved her, but it was a love mixed with sadness and pity when I was grown—and confusion and trepidation when I was little. I wanted her to be proud of me, but because she could be so critical, it was almost impossible to win her approval, and eventually I gave up, deciding I just didn't care. My own approval would have to do. My identity was mine and Joan Benny could not be Mary Livingstone. I wanted to make her happy, but eventually realized that was impossible. Her demons were too deep rooted, and it wasn't within my power to exorcise them.

Mom had a quick, clever wit, albeit of the sarcastic, biting, sometimes wicked variety. And I must admit she even had that most endearing quality, a sense of humor about herself. Unfortunately her humor stopped cold when it came to me. She laughed with her friends, I laughed with mine. That's not to say we didn't get along or have happy, friendly, mother-daughter conversations —we did on occasion—it's just that I don't remember our ever really laughing together.

She had so many good qualities—her sense of humor, her generosity, her loyalty to her friends. She had a famous, successful and adoring husband; she had famous, interesting and amusing friends; she lived in luxury; she was a celebrity in her own right. In short, she had everything a woman could possibly want. When I think of her it's with sadness because I wish she could have enjoyed it all more. I wish we could have enjoyed each other more. Loved each other more.

CHAPTER 17

As you know by now Daddy and I got along pretty well, but our relationship had its flaws, too— although to me they seemed minor. He wasn't always easy to talk to and we didn't have heart-to-hearts very often. It wasn't his style. Besides, it made him feel uncomfortable. Of course he was never, and I do mean never, aware that I couldn't talk to Mother, so I turned to Miss Vallance or inward to myself.

Was I disappointed? Hurt? Yes, because I wanted the closeness of a father-daughter relationship as I imagined it should be. Perhaps I had seen too many Andy Hardy movies. But since that was not to be, I settled for other forms of closeness. There were many things to share that more than made up for whatever hurt I felt because he couldn't deal with my personal problems. And happily during my late teen years our relationship blossomed due to our mutual love of music.

My passion for music—where did it come from? I can only suppose it must be something genetic. I was certainly not exposed to it at home. Yes, my parents listened to Bing Crosby, Frank Sinatra or Dinah Shore, and Dennis Day sang on the show, but as far as I knew, they had no interest in classical music, wouldn't know Bach from Bartok. Whatever interest Daddy may have shown in music, along with his violin playing, had been forgotten after the days of vaudeville and it would be a few more years before he took it up again.

As I mentioned earlier, when I was very young I loved to listen to records in my room and sing and dance along. *Pinocchio, Snow White* and *The Wizard of Oz* were my favorites. Then, one day —a day I remember vividly, a day that changed my life—I was engaged in one of my favorite activities, exploring cupboards and closets around the house. Usually my forays proved unrewarding, but on this day I hit the jackpot. On a high shelf in back of one of the library closets, I discovered something very unusual: three large twelve-inch record albums. Why would record albums be hidden away in a closet? I was positive that I'd happened on something forbidden, so of course my curiosity was overwhelming. Thick and heavy as they were, I managed to get them down and sneak them up the back stairs to my room. Unlike any records I had ever seen, no pictures or descriptions decorated the plain, drab covers. Only the black spines had gold-lettered titles, titles that had no meaning for me. What kind of records could they be? I could hardly wait to find out.

I put the first one on my phonograph. Within a few minutes I found myself transported to a world of glorious and beautiful sound I had not known existed. It was Beethoven's Fifth Symphony and my passion for music was born. The other two albums were Tchaikovsky's Piano Concerto and Tchaikovsky's *Swan Lake*. Now instead of dancing to Jiminy Cricket I could twirl and leap to real ballet. And I did. Incessantly.

When Mom asked me what I wanted for my birthday that year, I answered, "Another Beethoven symphony, please." She gave me a very strange look. I had quite astonished her. Music became my passion, my refuge and my escape. If I was depressed or unhappy, a Broadway show or Glenn Miller could cheer me up; if Mom had been nagging or lecturing I could go in my room, close the door, and retreat into my own world of Brahms, Schubert or Rachmaninoff—a world she couldn't enter. By the time I reached my teens I had amassed a rather large collection of 78 RPM records. When Daddy took up the violin again, a few years later, my knowledge and love of classical music would become the strongest bond between us.

When I was thirteen and a freshman in high school at Chadwick, every student had to participate in the school chorus. Throughout the fall term we practiced "The Hallelujah Chorus" and "For Unto Us a Child Is Born" from *The Messiah* to sing at our Christmas pageant. I sang alto. To this day I can remember every note. These were the first major choral pieces I had ever heard and I fell in love with them. I was not yet familiar with the complete oratorio, but that didn't matter. I wanted *The Messiah* for Christmas. I put it at the top of my list in bold capital letters. I told Miss Vallance, knowing she would tell my mother, that I wanted it more than I had ever wanted anything. And I crossed my fingers.

The tree was decorated, the gifts underneath; it was the day before Christmas. *The Messiah* at that time came in two enormous thick, heavy albums, six records in each, twenty-four sides in all—easy to spot. I had long since learned where Miss Vallance hid the presents from me at Christmastime—mostly in the closets in the powder room. I had also learned how to unwrap and rewrap packages without detection. This day I searched all the known caches, and even some new ones, but to no avail. No *Messiah*. I was crushed!

Our Christmas routine went as follows: On Christmas Eve we had our family turkey dinner in the dining room, which was festively decorated with holly berries, red candles and Santa Clauses. The table was set with our Christmas tree china. It was really beautiful. After dinner we all went into the library, where first my grandparents, Babe and her husband, Miss Vallance and Hickey with his family opened their presents. Next, Mother and Daddy opened theirs—not all of them, just the ones from family and friends. (The other gifts, the ones from business associates and agents, were opened the next day, kind of as an afterthought.) Then it was my turn. I was allowed to open the gifts from the family, not including Mom or Dad's, and one other—any one of my choice, but only one. The rest had to wait until Christmas morning. Those were the rules.

On Christmas morning I drank my orange juice, then went to the library where I impatiently waited, inspecting my presents until the magic hour of nine when my parents appeared. Finally, the time had come.

This particular Christmas morning when I went into the library I searched thoroughly; under other presents, under furniture, behind chairs, I even went back to the powder room. Again the search proved futile. When Mother and Daddy came in we wished each other Merry Christmas and I began the ritual of opening my presents. I oohed and aahed over everything, but with less than my usual enthusiasm. I opened their gift last as I always did, and though I no longer remember what it was, I hugged and kissed them and told them how much I loved it. Another Christmas was past.

As we were leaving the room to go for breakfast Daddy said casually, "Oh, we forgot something, Joanie—there's one more present. It's in the living room."

Daddy and Miss Vallance had outsmarted me. There sitting on the piano was my glorious *Messiah!*

For the next three years my record collection, both popular and classical, grew to the extent my allowance permitted. Then in 1950 when I turned sixteen I got my first job, as a salesgirl at the Beverly Gramophone Shop. Max, the manager, one of the most musically knowledgeable men I have ever known, paid me thirty dollars a week. He introduced me to contemporary composers, chamber music, German lieder and on and on. He recommended, I bought. Even with my discount, by the end of each week I had spent more than my salary and by the end of the two months I worked there I was in such debt it took me almost a year to pay it off. But I had acquired a great deal of knowledge along with a formidable record collection.

The following year Daddy decided to return to playing the violin. He did it with a vengeance, practicing three and four hours a day—in his dressing room. From the connecting door to his bedroom the long narrow dressing room, with its large bathroom at the far end, stretched clear across the inner U shape above the patio. On the side overlooking the pool there were small closets next to built-in bureaus, and in the center was a built-in brown leather window seat with a long window. On the other side, mirrors on closets covered the entire wall. Two small leather armless chairs, one on each end in front of the mirrors, completed the room.

Actually, he took his lessons there. He practiced in the bathroom! He was sent there like a naughty little boy by my mother because she loathed hearing those endless scales and exercises. By ensconcing himself in his bathroom with the door shut, no one in the house was forced to hear them— that is, no one except me. You see, my bedroom and his bathroom shared a common wall. Mom had a point. The sounds emanating from his violin were, to put it mildly, disagreeable, at least for the first couple of years. I tried to drown them out with some very loud Brahms or Beethoven, but that didn't work because I could always hear the faint sound of his violin penetrating even the full sound of a symphony orchestra on my phonograph. It was not a happy blend!

I finally solved the problem in two ways. One, I learned to ignore it and just shut my ears. Two, I joined him in his bathroom and tried to help him practice. His biggest problem was pitch. I think the violin is one of the most difficult of instruments. In order to hit a D and not a D-sharp or a D-flat, you must find the exact spot on the string on which to place your finger by hearing it. There is no other way. A violinist must have, in music parlance, perfect ears. Daddy didn't! He

347

really couldn't hear if he was sharp or flat, a problem most probably caused by not having played for all those years and possibly because he was now in his mid-fifties when a certain amount of hearing loss is common.

His intonation was terrible. He would be a little bit off on many notes. But by playing his scales slowly with me telling him when he was off pitch, he did improve, although he never acknowledged that the problem might be his hearing. I tried, in the kindest way, to tell him that he wasn't hearing properly, but he always said, "No, my hearing is fine. I just need to practice." There were times when he made a statement in a certain tone of voice and you just knew that the subject was closed. So I backed off and we continued slowly to correct the intonation problem note by note.

When he began taking an interest in classical music, I could hardly believe my luck. It was a godsend. Now, not only could I share my musical passion, but the problem of what to buy Daddy for his birthday and Christmas was solved. No more boring ties and shirts, of which he already had closetsful. I gave him scores of violin concertos, recordings of violin concertos and later, when I could afford it, two extra-special gifts—first editions of the Hill & Sons books on Stradivari and Guarneri. I even managed to get Jascha Heifetz to autograph the Stradivari one for him. Daddy was ecstatic. I, triumphant!

By now Daddy had an up-to-date stereo system in his bedroom. We spent many an hour listening to, comparing and discussing different violinists playing the same piece. Heifetz, Stern, Francescatti, Milstein, Oistrakh—it was interesting and instructive to listen to each of them play the same selection. They became his heroes.

Now that he was concertizing and had the opportunity to meet these artists he was as excited as a little boy meeting Superman. And he found it hard to believe that a great concert performer could be impressed to meet him. A close friend of mine, musician Artie Kane, remembers, "Once I made him angry. It was after a Rudolf Serkin concert, and Jack was telling us he'd been overwhelmed by his piano playing and had gone backstage to the green room. He couldn't get over it because Serkin ran to find a piece of paper so he could get Jack's autograph. I had had just enough of his humility and said, 'Jack, did it ever occur to you that he was twice as thrilled to meet you as you were to meet him?' He didn't like what I said. I didn't know why I'd made him angry because I was trying to compliment him. I realized later that he was right—he wanted to be impressed and I was spoiling it for him."

Daddy and I read scores together as we listened, discussing the notation. I introduced him to chamber music. I remember he particularly loved the César Franck violin sonata and the Anton Dvořák "Dumky" trio. Daddy was fascinated with this new world he had discovered—and so proud of his "brilliant" daughter. (Thank you, Max. I couldn't have done it without you.) He bragged about me to all his friends.

Daddy was too proud of his accomplishments: his many years of having the number one rated show in radio, his long career in television, the honor of having a junior high school named for him in his hometown. But if you were to ask him what gave him the most pleasure and pride, his answer would have been without pause, "My concerts." The public made a joke of Daddy's love of the violin. The fact was, it was the most important thing in the world to him. Here, in his own words, is the story of his music.

After so many years of ridiculing my fiddling, I became a serious violin player again. It didn't happen overnight. In 1944 when I was slated to appear at a benefit for Greek War Relief at the Hollywood Bowl, I was one of many radio/movie/concert stars scheduled to appear. The backbone of the program was the Los Angeles Philharmonic Orchestra and this gave me a wild inspiration. Instead of telling jokes or being master of ceremonies, I would play music. I went to Alfred Wallenstein, maestro of the Philharmonic, and told him the idea. He liked it. So on the night of the gala performance, with the full orchestra on stage, the announcer said the next performer was to be Mr. Jack Benny.

I walked out on stage in full dress, with tailcoat.

Nobody ever looked more like a serious violinist —not Mischa Elman, nor Heifetz, nor Stern. My face was solemn—as befitted a violinist. I had borrowed a fine Guarnerius for the occasion. I walked with dignity. I stood with dignity. With dignity I placed a handkerchief on my shoulder and fixed my violin under my chin. I got my bow into position over the strings. I nodded to maestro Wallenstein and the orchestra played an introduction to a rich and pompous arrangement of "Love in Bloom." Then I came in and we played "Love in Bloom" like a violin concerto. This arrangement I had commissioned was replete with trills, fast arpeggios and one crazy staccato passage. With a crashing of cymbals and a pounding of drums the number ended and I solemnly bowed to the audience, then to the maestro and then to the orchestra. The musicians stood up and applauded me—and I believe they meant it for I played well, way over my head that evening. And the audience—well, they went out of their minds because at first they had begun to laugh. Then as I showed I actually knew my technique, had a nice tone and really could play a violin, they listened attentively. When I finished I got a standing ovation. And I kept up my act. I didn't even smile. I was playing the role of concert violinist.

That night with the Los Angeles Philharmonic, I felt a strange gratification. The thought came to me that perhaps I could take up the violin and take a few lessons—purely as a personal hobby, you know. After all, man does not live by golf alone. Suddenly I found myself filled with a desire to hear violinists and to be with violinists. Whenever Heifetz, Szigeti, Ricci or Isaac Stern gave a concert in Los Angeles I was right down there in a good seat, drinking up the beautiful music, envying the violinist and imagining myself in his place.

February 3, 1946, was a red-letter day for me because that was the first time Isaac Stern was a guest on my radio program. To his surprise, I didn't make fun of him or of the violin or of music. It cost me $1,000 out of my own pocket to have Stern on the show. I was allowed $10,000 for guest stars on each show. We had already booked the Colmans, whose fee was $6,000. I heard that Stern was in Los Angeles and I said to Hilliard Marks that I wanted to book Stern on the show if he would agree to appear. Stern's fee was $5,000. I paid the difference myself—and never told Stern. But I got my money's worth. During rehearsals, I made him play about twenty solos for me, just for me, in my dressing room. I pretended I wanted to choose the best short number for him to play on the program. It was wonderful.

I just worship Stern, who is not only one of the greatest virtuosos now living, but who is also a man with a passion for life and eating and humor. He is wonderful company. And he became my friend. Can you imagine what it would have meant to my mother if she could have known that someday a man as great as Isaac Stern, a musician like him, would accept her son as a friend?

The next stage in the story of my fiddling on a serious level took place about five years later when I was beginning television programs for CBS. We did a program on the premise that a reporter is interviewing me and asks me how it feels to be a great comedian. I say I am not happy as a comedian—I am a frustrated violinist. If only I had studied harder and practiced the violin more as a child, I might have been a concert violinist now. Then by means of flashbacks there were scenes of me from my childhood, practicing the violin, then failing at it, then playing the violin in vaudeville and then later on in my life—not even using the violin as a prop. Finally, I said when we cut back to the interview in my dressing room, "So you see, instead of going out there and telling jokes, where I really belong is with the Philharmonic."

Then we dissolved to full stage and a full orchestra and I am giving a concert. The conductor is Wallenstein and I played a little of the *Zigeunerweisen* with them—the first difficult music I had tried to play since boyhood. Again, I felt that strange exaltation, feeling the strings vibrating under the caress of my bow, feeling the harmonies of my violin mingling with the harmonies of the orchestra. It was as though a small seed planted by my mother had lain dormant all this time and now, for no conceivable reason, had of its own volition decided that spring was here and it was time to sprout and it did.

After this show I was in my dressing room with

Mahlon Merrick, who for many years was the director of the band on my program. A decision had been forming in my mind and I said, "You know what I'm going to do? I'm going to give concerts and I'm going to do it for charity."

"But, Jack, why for heaven's sake?" Merrick asked.

"I don't know," I said, "but I just have this urge. It's something I have to do."

"You're crazy," he said, "to think you can give concerts. You haven't touched a violin in forty-seven years. How are you going to move your fingers—let alone interpret a piece?"

"I don't know how, but I'm going to do it. I'm *determined to do it.*"

In Merrick's group was a fine violinist, Larry Kurdjie. He played in many radio and television orchestras and in recording sessions. Larry became my first teacher when I resumed the fiddle. I started lessons all over again, but now it was with a different spirit. It wasn't the way it was with Professor Lindsay in Waukegan and Dr. Kortschalk in Chicago. Now I desperately wanted to play and I worked hard. I practiced two, three and four hours a day, day after day, driving poor Mary out of her mind, having to work in the bathroom so it wouldn't disturb her. I worked on my scales and the Kreutzer etudes and on even more difficult pieces.

Inside of a year, I gave my first concert with the Los Angeles Philharmonic. I did not accept any fees. Then I gave a concert with the Oklahoma

City Symphony Orchestra and began playing with symphonies in Chicago, San Francisco and Philadelphia. I played the first movement of the Mendelssohn concerto, the *Capriccio Espagnol*, the *Zigeunerweisen*.

And then—President Truman asked me to do him a small favor. We had been friends since 1945 when he was vice president. I met him while I was in Washington to be master of ceremonies at a National Press Club affair. We were introduced to each other informally before dinner. We sized each other up and immediately felt the flow of friendship. We had a lot in common: the same midwestern background, the same moral values, the same small-town childhood and a similar sense of humor. We talked the same language.

After this first meeting I visited with him whenever I came to Washington. We called each other Harry and Jack. I felt as though he was a guy I had grown up with. Our relationship became a good solid friendship and we wrote each other long letters. In 1953 Ed Pauley, Democratic Party treasurer and a San Francisco resident, gave a small dinner at his home for President Truman and I went up for this. Truman, being a amateur pianist himself, had been following the symphony concerts I'd begun playing. I had appeared for such charities as Greek War Relief, the Cedars of Lebanon Hospital and the City of Hope Hospital. Truman asked me if I really played the violin well enough to play with symphony orchestras and I assured him that while I was no Isaac Stern, I had been practicing hard and I even played some movements from the difficult violin concerti, like the Mendelssohn.

"Harry," I said, "all I know is that whenever I give a concert, it's completely sold out. Of course, I don't know for sure if people come to hear me play classical music—or to make a fool of myself."

The small favor that Truman asked me to do was to mention the Truman Library on my show. The library was about to open in Independence, Missouri, and he wanted all Americans to know about it and visit it. He believed it had an inspirational message for us all. I said I would do more than that. I would come to Kansas City and play a concert with the Kansas City Orchestra—and whatever money was taken in would be donated to his library.

He thought that was a fine idea. Then he called a few weeks later and said that the symphony orchestra needed the money more than the library and he wondered if I would give the concert for the benefit of the orchestra. I didn't have to think it over. I said I would. Not only that, I told him, from now on I would only give concerts for musicians—either for a musicians' pension fund or an endowment of a symphony or to build a new concert hall. "To think that with my rotten fiddling, Harry," I said, "I can help music and really good musicians—well, that means everything to me."

The largest amount of money I ever raised at

one time for the benefit of music was $838,000. I was in London when Isaac Stern called me. He was in Switzerland. He said he had just had a call from someone in Hartford, Connecticut, who said that if Stern could get Jack Benny to give a concert, they believed they could raise close to a million dollars to build a new conservatory on the campus of the University of Hartford. Alfred C. Fuller, the president of the Fuller Brush Company, had agreed to put up $400,000 if the benefit would earn at least the same amount.

When Stern told me this, I began laughing.

"What are you laughing about?" he asked.

"If you can't see anything funny in your being one of the world's greatest violinists, and they say to you, if you can get Jack Benny, who is one of the world's rottenest violinists, we'll take in a million dollars—if you don't think that's funny, then you don't know what funny is."

"Don't you see, Jack," he explained, "we real important violinists can only get $5.50 a ticket—but somebody as rotten as you—for you, they can charge a hundred dollars a ticket!"

Isaac Stern says, "Jack, when you walk out on that stage in your white tie and tails, holding the fiddle like an emperor, you look like the greatest violinist in the world. It's a shame you have to play."

Among musicians there are two schools of thought about my playing. Heifetz has told me I have an excellent tone and a good bowing arm. He sincerely thinks I purposely play bad to get laughs and I can play better than I really do. But I play the best that I can and, in fact, the humor of my concerts arises not from my making fun of music, but from the fact that I am really trying, struggling, fighting to play the violin like a Stern or a Heifetz, and I can't quite make it.

Of course, when I am not under pressure, when I am not giving a concert and when I am having one of those rare evenings when I am in good form, I do play well—once in a while. I am also a very quick reader and I can sight-read and play if the piece isn't too complicated. When there are many high notes to reach, I am in trouble. Reaching is my biggest problem. To do this proficiently you have to practice like a dog when you're a child and do finger stretching exercises so you can reach not only octaves but tenths. I started too late in life to reach properly.

One of the happiest experiences of my life was one evening when Stern asked me to play quartets at Gregor Piatigorsky's home in Los Angeles. Stern played first violin, I second violin, Leonard Rose played viola and Piatigorsky played cello. I happened to be having a very fine evening and was in splendid form. We played a Mozart quartet. I sight-read it and gave a good account of myself. Stern was impressed with my feeling for the rhythm, my following the notes, my staying with it to the end and my ability to keep up with the others and not get lost.

Piatigorsky, who was teasing me, said if I played like this all the time, I could put Stern out of business. Then he turned to me and said, "You know, you're the most fortunate concert artist because we others have to play under the pressure of having to be perfect every minute. We others don't make mistakes, but you, Jack, you can make a hundred mistakes and YOU BETTER MAKE THEM."

Which I thought was charming.

Isaac Stern recently reminisced about Daddy

"We first met at a benefit concert for the Philadelphia Orchestra about 1946. Shortly after, he invited me on his show and we quickly became close friends. A year after Carnegie Hall was saved from demolition we, the new board and operators of the Hall, found it necessary to raise a large sum of money very quickly. Thus in May 1961 we gave the Carnegie Hall benefit concert. It was the first benefit for the Hall and was the first large sum of money that allowed us to continue to rehabilitate the building and keep the place running. Other participants were Eugene Ormandy and the Philadelphia Orchestra, Van Cliburn, Benny Goodman and Roberta Peters. Jack and I played Bach's Double Concerto and Bach lost.

"We didn't rehearse very much. We played only the opening movement. Frankly, I have never said anything complimentary about Jack's violin playing and I find it difficult to break the habit.

359

"If he were a child brought to me for analysis as a young player I would have suggested he learn another profession. I think Jack was lucky in the way he used the violin—he had little talent but much desire. His talent, unlike certain Bordeaux wines, did not improve with age. Jack once told me himself that if he played better it would not be very funny. Generally, he had a good ear. He didn't know the notes that well, but he played in their general vicinity. Of course he studied the violin, but not in what I would call a serious way—I mean as far as professional standards are concerned. By the time he returned to studying it in his mature years, all his musculature was set—incorrectly. There was no suppleness, no strength in the fingers to produce the proper intonation or sound. The fingers in the left hand moved too slowly, too inaccurately. The bow control—the right hand—is like a throat. It creates your sound just as your throat creates your voice. It needs constant sensitivity to speed and pressure. He didn't have much.

"Aside from all the above, he was fine.

"His sense of rhythm was very good. One evening, I was surprised by Jack when he phoned and said he was in town. I told him I was playing quartets with some friends. I asked him to come over—'maybe you'll sit in'—and that one time Jack really amazed me. I played first violin and he played second. It was a quartet he had seen once long ago—a Mozart quartet. He wasn't thrown and we were all astonished. He stayed with it. He didn't play every note correctly, nor was every note perfectly placed—that would argue against the laws of probability—but he was never lost, knew exactly where he was supposed to be. It was the best performance I ever heard him give. And he was practically sight-reading. It was really remarkable and showed a surprising ability to watch, to read, to keep tempo, to play in unison and to follow the other players. It was one of the nicest times we ever had. Jack had such a nice smile.

"When I went on his show I learned a lesson. I had done other guest shots on popular shows and had had some very bad experiences. But Jack never made fun of music or denigrated me as a classical performer—other comedians made fun of longhairs and music, but Jack only made fun of himself. He always put the serious musician on a pedestal. He would put me in comedy situations, but he never ridiculed me, almost never. (Once I was concealed in a closet playing for him as he was trying to impress his sponsor.)

"Jack took the violin seriously. Which was why he went back to it after so many years. One must realize that for him to take it up at his age and still be able to use his hands and have them work as well as they did—with the stiffening of age and the lack of early training—is really astonishing. It's a rare example of what human will can accomplish. You know he had to go like sixty just to keep up. He would never get any better. But just to stay reasonably bad, as he was, wasn't easy. He had to run like the devil just to stay in place."

In 1956 I realized the first dream of every violinist. I played in Carnegie Hall. In 1961 Stern became the chairman of a committee to save Carnegie Hall from demolition, not only because it was a lovely piece of architecture with superb acoustics, but because it was also a symbol of art and music in the United States. In order to raise the maximum amount of money in one shot, Stern decided to make it a two-hour television special and sold the program to CBS for a large sum of money. In addition, the audience, who had to be admitted free because the Federal Communications Commission had ruled that admission cannot be charged for a sponsored television program, paid $100 each for tickets to a supper and ball at the Waldorf after the concert. The entire evening netted over $250,000 and enabled the committee to save Carnegie Hall. The evening was called "Carnegie Hall Salutes Jack Benny" because it was also a sort of thank-you from the musical world for the money I had raised for different symphony orchestras.

I didn't need any thank-yous. The happiness I got from playing violin with *real* musicians was all I ever expected and all I ever wanted. The American Federation of Musicians gave me an honorary gold lifetime membership card in the union.

In 1957 I realized the second dream of every violinist. I acquired a Stradivarius. I paid $16,000 for it at that time. Today in 1972, I am told by experts it is worth $50,000. Authenticated by the Rembert Wurlitzer people in New York and the famous violin house of William E. Hill & Sons in London, it was made in 1729 and the nature of the sound holes gives evidence that the violin was made by Antonio's son, Francesco, working with his father. I also play another fine violin, the Pressenda, which, while not as valuable as the Strad, is an equally fine example of the violin maker's craft.

In 1962 I returned to Waukegan once again—but now as a violinist. I played on September 29, with the seventy-five man Milwaukee Symphony Orchestra at a concert in the Waukegan High School. We raised $20,000 toward building a music center in Lake County, Illinois.

I had not played the violin in public in Waukegan since I had worked in the pit band of the Barrison Theatre. After the concert, I quietly evaded the crowds and the well-wishers. I turned down the brim of my soft black hat. I pulled up my coat collar. It had turned cold and the wind from Lake Michigan was knifing into my skin. I was thinking of the past and of my mother and her dreams of my being a concert violinist. I felt sad and happy all at once and I hoped that there was a life after death and she could look down and see that her dreams, in a way, had come true.

I was filled with an unbearable restlessness. Since I like to walk anyway, I walked along the quiet, darkened streets for maybe an hour. I walked from the high school to the downtown area. The Barrison Theatre was gone and there was a shopping center where it used to be. I went further along until I came to South Genesee Street and everything was gone—the house where we used to live and where I hated practicing and the store across the street where my father had the haberdashery business, everything was gone except the memory of those years and I still couldn't figure out how and why I had come to be what I was. And I knew that I would never figure it out, I knew that, sure enough.

Some years later when I was married to Bob Blumofe, who was coincidentally quite an accomplished violinist, we often played together for our own enjoyment—and once in a while even played for company. One evening as I recall, at a party in our home, everyone had consumed more than the average amount of cocktails and wine. After dinner—now the brandy was flowing—all the guests entertained; telling jokes, singing, and generally clowning around. Then it was our turn. Unable to do anything else and pretty well sloshed by this time, we stumbled through a Mozart violin-piano sonata. The room suddenly became dead quiet as though something important was happening. When we finished, Jack Lemmon, equally squiffed, with tears in his eyes, turned to the guests. "Aren't they sweet?" he said.

One day I had a terrific idea: why doesn't Daddy join us? So I took my book of the Mozart sonatas to his house, and suggested that he learn them. He did, and soon he was coming to my house almost daily, where we practiced, and occasionally entertained my children with our duets—or when Bob was home, trios. We played for company, too, but no one cried. With Daddy involved they thought it was a comedy act.

When Dorothy Chandler of the *Los Angeles Times* began raising funds for her new music center she came, naturally, to my parents. They immediately agreed to be founding members. Two years later when the symphony hall called the Dorothy Chandler Pavilion opened, we attended the gala opening night as a family and it was truly *gala!* We were then assigned season tickets in the glorious Founders Circle along with Founders Room privileges. Mom didn't care much about concerts and she rather enjoyed the few evenings she could spend quietly at home, so Daddy and I went together—not every week, but always if the program listed a violin concerto. He had at that time, about 1958, a magnificent navy blue Rolls-Royce, and on concert evenings he would allow me to be the chauffeur. Talk about feeling important!

He was so proud of the many friends he made in the concert world. As for me, I couldn't believe my luck. After so many years of listening to their records, I finally had the opportunity to meet some of my heroes. They may have originally been Daddy's friends, but later many of them became my friends as well.

In the 1960's three of those friends included Gregor Piatagorsky, Leonard Pennario, and the incredible Jascha Heiftez, and I was privileged to be in on their many informal evenings of chamber music. One evening when the music was to be at my house, I invited Daddy. He came into the living room, greeted everyone and settled into a comfortable chair. It squeaked.

"E flat," said Jascha

"E natural," said Daddy, looking wise and solemn. Was he putting him on? I wasn't sure.

Jascha looked imperturbable. I walked to the piano and played E flat. Daddy stood up, then sat down again. The chair let out an E flat!

The expression on Daddy's face was one of pure joy. He was happy to have been proved wrong, thrilled just to be in the same room with his idol and ecstatic to have had a demonstration of Heifetz's legendary perfect pitch.

CHAPTER 18

When Daddy first started in television I was a senior in high school. He only did two shows that 1950–51 season, both on Saturday nights, while continuing the regular Sunday radio shows. The following year he did more, and by the 1952–53 season he was on television weekly, and the radio show became history. During those years I was away at Stanford, concerned with my studies and college life, and less aware of or in on Daddy's career as I had been in the past, so I can only comment briefly, perhaps incompetently, about his feelings regarding television.

I think we all felt a sense of loss—I know I did—but Daddy was never one to dwell much on the past. Besides, there wasn't the time. There was simply too much to do. A weekly TV show took up so much more energy and time than radio—longer to write, longer to rehearse, longer to perform.

No, he didn't dwell on the past, but I don't think he was ever completely as happy or comfortable with television. Radio was truly his metier. "Funny" came naturally on radio—he'd been doing it for twenty years. Television was a different medium and "funny" was harder work. For instance it was harder to make the vault work visually than with only sound effects. (On the other hand I must admit there were some things, like his pauses, that worked just as well visually.) There was also more competition. It was almost like starting over, like starting as he had in radio with other shows already established, and having to work your way up the rating scale.

But he didn't have a choice. It was switch or retire and Daddy was not about to retire. He made the change, and to his credit he did the hard work with all his energy, and he did it successfully.

Although Bill Paley was a rich young man before he bought CBS back in 1929, he's a hard-driving competitor who has to be number one. CBS always made money. Some years it even made more than NBC. But in terms of ratings and the top shows, NBC had always been the foremost network. And that galled Paley. He couldn't do anything about it. NBC had always had the best programs and the public's favorite stars. In the pioneer years NBC had the Happiness Boys, Harry Reser and the Cliquot Club Eskimos, Jessica Dragonette, Amos 'n' Andy, Rudy Vallee and the Fleischmann Hour, Jack Pearl ("Vas you dere, Sharlie?"), Joe Penner ("Wanna buy a duck?"), Eddie Cantor and Ed Wynn.

During the golden age of radio (1932 to 1949) NBC broadcast me, Bob Hope, Bing Crosby, the Lux Radio Theatre with Cecil B. de Mille, George Burns and Gracie Allen, Edgar Bergen, Fred Allen, the Major Bowes Amateur Hour ("The number to call is Murray Hill 8-9933. A battery of operators is standing by to take your calls"), Fanny Brice's Baby Snooks, the Maxwell House Showboat and Fibber McGee and Molly. The primitive C.A.B. ratings had now been replaced by the Hooper ratings. Season after season, NBC dominated the ratings with eight or nine or ten shows out of the first ten.

Now with television looming on the horizon, it looked as if NBC would dominate television as it had dominated radio. By 1948, NBC already had the hottest television shows—Milton Berle and the *Texaco Star Theater* on Tuesday night and the Sid Caesar and Imogene Coca *Your Show of Shows* on Saturday night. Paley had the uneasy feeling that in a year or two, NBC would begin moving up its big radio guns into new television formats. And he didn't like it one bit. It made him very unhappy.

So he figured out a new tactic. He would raid the opposition. He would buy shows. CBS would own programs—the best programs that money could buy. Up to now, the leading radio shows had been owned or controlled by advertising agencies and sponsors. Many shows were originally created by advertising agencies. Networks sold only the time to sponsors. Now Paley decided CBS would own the shows and would sell both the time and such talent as it owned to sponsors. Advertising agencies would henceforth control only the commercials.

Paley's first move was tantamount to firing on Fort Sumter. He bought the Amos 'n' Andy show from Freeman Gosden and Charlie Correll, the actors who played the characters. They sold the show and all its characters to CBS for $2 million. CBS also paid $2,650,000 for Amusement Enterprises, Inc.—that is, for me. Here's how Amusement Enterprises came about.

In August 1946 I changed my agency representation to MCA Artists, Ltd. The president of MCA was Lew Wasserman, a dynamic gentleman who combines a shrewd business sense with a real creative show business flair and who takes a strong personal interest in his clients. Mr. Wasserman not only negotiated my contracts with the American Tobacco Company, but he advised me on the hiring of talent on the radio program and also got me better bookings at higher salaries in theaters and nightclubs.

The following year, 1947, a bright and aggressive young man, Irving Fein, joined me. He originally came to handle my public relations, but he quickly displayed a remarkable and unusual talent for showmanship and for spotting new singers and performers. In January, at the suggestion of MCA, we had organized Amusement Enterprises Inc., which owned the Jack Benny radio show. My own personal services were not owned by Amusement Enterprises. I had direct contracts with my sponsor, the American Tobacco Company.

Amusement Enterprises was also formed to invest money in discovering and exploiting new talent, in producing films and radio programs, in investing money in Broadway plays and in purchasing story properties, such as novels and dramas. Among the plays in which it invested was *Mister Roberts*, a smash hit. Among the talents I discovered was Jack Paar, a bright and brash young comedian, just a few years out of the service. I persuaded NBC to take him as my summer replacement in radio in 1947. He was wonderful.

The negotiations for the sale of Amusement Enterprises began in the summer of 1948. CBS made an offer for the stock. NBC also looked into it. Niles Trammell, NBC president, wanted assurances of my "personal services" if they bought A.E. MCA said they could not guarantee me and they threatened to break off negotiations with NBC. The question of my personal services had not been discussed during the previous negotiations with Paley and CBS. In other words, anybody who bought the company would be taking a gamble on whether they got me. CBS bought Amusement Enterprises on November 13, 1948.

On my show we did this joke:

Rochester: Boss, there's an airplane over the house skywriting, *Jack Benny moves to* . . .

Benny: Moves to where?

Rochester: I don't know. NBC's anti-aircraft just shot it down.

Despite dire predictions that I'd lose my audience, when I switched to CBS I took my entire audience along, and within the next few months other programs followed me to CBS. That's how they became the number one network in the ratings battle and William S. Paley won an exhausting war that he had been waging since 1929.

"I'd give a million dollars to know what I look like on television!"

This was the opening line of my first television show, October 28, 1950, on the CBS network. It was not a very historic moment except in my personal history. I continued with my weekly Sunday evening radio program. In those days, it seemed to most of us that radio would go on forever as it had gone on before. We didn't see that radio as it had existed between 1930 and 1950 was finished and done for. So every eight weeks after the first year I did a forty-five minute television show, using the familiar characters of the radio show and now, in addition, sound effects using props. I had a pay telephone in my house. In the living room was a soft-drink dispensing machine. The parrot was now a live parrot in a cage, though it was still Mel Blanc's voice off camera that reminded me to count the fruit in the fruitbowl.

Let me tell you about one of my favorite television shows—the first program of the 1951–52 season. It was just over when Mary told me that Mr. Paley was on the telephone from New York. I was kind of nervous when I answered the phone. In radio or television when you are on every week, the first show of the new season is the most important. It's the show that the critics review. It's the show that people talk about and if they like it very much, the chances are they will watch you the rest of the season. I had done something really ridiculous on this program. I had taken a big chance. It was the same old Jack Benny program —but it was without Jack Benny. Or rather, it was and was not without Jack Benny. I knew how

Mr. Paley must feel about it. He had not only taken a two-million-dollar calculated risk when he bought Amusement Enterprises, but he knew how much money the sponsor was paying me every week. I was afraid I was going to get scathing criticism from him.

"Jack," he said, "let me tell you right away, it was a good show. No, I'll correct that. It was a great show. It was one of the best shows you've done since you've come back to CBS. But, for heaven's sake, Jack—how did you have the guts to do such a thing on the opening show of a new season?"

Now I'll tell you exactly what I did.

The show opened with shots of the exterior and then the interior of a sightseeing bus. The bus is full of tourists who are taking the guided tour of Beverly Hills and Bel Air, seeing the homes of the Hollywood stars. The bus driver and guide is none other than my old tormentor, Frank Nelson, his voice as raspy and bitter as always. The camera kept cutting from shots of houses and streets and formal gardens to shots of Nelson in close-up and the tourists, Mr. and Mrs. Average Americans all, in the bus.

"And here we have the home of Esther Williams," Nelson said.

There was a loud splash as somebody dove into her pool.

"Now we come to the home of Dennis Day," Nelson said.

We cut to Dennis talking to his mother about

373

his troubles with me and his mother trying to persuade him to leave my employment.

"And here is the charming home of Mr. and Mrs. Jimmy Stewart," Nelson said.

You saw the Stewarts arguing with each other about how to get out of a social engagement into which I had coerced them.

At Don Wilson's home, Don did the middle commercial.

"And now we're passing the largest poolroom in Beverly Hills," the driver said. "The home of Phil Harris."

We cut to some repartee between Phil Harris and his uncouth musicians about what a terrible person I was.

And so it went—through almost the entire show—and the opening show of the season it was and nobody had seen a glimpse of Jack Benny. About thirty seconds before the show ended the guide called out: "And here we come to the home of Jack Benny."

And suddenly you hear my voice from the back of the bus saying, "Driver, I get off here."

That's all I said—just those five words and at the end of the show. That's all I said on the entire program and it was not only unprecedented but unheard of that the star of a program would not appear until the end of the show.

I didn't really think it was the crazy gamble that Bill Paley did. The idea of the show was so humorous to begin with that I just had to do it, once we'd got the idea. And then I was really on the show *every minute* without being physically present because everybody watching and knowing I was the star was naturally wondering *when* the hell I would come on. Also everybody was talking about me on the program—Jimmy Stewart and Don Wilson and Dennis and Phil. The suspense kept quietly building and we imagined the audience would keep trying to figure out what gimmick I'd use to get into the action. When I finally spoke my five little words, the suspense was broken, the audience was satisfied and we had had one hell of a good show—unprecedented and unheard of as it was.

My appearance on the bus was perfectly in character. Comedy as I see it comes out of character. The comedy situation arises from the incongruity between a certain character and a situation in which the character finds himself.

Since 1932, on radio and television I had done many burlesques of films. Our satires were always sharp and sometimes even a little nasty—as good satire should be. There wasn't a studio in Hollywood that wasn't eager for me to burlesque their films because it was such marvelous publicity. We were continually being badgered by publicity men and studio executives to kindly make fun of their latest movies.

One of the choicest burlesques we ever concocted was the one on *Gaslight*, in which Ingrid Bergman played the wife and I played the husband who is torturing her in order to drive her crazy so he can drive her out of the house into an insane asylum and find some valuable jewelry hidden in the attic. As a play it had run for two seasons in 1941 under the title of *Angel Street*. Patrick Hamilton, the author, was an Englishman. The play had been a smash hit in England. The movie, entitled *Gaslight*, was released by MGM in 1945. I was invited to satirize it and I did. Our version was called *Autolight*.

Then in 1952 I decided to do a new version of this travesty. The writers and I produced a completely fresh treatment. This time Barbara Stanwyck played the half-demented wife, I played the evil husband and Rochester played an English butler named Jeeves. Our parody took up fifteen minutes of a forty-five minute television program. We opened with Rochester asking for the day off to play cricket.

I gave him the day off. To play *cricket!*

Barbara Stanwyck entered, eating marinated salami. In the background, Dennis Day, playing a groom, was singing to the parlor maids. The house was so badly constructed that, as he sang, the plaster began to fall. Barbara coolly opened an umbrella and went on munching salami. There was no chinaware around because all the dishes were dirty and were in her bed. She liked to have breakfast in bed—also lunch, dinner and supper. She berated *me* for doing strange things around the house.

"Yesterday, Charles, you came back from the

fox hunt, hung your riding habit in the stable and put the horse in the closet."

I denied this and went away.

A detective from Scotland Yard arrived and began looking around. Barbara asked him what he was looking for and he said he was looking for rye bread on which to put the slices of marinated salami.

Finally, we got to the climax. I was arrested and tied to a chair by the detective.

Barbara turned on me and screamed, "You turned the pictures upside down. You turned the chairs upside down. You turned the table upside down. Once I made an upside-down cake and you *turned it right side up.*"

That show was one of my all-time favorites.

Marilyn Monroe only appeared once on a television show and it was mine. She was so charming. She said she didn't want money, but she would love to have a car, a really nice car. "Nobody has ever given me an automobile in my life," she said in that wistful, little girl voice, so of course I was delighted to play a fatherly role and give her a car. It was a black Cadillac convertible. She loved it and drove it until she married Arthur Miller.

The show was in 1953 at a time when Marilyn's stardom was on the rise, but she hadn't yet reached the height of her fame. 20th Century-Fox needed publicity for her as well as her new film, *Gentlemen Prefer Blondes*, in which she was co-starring with Jane Russell. They came and asked if I wanted her as a guest star and I said I would have her on the program *only* if we could work out an interesting idea for a sketch. I never used guest stars, no matter how famous they were, unless I had the right framework for them. I told my writers about the offer and together we came up with an idea. I told the studio yes.

I'm on the deck of a ship, dozing in a deck chair and contemplating my bad luck at having been assigned a seat next to a fat, messy woman. "Why couldn't she be someone glamorous and exciting like Marilyn Monroe?" I think. I fall asleep and dream that she really is Marilyn Monroe. When I awaken, still drowsy, I mistakenly grab the fat lady. She jumps up screaming and runs off.

"Don't leave me, Marilyn, don't leave me," I cry, running after her. She runs the length of the deck and disappears around a smokestack, emerging on the other side as the real Marilyn Monroe. I catch up with her and we do a comedy love scene.

She was delicious. She was superb. She read comedy lines as well as anyone in the business. She knew the secret—that hard-to-learn secret—of reading comedy lines as if they were in a drama and letting the humor speak for itself.

For television, we found an authentic Maxwell that looked miserable enough for our purposes. I remember one damn funny TV show we did in 1956 about the Maxwell being stolen.

Rochester and I hied ourselves over to the Beverly Hills Police Department to report a stolen car. As you may or may not know, in keeping with the high-class tone of Beverly Hills, our police force is probably the most snobbish group of gendarmes in the world. It is said that the Beverly Hills Police Department is so fancy that it has an unlisted number.

Rochester and I were seen entering a lavishly decorated office which resembled the reception room of a movie studio. There were no desk sergeants. A voluptuous blonde creature in a tight blue dress was smiling at us.

I can't resist interrupting here to tell you that I was the actress who played this part. I was twenty years old. Could I possibly have fit that description?

Rochester told her we wished to report a stolen car.

"Do you have an appointment?" she asked coolly.

"You mean you have to make an appointment to report a crime?" I asked.

While we were thrashing the problem out, the squad captain escorted a man through the reception room. He stripped the epaulets from this man, formerly a sergeant. He was being demoted to foot patrolman. It seems that while arresting a burglar this man had fired two warning shots and disturbed the sleep of the nearby residents. He was being punished for waking people up.

Another sergeant came through leading six beautiful white standard French poodles on a leash.

"What are they for?" I asked the receptionist.

"Escaped prisoner . . ." she murmured.

"You mean . . . ?"

"Yes, in Beverly Hills we use only French poodles to track escaped prisoners."

Finally, we got in to see a detective.

"What is it, my good man?" he inquired languidly.

"I'd like to report a stolen car," I said.

"What kind of Jaguar was it?" he asked, starting to fill out a vehicular theft form.

At the end of this scene a policeman told Jack and Rochester they would have to wait a few minutes before they left. It was teatime. An orchestra appeared, the policeman asked me to dance and the show closed with us waltzing around the station.

I appeared on the show twice. On the other show Jack dreamed he was married to Mary (that's as close as he ever came on the program). I was their teenage daughter. I guess I was a natural for that one. It was a live show done in front of an audience and I remember being very nervous about knowing my lines. The worst part was all the makeup they slapped on my face. Thank heaven today we can look more natural. Back then everyone wore three pounds of Max Factor's pancake and long uncomfortable false eyelashes that made me blink a lot.

While shaving one morning in 1959 a marvelous idea for a program with former President Harry Truman sprang into my mind. The idea haunted me all day, while golfing in the morning, all through lunch and then rehearsal in the afternoon. I didn't mention it to a soul. I just brooded about it. I didn't even mention it to my writers—I thought they would snicker. That night Mary saw I was troubled about something. She thought perhaps my game was off, but I assured her that it wasn't.

"Doll," she said, "something's bothering you. Out with it."

"Mary, I'll tell you." I paused and tried to frame what to say. "Well, I'll tell you," I said.

"I know you'll tell me," she said. "The thing is what will you tell me?"

"I'll tell you—I mean I have this idea for a show with President Truman as my guest. But how do you ask a former President of the United States to be on a comedy program?"

"Now, doll," Mary said, "I want you to go over there to that funny white thing on the table. You pick up that heavy part of it that's lying sideways.

381

You hold it up to your ear. Then you put your finger in those little holes and you dial his number. I mean right now, this minute. Don't say anything or think about it because you'll make yourself more worried. Just do it."

"He'll turn me down," I said.

She propelled me to the phone and I called Truman. When he finally got on the line, I was so nervous my hands were trembling. I was sure he'd turn me down.

"Harry," I said, "would you like to be a guest on my television program?"

And he said, "Why, certainly, Jack, I'd love to."

I was still so nervous I said, "Why not?" Then I caught myself and laughed and thanked him. I asked him if he had to consult with the Democratic Party leadership and he said he went his own way and did what he wanted to do.

"Well," I said, still nervous, "I promise you I'll keep the show in good taste and if it isn't— I'll kill myself."

"Okay," said Truman, "I've got an undertaker friend over in Kansas City who does darn good work."

"The show will be dignified," I said.

"Don't make it too dignified, Jack."

We brought three cameras down to Independence, Missouri. We could not light the exteriors or the interiors the way we wanted. You heard the distracting noise of chairs creaking and bells ringing off camera and voices that weren't in the scene. The film we shot was not clear and well lighted but it was very real and so was much of the dialogue. You saw me entering Truman's office and our making small talk. Then I asked him about his routine. He described the work of the library and showed me some of his mementos. He explained the educational purposes of the library and told about the books, papers and historical documents there. We walked from one office to another. In a larger room, known as the President's Room, Truman gave a little lesson in civics, describing the many functions of a United States President. When he showed me a photograph of General Marshall, he said that the Marshall Plan was "one of the greatest things that happened in the history of the world." (Well, it wasn't the *funniest* comedy show I had ever done.)

After a while, we came to some large portraits of former Presidents. Truman said the Presidents who most interested him were Jefferson, Polk and Jackson. "And Jack," he said, "I presume your favorite would be Abraham Lincoln."

"Abraham Lincoln, my favorite? Why do you say that?"

"Well," Truman said, "I just thought that any man who walked twelve miles to return a library book and save three cents would be your kind of President!"

Then we returned to his office and, before closing the door, Truman told his secretary not to disturb us for a while.

He closed the door. A few seconds later, she opened it slightly and you could hear the music of a violin and piano duet. It was actually myself and Harry Truman playing, but you didn't see us. We were off camera, playing "Tea for Two."

In 1963 I had another inspiration for a show, a show for which I thought the Reverend Billy Graham, the great evangelist, would be an ideal guest.

"Mary," I said one evening, "do you think Billy Graham would come on the show?"

"Billy Graham? What would he do?"

I told her my idea. She liked it.

"But he wouldn't accept, would he?" I said.

"Why not?"

"I know he wouldn't," I said. "A man of the cloth."

"Oh, Jack, you said the same thing about Harry Truman."

"This is different."

"Oh, he might love it."

"Not in a million years, Mary."

"At least you could *ask* him. I mean, the worst he could say is no."

"I can't stand rejection, Mary, you know that."

"Now you just go over and dial his number."

Billy Graham was holding a three-week crusade in Los Angeles and inspiring great crowds at our Coliseum. I called his number. I hoped it would be busy. I hoped the Reverend Graham wouldn't even speak to me. I hoped to get out of my own idea, if possible.

The line wasn't busy. And when I asked to speak to him, he got right on the phone.

"Hello, Jack," he said briskly, "how are you today?"

Gosh, he sounded real happy to hear from me, even though we had never met before.

"I'm fine," I said. "How are you?"

"Splendid," he said.

There was a slight pause for station identification. I pulled myself together.

"Uh . . . Reverend Graham . . . I better explain why I didn't call. I didn't call to say I've decided to become a convert to Christianity. What I wanted was to ask you if you could appear on my program."

"I'd love to," he said.

I told him my idea and he liked it. He asked only for twenty seconds in the beginning of the show to say why he had come and about sixty seconds after the show.

His opening twenty seconds were: "Some people have already asked me why I accepted your invitation to be on your show. I've never been on a comedy show before . . . I've always admired you. You've always had a clean, wholesome show and it's a great privilege for me to be here . . . And, incidentally, I want to thank you for inviting me to hear you play your violin in the Hollywood Bowl tomorrow night. You know I've always considered you a great violinist."

I looked at Billy Graham for a long long time. Then I faced front into the camera and smirked

385

my silly head off. "And you know, ladies and gentlemen," I finally said when the laughter subsided, "he's NOT ALLOWED TO LIE . . . ."

One of the Reverend Graham's wittiest lines came when I remarked that once, when I was drawing great crowds to the London Palladium, he had drawn about 500,000 people in one week to his meetings in London. This was true. We had both been in London at the same time in 1954. And he said he couldn't take the credit for his success: "Look at the writers I have, Jack."

"Writers?"

"Yes . . . Isaiah . . . Jeremiah . . . Matthew, Mark, Luke and John."

We talked about our ages and he said he was forty-four years old and I said that for years I'd made jokes about being thirty-nine but I didn't mind confessing that I was really forty-seven.

"Forty-seven?" he repeated, staring at me.

"Why, yes," I said.

"You know, Jack, I'd suggest you come to one of our meetings. We can't do much for your arithmetic, but we can ease your conscience a little . . . I'd like to ask you a question. Why do you comedians always use insults in order to make audiences laugh? Just now you called this fine young man you have on your show—Dennis Day—you called him a stupid kid. That seems unnecessarily cruel to me."

I said I had to say things like that to get laughs.

Billy Graham complained of my making the musicians whiskey drinkers and loudmouths and

"I'm sure there are other areas of humor without your always referring to Don Wilson's obesity."

"Well, Billy," I said, "if you want that kind of a comedy show where there are no insults and everybody is nice, I'll try it. I don't think it will get laughs, but if you'll sit right over there, you can watch. We're going to do a nice sweet show."

We put out a chair for Billy Graham and he sat on stage right and watched the proceedings. We started the whole show over from the beginning with a little "Love in Bloom" music. Three musicians came in late and I politely asked them why they were tardy.

"We're sorry, Mr. Benny," one of them said, just as politely, "but on the way to the studio we were thirsty and we stopped for a tall glass of orange juice."

"I had pineapple juice," another musician said.

"I had milk," a third one said, "because I always drink milk."

All this time I kept looking at Billy Graham as if to say, "Don't you see how unbelievable this is?" and all the time the audience laughed louder.

When I brought out Don Wilson, I complimented him on his thinness. "You're so un-obese, Don," I said.

Billy Graham nodded approvingly and the audience howled.

Don Wilson thanked me for the compliment and said, "I'd also like to thank you for the nice bonus you gave me. Yet, after all, it's only typical of your generous nature. There's no one, no one in the world, who's more un-parsimonious than you."

CHAPTER 19

Sandy Burns was beautiful. She was a beautiful child, a beautiful teenager—never even went through an awkward age or had pimples—and she became a beautiful woman. We were both blue-eyed blondes, but there the similarity ended. She grew rapidly to be tall and willowy; I made it to a chunky five foot three and that was it. She had long, shapely legs. Mine were short and I was, and still am, knock-kneed. Worst of all, she had lovely tawny skin, and when as teenagers we spent summers at the beach or by the pool, she got a gorgeous, golden tan. She was the California Girl the Beach Boys sing about. Not me—I had pale, white skin that only burned and blotched.

By the time Sandy and I reached high school, although we were still good friends, our interests had diverged. I loved to get dressed up and had discovered the high life of Hollywood: evenings at the Mocambo or Ciro's, dancing at the Cocoanut Grove and endless rounds of teenage parties. Sandy, on the other hand, liked nothing better than to put on a pair of jeans, stay at home, and cook for her boyfriend. Sandy went out with a couple of very good-looking, athletic guys during high school and then she met Jim Wilhoite. Jim was a male version of Sandy: blond, blue-eyed and tawny. They spent most of their time together at the beach. Jim was a surfer. George and Gracie were none too thrilled about this state of affairs. But Sandy was in love.

On one particular evening at about eight during the summer between high school and college, my phone rang. It was Sandy telling me to come over right away. I hopped in my blue Pontiac and within five minutes arrived at her place. Her parents were out for the evening. "Jim and I are going to elope," she said, "and you have to come to Las Vegas with us for moral support and to be a witness!" Since they weren't engaged, even I was surprised. But always game for adventure, I said, "Great, let's go." Off we went in Jim's car, along with a friend of his, a young man by the name of Marvin Mitchelson, who was then attending law school.

Somewhere between two and three in the morning we arrived in Vegas and went directly to one of those get-married-quick chapels. Fifteen minutes later Sandy and Jim were husband and wife. As we left the chapel we all looked at one another: "What now?" We were much too tired to drive right back to Beverly Hills and the newlyweds wanted to have a wedding night, but none of us had any money—and this was long before credit cards.

All of a sudden we remembered seeing the name "Tony Martin" on the marquee of the Flamingo Hotel. Tony was one of our parents' best friends. We had known him as Uncle Tony all our lives.

"Let's go to the Flamingo. He'll know what to do or maybe we can borrow some money," we decided. The only problem was that it was now about three in the morning, the late show had long since finished and he would probably be asleep. "I guess we'll have to wake him up." This was desperation time. All four of us marched up to his penthouse suite and banged on the door. A few seconds later it was opened by a groggy, bleary-eyed, pajama-clad Tony Martin. It took him a long befuddled moment to recognize us. Then he sleepily invited us in. Sandy explained the circumstances. Tony looked dumbfounded. When he recovered his wits, he was furious. No help, no handout. "You mean you didn't tell your folks where you were going? How could you have been so thoughtless?" He picked up the phone to call George and Gracie.

Back in Beverly Hills, heedlessly unimagined by us, the Burnses and the Bennys had spent a frantic night. The Burnses had arrived home after dinner to find their daughter gone. No note, no nothing. They immediately called my parents. "Is Sandy at your house? Is Joanie there?" "No," replied my mother, "we were just about to call *you*. We'll be right over."

They spent the next few hours calling the police, the hospitals and anybody they could think of who might know our whereabouts. When Tony called they all breathed a sigh of relief. But once they knew we were safe, anger and George took over. He was apoplectic. Fortunately, it was Sandy who had to talk to him, not I—my own parental showdown came later. She was told to drive back home immediately—drive carefully, but GET HERE! NOW!

Back we went for the confrontation, and what a confrontation it was! First, George lit into Sandy for deceit and dishonesty; then into me for aiding and abetting the crime; then into Jim for everything else he could think of. Only Marvin was left out of the tirade. (However, it undoubtedly impressed him. As the world knows, he became a successful divorce lawyer who established the principle of palimony.)

Gracie echoed George's words. Then my mother got into the act, her anger directed almost totally toward me, of course. Daddy as usual said very little—just a nod of agreement here and there, or a repeat of a sentence for emphasis.

It was by now the next morning, the marriage a fait accompli, the anger finally spent. We all went into the dining room and ate a reasonably peaceful, if not celebratory, breakfast. The Burnses soon accepted Jim as their son-in-law, and a few years later were absolutely gaga over their two beautiful granddaughters, Laurie and Lisa.

That September, with great excitement and anticipation, I drove the blue bomb to Stanford. After a seven-hour drive I reached Palo Alto, turned off at Palm Drive and from the moment I saw that beautiful Romanesque-style quad with the chapel glittering in the center I knew I was in the right place. It was every bit as wonderful as I had dreamed and hoped it would be. But for the first time in my life I did not feel just one of the crowd. Gary Crosby was in my class, too, and, although we had not met before (apart from the long-ago birthday parties), being in the same boat made us very good friends. The San Francisco papers occasionally ran stories about us, reporters would sometimes show up on campus to interview us. We were the only two celebrity kids among five thousand undergraduates, and we were different.

It wasn't anything overt or obvious, but I would notice a group of girls down the hall whispering and glancing my way and could sense a conversation something like, "That's Jack Benny's daughter—I wonder what she's like—do you think she's a snob, stuck-up?" It was just a feeling and maybe I was being paranoid. Fortunately, the novelty of having a quasi-celebrity in their midst faded quickly. Possibly as a little joke, the rooming office assigned a freshman named Judy Garland as my first roommate. I soon made many friends, learned to play bridge, tried out and made it as a cheerleader (we even got to the Rose Bowl my sophomore year where I had the thrill of showing off in front of my old L.A. friends), and became what I had wanted most: Joan College.

From Palo Alto it took only forty-five minutes to drive on the then extremely dangerous Bay Shore Highway to San Francisco. I went occasionally to shop or for dinner at the Mark Hopkins with a boyfriend. The best times there, though, were when Daddy played the Geary Theatre. It was 1952, and the Will Mastin trio, starring Sammy Davis, Jr., was the opening act! For those two weeks I commuted daily. After the show we, my parents, my date when I brought one, Sammy and other assorted friends went almost every night to Trader Vic's where the food was sensational and where, incidentally, I learned to drink navy grogs. Then a harrowing drive back to Stanford in the wee hours.

By the following year Sammy was a major star, a headliner. He played the Fairmont Hotel doing two shows a night, and I repeated the frequent trips north. This time instead of Trader Vic's after the late show we all headed for Sammy's suite in the hotel where along with carts of food and drink there was a running Monopoly game. It went on until four in the morning almost always ending with someone throwing the board across the room after a fight over the price of a house or hotel! Some nights Eartha Kitt, who was in town at the same time playing *New Faces of 1952*, would arrive in the middle of all the commotion and fall asleep on the sofa. She and Sammy were an item then, and a stormy romance it was!

In the spring of my senior year at Chadwick, Vic Damone was drafted, sent to Fort Dix, New Jersey, for basic training, and by the time I graduated had been posted to Germany. We kept in touch by letters and an occasional phone call throughout my freshman year at Stanford. Those calls from Germany created great excitement among my roommates, and word quickly spread up and down the halls.

And then in June of 1952 my parents were again in London for Dad's third engagement at the Palladium. I was to join them as soon as I finished my final exams. I came up with a wonderful idea: during my stay in London I would fly to Germany and surprise Vic. But the day before I was to leave Stanford, as I emerged from the shower wearing a bathrobe and a towel around my wet head, our dorm supervisor came running toward me waving frantically. "Joan, there are a bunch of reporters and photographers in the foyer, and they want to see you. What should I do?"

I couldn't imagine what this was all about, but with my usual equanimity, still in robe and towel, I went out to see them. It was pandemonium! The photographers were snapping, the reporters yelling, "Joan, what about you and Vic? Are you two getting married? Are you engaged? Now that Vic is back, what are your plans?"

Vic is back? When? Why haven't I heard from him? That rat! All this was going through my mind as I calmly answered their questions, "Yes, of course I've spoken to him. No, we have no immediate plans. No, we're not engaged. I intend to finish college first. Etcetera. Thank you, gentlemen, I have no further comments." I was steaming!

What I didn't know was that Vic had planned exactly the same thing. He hadn't called because he was going to fly to California to surprise me! In my anger, not knowing this, I didn't even try to reach him. I just left. Unfortunately, by the time I returned from Europe four weeks later and all this scheming was cleared up, it was too late. The romance was over.

But the trip to London had its highlights, the highest of which was Dad's opening night, which coincidentally was also the evening of my eighteenth birthday. After the show Mom and I went backstage to his dressing room. Amidst all the commotion of congratulations, telegrams, flowers, fans—all the typical opening night frenzy—Daddy spotted me in the crowd, rushed over, kissed me Happy Birthday and presented me with a beautiful diamond heart on a platinum chain. I was thrilled—and there was more to come . . .

After Dad changed into a fresh dinner jacket we went on to the Café de Paris to see Noël Coward. It was his opening night, too. I had heard for so many years how wonderful Mr. Coward was as a performer. I had seen some of his plays and I knew some of his witty, clever songs, but this was my first opportunity to see him in person. I hadn't realized a party had been planned so when we arrived at the club I was surprised to be shown to a ringside table for twelve. No one had yet been seated, people were milling around the tables in little groups, and it took me a moment to get my bearings and figure out which was for our group. Could it be true? The one that included Douglas Fairbanks, Jr., Laurence Olivier and Vivien

Leigh? Yes! Mother and Daddy were greeting them and there were kisses and hugs and congratulations and all those show business enthusiasms, and then I was introduced. When a few minutes later we were seated at the table, I found my two dinner partners were Sir Laurence and Mr. Fairbanks. I don't know who was responsible for that seating arrangement but whoever it was he/she is on my "lifetime gold page." Sir Laurence was every bit as charming as I had known he would be. After all, how could Admiral Nelson be anything but? (When I was eight years old *That Hamilton Woman* played the Beverly Theatre. I saw it every day for one week, and with the patch over his eye, his Admiral's uniform, his love for Lady Hamilton and his death scene on his ship—"England expects every man to do his duty"—I thought it was his most romantic role, and I include his much better known Heathcliff. Lord Nelson will always be Laurence Olivier and Emma Hamilton, Vivien Leigh.) I remember that both men impressed me with their charm, and that Mr. Fairbanks was an excellent dancer and raconteur. When I danced with "the Admiral" I was too busy trying to keep my legs from wobbling to notice what, if anything, he said. I don't recall another thing about the supper, Mr. Coward's show or the other guests, except thinking how sorry I felt for anyone who didn't spend their eighteenth birthday the way I did.

After Daddy closed that engagement we went to Paris for a week. One day while I was out shopping by myself on the Avenue Montaigne I spotted a pair of gorgeous black suede shoes in a store window. I had to have them. I marched in, and was told by the saleslady that their shoes were handmade. She would draw a pattern of my foot and the shoes would be ready in five days. "Combien?" I inquired in my best high school French. She gave me a figure which I quickly translated as about thirty dollars. "Wonderful," I said.

Five days later I returned to pick up my shoes. The saleslady greeted me with a smile. "Voilà, here they are," she said. "That will be fifty dollars American." I somehow managed a smile, mumbled that I was in a hurry, would return to get them tomorrow and fled from the store. I had obviously misfigured the exchange rate. I didn't have fifty dollars. Where was I going to get fifty dollars? I couldn't ask Mother. Despite the fact that she was the Imelda of her day, she would kill me for spending that much on a pair of shoes. Asking Daddy was definitely out. Then I thought of my parents' good friend, Milton Berle, and his then girlfriend, later wife of thirty-six years, Ruth. They were staying at our hotel. I went to their suite, told them what I had done, and asked if they would lend me the money. Of course they did, of course I paid them back and luckily my mother never found out what I had paid for my beautiful Paris shoes.

But the Berles never let me forget it.

During that stay in Paris I met a soon-to-be-famous man. But in 1952 he wasn't all that well known, and our meeting—where, when and how—was soon forgotten, at least by me. Ten years later, in the spring of 1962, I attended a Democratic fundraising dinner in Los Angeles, and because my husband was co-chairman of the event I found myself seated next to President John F. Kennedy. He turned to me, all smiles and charm. "We've met before," he said.

"We have?" I replied, with a blank look. (I've told you about many of my shortcomings—did I mention lack of diplomacy?)

"Yes," he said, "in Paris in 1952."

"Really? I'm sorry, I don't remember. Where?"

He then recalled the occasion, what I was wearing, and what we talked about. Amazing! How could he remember such a minor incident from so many years ago?

I was extremely flattered, and by now realized how crass I had been. "Of course, *now* I remember," I said, adding bits of trivia about Paris, telling him the story of my fifty-dollar shoes and in general trying to make up for my previous tactlessness. His enormous charm and my lack of it during that conversation embarrass me to this day.

CHAPTER 20

Christmas vacation of my junior year at Stanford I went to New York to be a bridesmaid at Gwynne Hazen's wedding at the Pierre Hotel. Gwynne was a niece of Walter Annenberg (her mother was one of Walter's seven sisters) and we had been close friends from the time we met in Lake Arrowhead when we were thirteen. Her parents rented a bungalow at the Beverly Hills Hotel every summer and our friendship continued. She was marrying a local boy, Stanley Cherry. At the wedding dinner I was seated next to one of the ushers, a very tall, dark and handsome young man related to Gwynne on her father's side. He asked me for a date the next evening.

For seven days and nights, until I had to go home, Seth Baker and I went to the Plaza for tea, "21" for dinner, the Copa to see the show, El Morocco for dancing and Reuben's at four in the morning for breakfast. We went to Broadway shows, took long drives to eat at country inns and saw *Die Fledermaus* at the Met on New Year's Eve. It was a whirlwind courtship. When I boarded the Los Angeles–bound plane I was sporting an eight-and-a-half-carat marquis-cut diamond and Seth and I were engaged. How could I have turned it down? I had been swept off my feet. The glamour that had always just reflected off my parents onto me was now my glamour.

When I arrived home I requested a family conference. It took place, as our conferences always did, in the living room. I announced my engagement. My parents reacted traditionally. "Are you in love with this man? Who is he? What do you know about him? What does he do? How old is he? You should finish college" and on and on.

The fact was I really didn't know a lot about

him. I had met his parents, Gladys and Harry, and his sister, Renee; a very nice upper-middle-class Jewish family living in a lovely apartment on Park Avenue. (Renee and I are still good friends.) I knew he was twenty-three, a graduate of Amherst College, had a seat on the New York stock exchange and was about to be made a junior partner in his firm, one that dealt in odd lots. He, or perhaps his family, belonged to a fashionable country club, although he was not a golfer or tennis player—in fact he wasn't much of an athlete. He drove a Jaguar convertible, went to all the "best places," and had quite acceptable manners. That's about all I knew—then.

I answered Mom and Dad's questions as best I could, but was determined. I had dug in my heels. After all, Gwynne was married, Sandy was married and two other close friends had married a few months before. Everyone was doing it. It was time for me to get married, too. I was infatuated with Seth and the idea of living in New York, a city I had loved since childhood, doing all those exciting things, being grown-up and on my own, was so much more appealing than going to classes, writing papers, studying for exams and waiting for my allowance—which depended on my being good. Whether or not I was really in love didn't seem important—at the time.

Daddy looked very unhappy and, in his usual discomfort when confronted with a family crisis, left the room. Mom didn't look too thrilled either, but since I was so determined to make this drastic move, thought we should go ahead and plan a wedding. "How about the end of March?" she asked. "Fine," I said. And the die was cast.

We agreed that it would be a relatively small wedding, just family and close friends—perhaps about a hundred people—in one of the small banquet rooms at the Beverly Hills Hotel. The next day I returned to Stanford to say goodbye to my friends and collect my belongings. I wish I could remember my feelings then—the farewells and leaving my beloved campus behind, but it was a long time ago and not only is my memory fuzzy, it tends, like most people's, to be selective. I can't recall any unhappiness, only the events. I went through it like a horse wearing blinders (not unlike Dad's)—galloping straight ahead with determination and resolve. It's as though I'm telling a story that happened to someone else.

I was in no particular hurry so I lingered at school for about ten days, showing off my ring, packing cartons, canceling classes, returning the fraternity pin to my now past-tense boyfriend, and then with my car stuffed to the roof I drove back down Palm Drive for the last time and headed for home. As I walked in the side door my parents' doctor was coming down the front stairs. "What's happened?" I asked.

"Your mother threw her back out. It's nothing serious. She should be fine in a couple of days," he replied.

I went immediately to her room where I found her lying prostrate on the bed. "What am I going to do? I have the wedding to plan, and my back is killing me," she said.

"Not to worry, Mom—the doctor said you'd be fine by the end of the week," I said, never suspecting what was to come.

She then proceeded to tell me what she had done so far—and she had done a lot! Don Loper, one of the top Beverly Hills dress designers, would make my gown as well as the bridesmaids' dresses; the flowers, the orchestra, the rabbi, the invitations, the cake—it was all in the works. She had also made arrangements, not for the small banquet room, but for the Crystal Room. "Wait a minute," I said. "I thought this would be a small wedding."

"Joanie, I went through my phone book, and we can't invite so-and-so without inviting so-and-so, and you really should invite so-and-so, and then there's Seth's family and their friends, and we have to ask the cast and the writers and all Daddy's business associates." And on and on and on it went. By the time the lists were finished and engraved invitations were in the mail, 1,200 people had been requested to attend the wedding of Jack Benny's daughter. Of course there were a few more who called to say, "You must have overlooked us—we never received an invitation."

I guess you could say it snowballed. It became the social event of the season, the gala wedding of the year, an incredible extravaganza. It happened thirty-six years ago, and to this day I run into people who say, "I remember your wedding."

For two months our lives revolved around it.

402

Fitting the gowns, shopping for a trousseau, attending to details. Mom took part in every aspect, but her back didn't improve and she walked as though in pain—at least, when someone was watching. I caught her once when she didn't know I was there. She was walking just fine. Nor did she stop playing the martyr and complaining about it—not until the day after the wedding. (For a change I was the center of attention. Could she have been jealous?) She was never without her back pillow, which Deedee or Sandy or I had to carry—into the car, out of the car, into the store, out of the store. We made a pact: the afternoon of the wedding we would light a pillow bonfire on our front lawn. (Of course we never did.)

The gifts began to arrive. Two or three a day at first, then ten or more. I wrote thank-you notes each night—I had to, otherwise I could never have kept up. (My daughter, Joanna, did the same last year when she was married. It's good advice.) We set up a huge table in the library to display the loot. It soon became crowded. Granted prices were different in 1954, but the gifts were extravagant even so. In silver, never less than a place setting, usually more; in Steuben crystal, a dozen; in Wedgwood china, the same; silver platters and serving dishes. I could have opened a store.

In the meantime, Seth and I spoke on the phone daily. I told him all that was going on, and I think he was as nervous about it as I. In late February he came to Los Angeles for a week to see me and to meet my parents. I wasn't sure what to expect.

After all, I had spent only seven days with him and that had been almost two months ago. I drove to the airport to fetch him, and when I spotted him coming down the ramp I looked at him in horror: Who is this strange man? I'm not in love with him. I don't even know him. How can I possibly marry him?

I did know I was about to make a dreadful mistake. Our backgrounds were so totally opposite we might have come from different planets. His was East Coast, Ivy League, Brooks Brothers, formal, uptight, Wall Street oriented; whereas mine was California, outdoors, athletic, easygoing, casual, show business. Seth and I had virtually nothing in common. All the excitement suddenly turned into a nightmare. What was I going to do? Mom's grandiose wedding plans had reached a point where I no longer had control of anything. I was caught between the proverbial rock and the hard place. I had two choices. One: I could go through with it and get a divorce later, or two: I could call it all off, return the three hundred or more gifts already received, cancel everything including the already-paid-for gowns, trousseau, invitations and stationery, forfeit the deposits on the Crystal Room, the orchestra and have to listen to my mother say daily for the rest of my life, "All the money we spent on you . . ."

I chose One. My nineteen-year-old mind said, "At least in a couple of years I could put an end to it, whereas choice number two would never end." I didn't have the guts to cancel it, in spite of the fact that Daddy kept asking me if I was sure. I think he was as unhappy as I, and knew how I felt, but as long as I went on repeating, "Yes, I'm sure," there was nothing he could do about it.

So, with clenched teeth, a phony smile, and a sinking heart, I married Seth. Eight hundred and fifty people attended my magnificent wedding, and even from my point of view, it was indeed magnificent. The Crystal Room was a spectacle of white—flowers, vines, trees, centerpieces. It was breathtaking.

My gown was ravishing: the material was dead-white French satin, brocaded with lilies of the valley, the skirt, with its long train, was cut on the bias and contained what seemed like hundreds of yards of fabric; the bodice was tight-fitting with a thin belt around my nineteen-inch waist; the sleeves were long and tight coming to a point over the hand; from the tip of the shoulder the neckline curved down to a low point in the center, and a stiff cuff about three inches wide at the shoulder that narrowed to nothing in the center framed my neck and shoulders. A seven-layer net and tulle petticoat with a wide blue satin band went underneath. On my head I wore a tiny cap of seed pearls with a long three-tiered net veil flowing all the way to the end of the dress.

The bridesmaids wore short-sleeved blue taffeta covered with a layer of white lace. My maid of honor was Seth's sister, Renee. The bridesmaids included Gwynne; her cousin, Paulette Ames; a local friend, Jane Gordon; my Stanford roommate, Ann Schuette; Sandy and Deedee. The ushers were Seth's friends from New York.

I remember walking down the aisle on Daddy's arm, both of us toughing it out. I don't think anyone there suspected for a moment how we really felt. I don't remember the ceremony, only that it must have happened because all of a sudden we were walking back up the aisle, and then accepting congratulations in an endless reception line. The guests had dinner. We didn't; we were still receiving. By the time we finished shaking hands and kissing it was time to cut the gargantuan cake. Then the press was allowed in and for an hour we posed for pictures. Then it was over. I changed into my going-away suit, threw my bouquet (I don't remember who caught it), and because we hadn't eaten and were starving, we went with Johnny Green and his wife to C.C. Brown's in Hollywood for a hot fudge sundae. I do remember that because it was the highlight of the evening.

From there it was downhill most of the way. Sitting on a chair in our honeymoon suite at the Beverly Hills Hotel I cried through most of my wedding night. The following morning, feeling a bit better and determined to stick it out, at least for a while, I left with Seth for the Hotel Hana-Maui in Hawaii. The hotel was lovely, the weather gorgeous, the beach divine. Still, the less said about our honeymoon, the better. Two weeks later we flew to New York to set up housekeeping in our newly rented apartment on East 56th Street. After six months there, missing the California outdoor, sports-oriented lifestyle, and complaining a lot, I joined a tennis club, started playing bridge again, made many new friends and decided New York was okay. I spoke to Mom and Dad almost daily, but didn't see much of them.

Then in July 1955 the time had come. Mother and Daddy were about to be grandparents, and with great excitement they flew to New York for the big event. As is often the case with a first baby we didn't know exactly when he/she would decide to make an appearance so they arrived shortly before my due date. And waited and waited and waited. Finally, two and a half weeks later, at about five o'clock in the morning on July 16, after eating a huge dinner with my husband, my parents and Mr. and Mrs. Paul Hahn (the president of American Tobacco) at the Pavillon the previous evening, I awoke with an odd little pain. By now I was so tired of waiting I had almost forgotten about the baby. I attributed it to all the rich French food. Then I had another pain, and another. Not knowing what labor pains were supposed to feel like and still thinking I had just eaten too much, I reached over for a cigarette. On the first puff I started to choke, and the next thing I knew a rush of water had flooded the bed. Oh, my god—this is IT! While I got dressed Seth called the doctor, his parents and my parents. And off to the hospital.

I was later told that Daddy had answered the

telephone and awakened Mom, who, when she heard the news, shot out of bed and flew to the bathroom to get dressed. She ran the bathwater and jumped into the tub—still in her nightgown.

Michael was born about nine in the morning. Mother and Daddy went nuts, the press went nuts, the maternity wing of Mt. Sinai Hospital went nuts. Between the photographers, reporters, visitors, flowers and telegrams it was bedlam.

Just recently I was sitting in the green room at Michael's Pub where Joan Rivers was playing. We were chatting together before her show when some friends of hers came in and joined us. I was introduced to a woman, who when she heard my name gave me a strange look and exclaimed, "I can't believe it. You're Joan Benny! You have a son who was born on July 16, 1955."

I said, "Yes—why?"

She answered, "For thirty years I've wanted to meet you to tell you how much I hate and resent you! You see, my first baby was born on the same day in the same hospital. I even had the room next to yours, and I feel sorry for anyone who was there at that time. All I heard was Jack Benny's grandson this, Jack Benny's grandson that—you would have thought it was the Second Coming. When I rang for a nurse, no one answered; when I wanted to ask about my baby or get a drink of water or get my wastebasket emptied, no one came; when I wanted some attention, no one bothered; they were all in your room."

I apologized, saying, "I'm really sorry. I had

no idea. If I had known—if you had asked me, I would have been happy to come in and empty your wastebasket or get you a drink." We had a good laugh about it.

My parents stayed in New York for another week. Six weeks later, as soon as I was allowed to travel, Seth and I took Michael to California to spend some time with his doting grandparents. After two weeks Seth went back to New York. I didn't. The marriage was over.

Actually, it was hardly a marriage to begin with. I had gone into it frivolously with not even a vague idea of what marriage was all about. I was much too young, I wasn't ready to settle down, I was living in a strange city with few friends and no family. I missed my friends, I missed California, I missed Daddy, I even missed Mother. Besides, I wasn't in love. From the beginning I never tried to make it work, not expecting it to last, not giving it a chance. I wish I could put the blame on Seth, but that wouldn't be fair. He was a perfectly nice man, but he was, in spite of a previous marriage, young and inexperienced, too. We were like two acquaintances sharing an apartment. We didn't even play at marriage—there was no marriage. It only lasted as long as it did because after that enormous wedding I couldn't call it quits too soon, and then just when I was getting up the courage, I accidentally got pregnant.

I didn't tell anyone my plans until Seth left for New York. Even he didn't know. He thought I was going to stay another week or two and then return east. First I decided I had to tell my parents. I was scared to death. When I finally got up the nerve to confront them and plunged in, much to my astonishment they weren't surprised. It came as an anticlimax. I thought I had been so cool pretending to be happy, but they had suspected all along. (Parents are sometimes amazing!) Even Daddy, with his mind often elsewhere, knew I had been putting on an act.

My father didn't particularly like Seth. He didn't dislike him either, it was just that Seth and Daddy were as incompatible as Seth and I. They too had little to talk about. The financial world was not only foreign to Daddy, it didn't interest him. Comedy was foreign to Seth. And his formality, his stiffness—he was never without a tie —made Daddy uncomfortable. His own feelings aside, he had felt from their first meeting that Seth was the wrong man for me. And how right Daddy was. If he was at all disappointed in me he didn't show it. He joined in the discussion of what to do now and didn't, as he frequently had done in the past, suggest I talk to my mother. We would work it out together. Both of them rose to the occasion and were entirely supportive. Even Mom never said a word about "and after all we spent on the wedding." In short, they were wonderful.

My son and I lived at home where a nursery was set up in the old guest room. My parents acted just like all new grandparents—they went bazooey! Daddy went back to his old tricks; putting paper on his eyelids, making funny faces, crawling on the floor with rattles and toys. Of course Michael was too young to pay attention to any of this silliness, but Daddy didn't care. He went right on doing it. He took him for drives to his office, to Hillcrest, to the Friars—anywhere he could think of to show off his new grandson. Mom got up early—for the first time in my memory—to see him. She took him for walks in the pram. She even changed his diapers and fed him a couple of times. I hardly had a chance to see him myself!

In January, knowing Michael was well taken care of, I went to Reno to ski and get my divorce. When I returned in March, six weeks later, I was already remarried!

I met Buddy Rudolph on a blind date arranged by Deedee (he was her cousin-in-law) shortly after I arrived home from New York, and had been seeing him steadily ever since. He was twenty-six, tall (six feet one), slim, with an athlete's build, half blond–half bald. At the time he was in the airplane parts business. Maybe this time I was looking for a father figure because Bud was remarkably like Daddy. He even walked with that same purposeful stride. The antithesis of Seth, he was easygoing and casual, he liked everybody and everybody liked him. Although not in the business himself he had been around show people all his life. Unlike Daddy, he was a sensational golfer, a two to scratch handicap, the Hillcrest Club champion. They played together frequently, and my father loved to brag about how badly he was beaten

411

by his son-in-law. Bud also had a delightful dry sense of humor. The two of them got along famously.

Buddy loved and adored me, and he was crazy about Michael. Since I was convinced I was a fallen woman, having come home with my tail between my legs, twenty-one years old, divorced and with a baby, I thought no one would ever want to marry me again. And along came wonderful, funny, sweet Buddy. What more could I have asked for? I stupidly thought it didn't matter that *I* wasn't in love, it was only important that *he* was. I still had a lot to learn—the hard way.

Buddy flew up to Reno, and we were married by a justice of the peace within hours of my divorce decree. We bought a small house just outside of Beverly Hills, settled into married life, and a year later Michael had a baby sister, Maria, named after my mother. She was born early on a Tuesday morning at Cedars of Lebanon Hospital. Again, Mom and Dad were there.

Remember Dad's absentmindedness? After Maria's birth, he spent most of that day with me. He came to the hospital again on Wednesday. I was due to go home on Friday. Thursday around six in the evening my phone rang. It was Daddy, who said, "Joanie, I just did the dumbest thing."

"What did you do that was so dumb?" I asked.

"No, really, sometimes I'm so forgetful and dumb," he repeated.

"Okay, Daddy, what are you talking about?" I asked again.

"Well, I came down to the hospital to visit a friend today and forgot you were there and didn't come to see you. Wasn't that silly?"

"Not really," I replied. "First of all, you were here yesterday and the day before and I'll see you tomorrow when I come home, and secondly, the maternity pavilion is a long way from the main hospital. It would be easy not to connect them in your mind."

"Yes, but I should have remembered."

"Daddy, it's *okay*," I said, beginning to get exasperated. "Honestly, don't worry about it."

"Well, it was stupid. My friend and I came all the way downtown to visit a pal who is recovering from surgery, and we should have come over to visit you, too."

"DADDY, IT'S OKAY!"

"No, it isn't."

"YES, IT IS!"

"It isn't okay. Harry Truman and I came to see—"

"HARRY TRUMAN, HARRY TRUMAN?" I screeched. "You were here at the hospital with Harry Truman? The President? And you didn't come to see me? How could you do such a thing? You're right. You *are* stupid. You *are* dumb! How could you do this to me? I would kill to meet Harry Truman."

I never did.

I had listened to golf stories from my parents all my life and now I was married to a golfer. I just

413

couldn't hold out any longer. The time had come for me to learn. So I started going to Hillcrest every day for lessons. It didn't take me long. With Buddy's help and some natural athletic ability I was playing the course in no time. I could hardly wait to surprise my parents with my newfound talent, but I didn't want to disgrace myself so I kept on practicing until I thought I was good enough, at least good enough to beat my mother —who was not very strong or much of an athlete. One day when I felt I was ready to compete I told Mother I had learned the game and asked her to join me. We had lunch together and I told her all about my lessons and how I had wanted to surprise her. "I can't wait," she said.

We teed off. I hit the ball a mile. "Wow, what a drive," Mother exclaimed. She hit her typical dinky little drive, and off we went down the fairway. To make a long story short, her dinky little shots just went straight ahead and into the hole, while my tremendous long ones were all over the course. She beat the hell out of me! I played golf for four or five more years and I never ever won a game from her. Guess who was smirking now!

But during those golfing years I played a lot with both Mother and Daddy, their golfing friends, and mine—particularly in Palm Springs. And it was through golf that I got to know Clark Gable. As you remember I had met him briefly, though memorably, when I was fourteen. I was now in my early twenties, he was married to Kay, and they had a home on the Bermuda Dunes golf course in Palm Springs. One day while shopping I ran into her. We greeted each other like long-lost friends, and somewhere in the course of conversation she asked if I played golf and would Buddy and I like to join them at Bermuda Dunes for a game. I eagerly accepted. And that's how we became friends. We played and lunched frequently at their club and at ours, Tamarisk. They were both average golfers and, unlike my husband, who occasionally lost his temper and once threw all his clubs in a tree, didn't take the game too seriously.

Clark Gable was even amiable on the golf course! He never let me down. He had a quality rare among men—or women for that matter: he paid attention to you. When he talked to you he focused on you, when he listened to you he listened with both ears and both eyes. He made you feel as if what you were saying, no matter how trivial, was the most important thing he had ever heard. Unquestionably, Clark Gable was the most charming man I ever met.

Buddy and I enjoyed playing golf together, or should I say he enjoyed teaching me. We also learned to fly together—he got his license, I only went as far as soloing. We even had our own plane for two years: a Cessna 140, which we frequently flew down to Palm Springs. Still, in spite of our interests in common, in spite of Bud's easygoing nature, our marriage wasn't working. I had again married for the wrong reasons—different ones, but wrong nonetheless. This time there was no family conference, just an announcement. I think Mother and Daddy were disappointed because this time they liked my husband (So did I. If only I had been in love with him), but had given up on me when it came to marriage. I think they also realized that their daughter was pigheaded, stubborn and it was too late for them to do much about it. They just sighed and said something like, "If that's what you want—we love you no matter what. Joanie, *please think before you do this again.*"

CHAPTER 21

In the early 1960's I decided to try my hand at show business. Daddy had been asked to appear on *Password* with me as his partner. We were a sensation. Shortly afterward I was asked by Goodson-Todman to appear on the daytime version of that show as well as another of their shows, *To Tell the Truth.*

One day during this time I was at CBS Television City on some business of my own. I was walking down the long hallway there when I saw my father approaching from the other end. As we came closer I could see he was lost in concentration. He walked right past me! I let him go for a few seconds, then turned around and followed him. "Mr. Benny," I called out. He turned, looked at me blankly, then: "Oh, Joanie, what are you doing here?"

416

"Nice of you to recognize me," I said.

For the next four years I appeared frequently on game shows, talk shows and even did a pilot for my own interview show, *Joan Benny's Hollywood*. It didn't sell. I did magazine ads and TV commercials. Most of the shows were out of New York, so I did a lot of commuting.

I was staying at the Sherry-Netherland once doing two weeks of *To Tell the Truth* when, coincidentally, Daddy was staying there, too. One day he asked me if I would accompany him to a charity affair. He was to be the emcee. "I'd love to," I said, "but I didn't bring an evening gown."

"That's okay, honey. We'll go to Bergdorf's and I'll buy you one." And with that we marched across the street to Bergdorf-Goodman. And up to the third floor.

Daddy was adorable. Although he enjoyed shopping in general and couldn't have been sweeter about it, he looked a bit sheepish and discombobulated to find himself in Ladies' Evening Gowns. As we stepped off the elevator a saleslady, recognizing him immediately, rushed over to help us. She showed him a comfortable sofa in the middle of the salon. He sat down and put his overcoat beside him. She brought out an armful of size 6 evening gowns. By now a small crowd had gathered, discreetly watching us from a distance. I briskly picked out three or four dresses, trying hard not to prolong Daddy's obvious discomfort. He was sitting straight up on the edge of the sofa with his hat on his lap, trying to look as if he belonged there.

In the fitting room I narrowed the choice to two; one a tight-waisted, full-skirted, rather demure blue taffeta, the other quite the opposite—a slinky, tight, sexy, backless silver lamé. It had a high neck in front, cut at an angle, it was sleeveless and totally backless down to the waist. I walked back into the salon modeling the taffeta. I was afraid to show him the lamé first. He loved the blue gown. Then I stammered, "Uh, Daddy, there's another one. It's kind of silly—not the sort of thing you're used to seeing me in—but . . ."

"Well, let me see it."

A few minutes later I emerged in the slinky number. "Here it is!" I said, wondering what his reaction would be as I turned slowly around with a slink to match the dress. "How do you like it?"

He loved it, too.

Even though I was still "Daddy's little girl," he loved sexy women and sexy clothes and he loved that dress. Even if it was on his own daughter.

"I can't decide, Joanie. Let's take them both." Maybe he was just anxious to leave, but I don't think so. I think he genuinely liked both gowns and wanted me to have them. I told you he was a generous man! He was such a gentleman, such a delight, so sweet that afternoon, he must have made many fans among the sales force at Bergdorf's. After he signed some autographs, we left the store—but not before buying shoes to go with the dresses.

The following night I wore the blue taffeta. Even though we both liked the silver, I thought it a bit much to wear with my father. A short time later, back in Beverly Hills, I wore it to a party with my friends and contemporaries. Remembering my lesson from Marilyn Maxwell, I bought a roll of adhesive tape!

After four years of playing the Gay Divorcee, flying back and forth between jobs in New York and my children in Los Angeles, pursuing my so-called career halfheartedly and jet-setting around the world, I decided it was time to settle down again. At home between trips, I had been going out with Bob Blumofe, who was then head of production at United Artists. We had been seeing each other for about a year when one morning he called me. I was in New York.

"What are you doing?" he asked.

"I'm leaving for the south of France tonight," I replied.

"That plane's going in the wrong direction." he said. "Get one heading west. Come home and marry me."

I did. Would I never learn? This time I really thought I was in love. Bob was much older than I—twenty-five years to be exact—a settled, solid, law school–trained businessman, who would be *good* for me, who would keep me and my capricious tendencies in line. Unlike my previous husbands he was in show business. That was a plus. He was enormously bright, well read and knowledgeable. (I used to laughingly say, "He's the only person I know who can spell all the 'twenty most misspelled words in the English language' correctly!") He played the violin, loved going to concerts and owned a record collection more extensive than mine. We had so much in common.

Mother and Daddy thought I was making another mistake. "He's too old for you," they said, but again they knew I would do exactly what I wanted. Mother arranged a small wedding—and this time it really was small—at their house, with just the immediate family and my two children. My favorite memory of the event is of six-year-old Maria, who was standing next to me holding my hand, announcing right smack in the middle of the "I do's" that she had to go to the bathroom. The ceremony came to a dead halt, as though someone had said "Freeze," and resumed when she returned. Daddy fell on the floor laughing—and never let her forget it!

Less than a year later we had a son, Robert. He was born on Mom's birthday, June 23. She said it was her best birthday present ever. Almost exactly a year later Joanna was born, this time on my Uncle Hilliard's birthday, June 29. I was now the very happy mother of two boys and two girls. The symmetry, I've always believed, was the result of my mathematical mind!

The next ten years went by quickly. I was busy raising my children, working for charities, playing tennis (no more golf—I didn't have the time), traveling with Bob, entertaining and generally trying to act like your everyday ordinary house-wife. We saw a great deal of my parents, partic-ularly my father, who took to dropping in almost daily, now that he had four grandchildren. It was also a chance for him to eat some of the things he loved that were denied him at home. Since Mother had all but given up traveling I still accompanied him, whenever possible, on one- or two-day trips to his concerts or various special appearances.

One afternoon Daddy called to ask if I would like to go to Las Vegas with him for the evening. He had agreed to play a benefit there after the late show. We would return the following morning. I could tell by the tone of his voice that he wanted company. Of course I said yes—Bob wouldn't mind.

In Vegas we stayed at the Hilton where Danny Kaye was headlining, and after showering and changing we attended his dinner show. I didn't realize until the end of the show when Danny introduced him from the stage that Cary Grant was also in the audience. I had never met Cary Grant, and I reacted no differently from any other red-blooded American female. Wow! I was in the same room with Cary Grant!

After the show, we went back to Danny's dress-ing room, and there he was again. We were in-troduced. After the usual bravos, compliments and praise for Danny, we all sat down to talk and the conversation turned to general topics while Danny changed his clothes. When Cary (Mr.

Grant to me) casually asked, "Jack, when are you going back?" Daddy replied, "Tomorrow morning."

Cary said, "How?"

Daddy replied, "On Western Airlines."

Cary said, "Why don't you and Joan fly back with me on my private plane?"

Daddy replied, "That's okay, Cary, we don't want to trouble you, and besides we have our reservations. No, but thank you for the invitation!" Daddy was sitting across the room from me, so I had no opportunity to kick him. Could you die? There I was, not able to say a word.

After Daddy and I left the dressing room I said to him, "DADDY, I want to fly home with Cary Grant!"

"You do?" he asked, looking puzzled, as though he were thinking, Why would anyone want to do that when they can fly on a commercial airline?

"Yes!" I cried.

"Okay, honey—sure, if you want to. We'll be seeing him again later at the charity affair and I'll be happy to arrange it."

(Dad was a true egalitarian. His friends were his friends; movie stars, writers, guitar players—they were all the same to him. He didn't separate them into categories. He didn't rate them. It didn't occur to him that others, me for example, might feel differently, that they might be more excited to meet Cary Grant or President Truman than one of his golfing cronies.)

When we next saw Cary Grant, my father said, "I've changed my mind, and Joanie and I would love to take you up on your invitation to join you flying home."

Cary was delighted and turning to me said, "May I telephone you in the morning to let you know what time the car will come to fetch you?"

"Me? Yes, of course," I replied eagerly.

I am a very sound sleeper under any circumstances, but since we hadn't gone to our rooms until after the benefit and a late snack, it must have been 4:00 A.M. before I went to sleep. At 9:00 A.M. when I was still dead to the world the phone rang. After many rings I finally reached over, took the phone off the hook, and grunted, "Uhhh."

A voice on the other end said, "Joan?"

I repeated, "Uhhh."

"Good morning, this is Cary Grant."

Can you imagine being half asleep, not knowing where you are or what day it is, picking up the phone, and hearing the unmistakable voice of Cary Grant talking to you? My first reaction was to say, "Sure you are!" and hang up. But before I could make that terrible blunder, I slowly remembered and realized that he was really who he said he was.

He told me the car would be at our hotel at eleven. I said we would be ready. I was so excited that as soon as we hung up I called my three closest friends in Los Angeles to say, "Guess who just called me on the phone?"

His plane was actually the Faberge plane (the

423

company to which he was under contract), a beautifully furnished converted DC-3. Wonderful! It wasn't a jet and that meant the trip would take longer! Daddy was typically Daddy. He climbed on board, sat in the nearest seat, opened a newspaper and never looked up throughout the flight. Mr. Grant showed me to the other end, nearest the cockpit, where he immediately sat down at a spinet piano and began playing the *Rodgers and Hart Songbook*. I was in such a state of enchantment that I, who can't carry a tune, I, who have never before or since sung except alone in my room or in the shower, sang Broadway songs off-key all the way back to Los Angeles.

Daddy couldn't get enough of his grandchildren, but Mike, the firstborn, was his pet. By the time he was six years old he had usurped my place— now the gin games and baseball games and traveling were no longer with me, they were with *him*.

Mike recalls: "We never talked very much but I liked to be with him. I loved traveling with him. I spent Christmas vacations and parts of summers with him in Tahoe or Vegas. Sometimes Maria would go, sometimes the rest of the family. I remember in Las Vegas—I must have been eight or nine and I was put in charge of his makeup—I don't remember what I did but it made me feel important to have a responsibility. I do remember the stuff he used—something black—to cover the thin spot on his head. And it came off on everything. One thing I had to do was make sure his cue cards were in his pocket with a little black rubber thing—maybe a bow stop that he would sometimes keep in his hand and play with, kind of like Captain Queeg.

"I remember once I made him almost apoplectic. It happened in his dressing room at the Sahara Hotel in Vegas. I had been told to 'watch the Strad—don't leave the room, or if you do, lock it.' I left the room, but because I wanted to return and didn't have a key, I didn't lock the door. Instead, to be sure the violin would be safe, I hid it in the shower. No—no one turned on the shower, but what did happen was that Granddad came back early, and when he couldn't find the Strad, called the security police. So when I walked in, I was confronted by Granddad's anger and the policemen's grim faces. I had to sheepishly confess what I had done. He ranted at me briefly and then started to laugh. He decided his grandson was really quite clever. And bragged about me to his friends.

"He took me with him to Expo 67. I loved it. Being with Granddad meant I didn't have to wait in line. Because I was his first grandchild I had a special position in his life.

"I liked listening to him and his friends. The people who were around him were funny people, though he himself wasn't generally—Uncle Hickey, Fred De Cordova, and his wife, Janet— she was good with children, always making funny noises and telling stories. But he wasn't funny. I never thought he was very funny—even on stage.

Maybe because I heard everything so many times—the same show twice a night, night after night.

"The trip to Cape Kennedy to see the launch of Apollo 11 was and probably still is the highlight of my life. I remember Mom being mock-jealous because she had always been his traveling companion and the moon launch was a trip she was dying to take, but now his grandson had taken her place. (Actually she was thrilled for me.) Since I was a science and math nut, it was just unbelievable. And Granddad was real excited about it, too, even though he didn't understand any of it —that is, the technical aspects. He was always asking me questions and I tried to explain it to him in layman's terms he could understand—he was still fascinated by all of it and loved it.

"We flew there. I remember about three in the morning of the launch having breakfast with a group of astronauts. And then having my choice of being able to watch the launch from the V.I.P. stands or the control room. Naturally I chose the control room. The only trouble with the control room was you couldn't see the launch because all the windows were covered. I got to sit next to Wernher von Braun. Granddad went to the V.I.P. stand a couple of miles away. We were right up close to the launch, but I could only see it on the monitor. After the launch we were taken to see Apollo 12. It was still in the building where the rockets were built. I just remember that it was so huge that—you'd go up to one of these things and

426

it was like looking at a wall—you couldn't even see the curvature. You had no idea of how they could get off the ground, let alone get to the moon. In layman's terms, certainly Granddad understood what it was all about.

"From there we went to Indianapolis (he was performing there) and together we watched the walk on the moon. It was late afternoon and all activity stopped. That was really exciting.

"I know he liked me—loved me—but he didn't show much emotion. We never really talked. Maybe he didn't know what to say to me—I didn't know what to say to him either. Perhaps as a little boy it was because our worlds were so different. I didn't understand show business and he didn't understand math and science. And I was shy—never much of a talker. I know, mostly from others, that he was proud of me.

"My most treasured gift from him is the money clip. [A local Beverly Hills jeweler custom-made them for him. They were fashioned of fourteen-karat gold with the famous Jack Benny line drawing by Bouché etched on top. He gave them to his closest friends.] Granddad gave it to me shortly before he died. I was at Stanford then. I love it because he gave it to me. I always think that if there were a fire it would be the first thing I'd save."

Although most of my life now centered around home, husband and children, I still occasionally went to New York alone—for a game or talk show.

427

During those years Daddy was traveling a lot, too, so we didn't always know about each other's comings and goings.

Once I was again staying at the Sherry-Netherland. As I was leaving the hotel, much to my surprise, Daddy was coming in.

"What are you doing here?" we asked each other. After brief explanations, Daddy said, "My friend, Kenneth Tynan, called me and wants me to see his new show, *Oh, Calcutta!* I have tickets for tomorrow night."

When it first opened, *Oh, Calcutta!* was considered the most shocking production ever to hit Broadway. Comprised of risqué comedy skits, all the actors appeared in the buff—totally. It received mixed reviews, but because it was so controversial I was dying to see it. "Daddy," I said, "please take me with you."

"No, I can't," he said. "I would be embarrassed to take my daughter to see a show like that."

"Don't be silly. I'm a grown-up sophisticated woman. I've been married three times. I've seen nudity before, and after all, this isn't the Dark Ages."

"Well, I'd be embarrassed—but if you really want to go—well, I'll call your mother and see what she thinks."

Mom said pretty much what I said, so Daddy relented. The following evening we went to see the show. In the lobby of the theater he looked terribly uncomfortable, not introducing me to anyone and pretending he was alone. We went to our seats separately, Daddy buried his face in the program. We didn't exchange a word. Finally, the lights went down and the show began.

I didn't find it particularly shocking, or particularly funny. Actually, I was rather bored. As it turned out, so was Daddy. During the first act I caught him a few times surreptitiously glancing my way to check my reactions. By the time the lights came up for intermission, he was totally relaxed and pretty bored, too. We both agreed we would like to leave. But because he was a friend of the producer and so easily recognizable, Daddy couldn't walk out. Reluctantly we stayed to final curtain.

To the end of his life—I guess like most fathers—he thought of me as a little girl, sheltering and protecting me—except in one way that I remember well.

In 1965 my parents sold the house on Roxbury Drive. I was still married to Bob at the time and when my parents told me their plans, I thought how lovely it would be to go back home and live in that house with Bob and all four children. I talked to Daddy about it, not to Mother. I wanted that house very badly and would have moved there in a minute. The house Bob and I were living in on Walden Drive was not worth as much as the Roxbury house. I talked with Daddy and his lawyer and said we would give them the money from the sale of our house and they would lend us the money as a second mortgage for the amount over and above what ours was worth.

We waited a long time for the answer, which was finally yes—they agreed. I was so excited. I couldn't believe I was finally going to live in my house again! I went over there day after day. I measured every room to see where my furniture would fit. Mother's room would have been our master bedroom, Daddy's room would have been one of the kids' rooms—it was a little difficult, because there were only two other bedrooms (mine and the guest room), but we could have turned Daddy's dressing room into another bedroom. It would be a bit complicated to squeeze in four kids, but it could be managed. This paradise I was living in, this great joy lasted for two or three weeks.

Then one day I received a telephone call from Dad's attorney to say they could not let me have the house after all. They couldn't afford it. Because my mother had overspent so drastically on reconstructing and decorating their new penthouse apartment, they needed all the money the sale of the Roxbury house would bring. I was devastated. I had wanted that house more than I had ever wanted anything (except perhaps *The Messiah*) and I was terribly hurt that it was not to be, but the worst hurt was that my father hadn't told me himself. I think his leaving it to his lawyer was the single most painful thing my father ever did to me. Knowing Daddy, of course, I can see now it was something he just couldn't do. It would have been quite beyond him. He always had trouble being the heavy. I think he knew, although I had never told him in so many words, how strongly and emotionally I felt toward that house, and he just couldn't face me. Afterward, I never said a word about it to him, nor did he ever mention it to me. The case was closed.

For years it was something I couldn't think about or talk about. It would just make me cry. For a very long time I couldn't even drive by the house. I would go out of my way, rather than pass 1002 North Roxbury. Ten-oh-two—that number stays with me. Sometimes when I glance at a digital clock or wristwatch and it says 10:02, I feel it—not a pang, not even a twinge anymore, but it's there. My life will always be somehow wrapped up in that number, that house.

CHAPTER 22

In 1955 Daddy laid the old Sunday evening weekly radio program to rest. For the next ten years television was his full-time occupation. During that period I was busy with my own life—getting divorced, remarried, divorced, remarried and having babies—so there were times when I just didn't know what Daddy was doing professionally. Also, he kept things pretty much to himself, and we never talked about how he felt, but I do think he had a kind of love-hate relationship with television. I think—and this is solely my own opinion —that his age was the primary factor. Daddy was in his sixties. He had been doing the same kind of comedy for almost twenty-five years, and here he was plopped into a new and young medium, competing against younger and fresher comics and a younger audience. Times had changed. That's not to say that he was old or that he even thought old. As I said previously, he didn't dwell on the past, he did try to be contemporary, and to a great extent he succeeded—he couldn't have lasted for ten years had he not been—but the competition got rougher and rougher as the years passed, and by 1965 he was seventy-one years old. It just couldn't go on forever.

In 1965 I had had a fifteen-year run in television, which for television is not bad. It was the ratings that did me in. In our business you live and die by ratings. We are in what Goodman Ace has called a "rate race." Now when my ratings went down, this did not mean that people stopped watching me and my cohorts. Oh, no. Millions of people watched. About eighteen million—which is an awful lot of people. What's so terrible about an audience of eighteen million?

Let me explain. Those of you who do not understand these things (and that includes me) should know that it costs a sponsor about $250,000 to put on a show, including the costs for the talent and the network "prime time." In order to make any money, he has to sell a great deal of mouthwash or gelatin dessert so he wants to reach the maximum millions of listeners. He is interested in the "cost per viewer." If it costs him, say, $2.80 for a viewer of Jack Benny, and only $1.98 for a viewer of *Hogan's Heroes*, he will get a bigger bargain with *Hogan's Heroes* so that's the show he will sponsor. About comedy as a fine art and the glory of satire—well, he couldn't care less.

By my second year in television, I saw that the camera was a man-eating monster. It gave a performer a close-up exposure that, week after week, threatened his existence as an interesting entertainer. I don't care who you are. Finally you'll get on people's nerves if they get too much of you. I don't care how wonderful or handsome or brilliant or charming you are—if the public gets too much of you, they'll be bored.

Given the kind of magnification combined with intimacy that's characteristic of television, the essence of a comedian's art becomes inevitably stale. The audience gets to know you inside and outside. Your tone of voice, your gestures and your little tricks, the rhythm of your delivery, your ways of reacting to another performer's moves, your facial mannerisms—all of these things at first so exciting to an audience when you are a novelty, soon become tedious and flat.

George Jessel once said that television is like having seven brothers-in-law living in your house.

In radio people loved me in a different way. I came at them gently—quietly, through their ears. I suggested subtle images to them, picture jokes. I was like a friendly uncle, a slightly eccentric mad uncle—now I became something else, too much.

The television camera is like a magnifying glass and you can't enjoy looking at anything so blown up for too long.

In vaudeville a great act could last a lifetime, because people saw you once a year. A good standard act, like Smith & Dale, Joe Jackson, Cardini, W. C. Fields, Fred Allen or Julius Tannen, never had to change its foundation. Some vaudeville acts didn't even change a jot or a tittle in fifty years —and audiences loved them the way they were.

In radio the longevity was briefer. But you could still survive if you kept your program fresh and you had original and creative writers—if people liked you. My lifespan in radio was exactly thirty-three years. Fred Allen, whose program was literate and satirical and biting, survived for seventeen years. Bob Hope, Edgar Bergen, Fibber McGee and Molly—all held on in radio for twenty years or more.

But television! To survive even five years with a regular weekly program is damn near impossible. The first two great new faces of television— Milton Berle and Sid Caesar—eventually began losing audiences and falling in the ratings. You could become the king or queen of television— but your reign would be all too short. Sometimes there were great clowns, like George Gobel and Red Buttons who were sensational—and then, after one season, after two seasons, were not sensational.

Afraid of weekly exposure, I first tried doing television every four or six weeks. Then we did a

Friday evening thirty-minute television show for CBS. Then in 1963—guess what?—I was back in the arms of NBC with a regular weekly program. I could have gone on, week after week. I didn't want to. When it came time to renew the contract in 1965, I told NBC I had had enough of this weekly program.

From now on, I will do one or two sixty-minute specials of my own each year and will be happy to go on anybody else's program as a guest star, if they want me. I will do plays if I can find a play and I will do movies if I can find the right part in a movie.

Now I know that this may sound like sour grapes—but I don't believe in the ratings. Having been in the first five in radio and later in television for so long, let me tell you I didn't believe in the ratings then either and said so whenever I was asked. I don't care what system of projection is used, you'll never convince me that 1,500 people, no matter how ingeniously chosen, can accurately represent a nation of about 180,000,000 citizens, with such diverse tastes and educations and backgrounds.

And I'll tell you something else. No rating system can ever tell you how a person watches and how he reacts. All they tell you is maybe so many millions are watching the show because 22 percent of the 1,500 Nielsen samplers had their sets tuned in to the channel. Maybe the set was turned on and tuned in, but the viewer was asleep or in a trance in front of that tube? A lot of people put on the television and just watch it absentmindedly, going in and out of the room. You can't tell me any human being can intelligently watch anything for six or seven hours. Television is free and available at the twist of a knob. Doesn't the quality of the viewer and how he watches mean anything?

I'll tell you the kind of a rating that impresses me. In his book about JFK, *A Day in the Life of President Kennedy*, Jim Bishop tells how toward evening he asked President Kennedy, "What do you do for relaxation? For instance, do you watch television?"

"No," he answered. "I haven't got much time for television. The only shows I'll put away my portfolio for are *The Jack Benny Show* or a good documentary."

Daddy had no reason whatsoever to want to move. He adored the Roxbury house. Lucy was next door; Jimmy and Gloria Stewart were just down the street; his crony Eddie Cantor was up a few houses, the Burnses were nearby—there were so many friends to drop in on. He was comfortable there. It had been home for thirty years. Why leave? Selling it was Mother's idea, and I no longer remember why. Perhaps because I was gone, she thought it too big for them—I really don't know. All I do know is that she wanted to move, and what she wanted she got!

Why didn't Daddy fight for it? Again I can only

guess. He wasn't a fighter—he must have argued, perhaps even pleaded, but Mother was strong and persevering. He was easily talked into things. He hated arguments and unless it concerned his show, would usually take the path of least resistance. I think, A: she wore him down, B: she convinced him that he would be near Hillcrest where he spent so much time, and C: smaller was better and apartment living was simpler. In the end, he would do anything to please her.

So they sold the house and moved to a penthouse in a high-rise apartment building in Century City. Daddy never totally recovered. For the rest of his life he spoke lovingly and longingly about our old house. He missed it terribly, and in a sweet, kind of melancholy voice, would frequently say, "Doll, why did we have to sell that house?"

The penthouse was really two penthouses which they joined together. Mother hired Bill Haines to decorate it, and in typical Haines style it turned out very pastel, crisp, chic, elegant—and impersonal. Mom had a suite: bedroom, dressing room and large bathroom, while at the end of a hall Daddy had a little bedroom and bath, the size of a maid's quarters. (Wait a minute—who was the big breadwinner?) The dichotomy in room size, as well as "Mary's spending habits" became a source of laughs at Hollywood parties.

The apartment didn't last long. Although it was conveniently across the street from Hillcrest he could no longer drop in on his friends or walk to his office, and they both missed living in a house.

According to Irving Fein, they loved it at first: "It was a corner apartment with a terrace all around it on the thirty-ninth floor. You could look out over the whole city, to Catalina and the ocean. Mary said, 'It's so great—there are no problems. If the sink stops up, you just press a button and the engineer is here. Your car is waiting when you come down and you just leave it when you drive home later.'

"Bill and Edie Goetz had been away when they first moved in and when they came home a few months later, Mary gave a party for them—she was so proud to show off her lovely new home. Edie agreed that it was beautiful, but she said to Mary, 'It's wonderful for you, Mary, but I couldn't live here—I couldn't live in an apartment. I have to be able to walk out into my garden—out onto my lawn.' "

Whether or not Edie had anything to do with it, after two years they moved again. This time to Holmby Hills. I remember my mother with two or three real estate agents in tow, searching for the perfect place: convenient location, fairly small (just two bedrooms—they could always add servants' quarters), easy to care for, in short, a cozy little cottage for two. It seemed to take forever, but about a year after she began looking, I received a telephone call. "I've found it! The perfect house. Do you want to see it?" Mom gave me the address and said to meet her there.

I hopped in my car and drove to 10231 Charing Cross Road where I found only a driveway. No house—just a driveway. I turned in and followed a straight uphill road, bordered on the left by woods and on the right by a cement wall. The drive then took a wide curve to the right and opened up on a giant courtyard, large enough to park thirty or more cars, and voilà! There was the house, along with three acres of grounds. What happened to the cozy cottage for two, I wondered. Here stood an enormous, imposing Mediterranean villa. Run-down, paint peeling, overgrown weed-strewn gardens, cracked-tile pool; in short, a mess.

"This is your dream house? Your cozy little cottage for two?" I asked.

"Yes. Just wait," Mother said.

She was right, of course. She always was in matters of dress, decor and style. A year later, with her taste and the expert eye of Bill Haines, the mansion was completed and they moved in.

Jimmy Stewart's wife, Gloria, said recently, "I was sorry when they moved away. Did they want a bigger house? No—the house on Charing Cross was really smaller than the Roxbury house. After they moved, Jack was never as relaxed. Your mother seemed to enjoy it, though. I was sur-prised, I remember, very surprised when they moved. And we didn't see as much of them after that—you couldn't just drop by." Incidentally, the Playboy mansion was right across the street from my parents' "little cottage" and during the years they lived there an occasional animal would get loose and stray to neighboring homes. Can you

439

imagine driving up that long driveway and being greeted by a huge peacock?

As far as the number of rooms was concerned, it really was a place for two; its dimensions, however, were gigantic. The entry with its magnificent dark parquet floors, repeated throughout the house, led to a long gallery. One end opened onto a huge dining room with a breakfast alcove overlooking the patio and completely redone pool. At the other end was a library-den. Half of the room was for TV watching, conversation and informal entertaining, and the other half with an oval table and six red upholstered chairs was used for family dining. Across from the den, down three wide stairs, was one of the largest living rooms I've ever seen. And except for the kitchen, pantry and maids' rooms, that was the downstairs. Not a lot of rooms, but very spread out.

The upstairs was smaller, but again, covered lots of space. My mother's suite consisted of a big bedroom, big dressing room, big bathroom, an enormous walk-in closet and a second small bathroom set up as a hairdressing parlor. At the top of the staircase an open sitting area turned out to be the most accessible room in the house. It only had a sofa, an armchair and a small square table with four chairs, but it became Mother's "perch." In the afternoons when I and/or my children visited, that's where we sat: Mother on the sofa, I in the armchair and the kids on the dining chairs. If we wanted something to eat, we ate it there; when Daddy came home, that's where they discussed the day's events. When Mom was alone, she read, watched TV and had her meals brought there. If Daddy and I were there together I, of course, conceded the armchair to him.

The "joke" continued. Daddy's room—at the other end of the hall—was about the size of Mother's walk-in closet. Comfortable, nicely furnished, plenty of closets, a lovely bathroom, naturally—but not exactly what you would expect of a "star's" living quarters. Dear Daddy—it didn't bother him one bit. He had everything he needed for his comfort and seemed perfectly content with the arrangement.

Artie Kane remembers "when they had moved to the Charing Cross house and Jack wanted his pictures displayed in the foyer. He had all these wonderful photographs—portraits of famous people autographed to him, pictures of him with famous people: kings, queens, presidents. He was kind of pathetic about it. He asked Mary if she could find a table to put downstairs in the gallery for these pictures. I thought, 'Would you give this man his f——ing table? He lives in this little room and bath and at the other end of the hall is the queen with a drying room and a wet room and a sleeping room and a side room and a dressing room and a sitting room and he's there with his fiddle on the chair watching a baseball game on his built-in TV. All he wants is a table downstairs so his friends will be able to see his pictures that he's so proud of.' So, I remember, Joanie, you and I went to Carmel and you found the perfect table in an

441

antique store there and we sent it to him and he finally had his table. He would ask your opinion or my opinion—'Don't you think it would be nice if . . .' Can you imagine another star doing that? Anyone else would say, 'I want . . .' It was absurd!"

When my parents moved in, Bobby and Joanna were quite small—at birthday party ages—so for the next four or five years parties were held, by their request, at Charing Cross. It was kiddie heaven. Hide-and-seek in the woods, running games along the flower-bordered paths by the pond, ballgames on the lawn, swimming in the pool and lunch on the patio. Bobby remembers his grandfather joining the party for ice cream and cake and playing "Happy Birthday" to him on the violin.

Mom and Dad's own parties were as grand as ever. I know—I was there at most of them. No longer on New Year's Eve, they occurred on an anniversary or a birthday, or sometimes for no reason at all. The guest list, now updated, was as star-studded as ever. Some of the "old-timers" remained: George Burns, Frank Sinatra and his current wife Barbara, Jimmy and Gloria Stewart, Danny and Sylvia Kaye. Others were replaced with such luminaries as Gregory and Veronique Peck, Jack and Felicia Lemmon, Johnny Carson, Walter and Carol Matthau, Sammy and Altovise Davis, Cliff Robertson, Henry and Ginny Mancini, Billy and Audrey Wilder. Cristal champagne flowed, and great mounds of caviar were consumed. (I always returned the following day to eat whatever was left over, down to the last little bead.) With that enormous living room and elegant wide gallery it was a sensational house for entertaining.

But it was a cold and formal house, lacking in character and charm. Perhaps because there were no children, no animals, no real family. Only two people lived in this huge place; one reclusive, the other frequently traveling. The downstairs rooms were hardly ever used except for parties or occasional company or when I came to dinner with my children. When I would sometimes visit my mother in the afternoon, as soon as I came in the front door, I could hear my footsteps echoing on the parquet, feel the hollowness of empty, unused rooms. Even the upstairs seemed deserted, save for Mother's presence on the sofa in the sitting room.

When they were alone my parents ate their meals upstairs, either together in the sitting room or alone in bed each in his or her own bedroom. Irving Fein recalled, "Jack always had a little teeny room. Her bathroom was bigger than Jack's bedroom. Jack used to call me at the end of every television broadcast. It was sad. The show would be on at nine o'clock at night and when it was over, around nine forty-five, Jack would call me and say, 'Mary just buzzed me and said she thought it was a good show—and she especially liked this and that . . .' Here they're both watching the same show in separate bedrooms. To me that was so sad. Here he does a show—wouldn't you think they'd want to see it together?"

Actually, this lack of togetherness was nothing new. As far back as I can remember my parents lived in separate quarters, and spent time alone and apart. Daddy would be in his room listening to the fights and Mother would be in hers listening to a detective show. At Roxbury, though, their bedrooms were across the hall from each other and could be locked off together from the rest of the second floor, whereas at Charing Cross they were at opposite ends of an open hallway. Even when they traveled they never shared a bedroom. That was one of the many enigmas of their relationship I found curious, yet never had the nerve to ask about.

One day during the preparations for my first wedding, Daddy asked me to drive him to the airport (a rare occurrence in our family) because he wanted to talk to me alone. He told me I had done some things to upset Mom, and that he expected me to "shape up." I don't remember now exactly what my sins were—I do remember that what he said wasn't true—and I said as much to Daddy.

"Are you telling me your mother *lied?*" he said in a threatening tone.

I backpedaled fast! "No," I replied. "Of course she didn't lie. I didn't mean that at all!" Then I rambled on about how there must have been a misunderstanding. I was sorry and didn't mean in any way to upset her. After all, with her bad back and everything . . .

I had learned never to contradict anything Daddy said about Mother.

Once when I was starting my own career, I had an offer to do a commercial or a game show—I don't remember exactly what it was, but I thought maybe I ought to have an agent. Of course I decided to go to my father to get his advice. I went to his office and told him the situation and I said, "Daddy, I really want your input—I need to know what you think. What should I do?" And he said, "Go ask your mother about it." I really wanted to know what *he* thought about my career. I remember that tears came to my eyes. He didn't want to be a part of my life in that way. He didn't want problems.

Another time I incurred Mom's wrath. One night we were sitting with a group of people at Sardi's, and someone said he had been at the opening night of *The King and I*.

My mother popped up with, "So were we!"

Daddy said, "No, we weren't, doll. Don't you remember? We saw it the following month."

I guess Mother was trying to impress these people because she kept insisting that Dad was wrong—they had been there on opening night.

Somehow I was pulled into arbitrating and stupidly told the truth: "Daddy's right, you saw the show later. I know because I was with you." If I'd been smart, I would have said, "I don't remember." Mother looked daggers at me and didn't speak to me for days.

I never came between them again!

Estelle Blanc saw an amusing side of their relationship. She said, "Jack wanted her with him all the time. But Jack did funny little things in spite of it. We were all in San Francisco for the opening of a new radio station and staying at the same hotel—the Fairmont at the top of the hill. At that time they had a Blum's candy store and ice cream parlor there. Mel and I were sitting and having a soda before bed. We had just ordered when Mary and Jack came in with Gracie and George. They all had to work the next morning, but Jack says, 'I'll go over and sit with them.'

"Mary says, 'No, you won't Jack. You're not going to have any ice cream.'

"And the four of them walked to the elevator. Five minutes later, Mel and I were just getting our order—they had just put our sodas on the table—when Jack comes down. 'Quick, give me some ice cream.' He was like Peck's Bad Boy."

My favorite story about them is told by Lenny Gershe: "The only thing I can think of to say 'bad' about your dad was something he told me about himself. We were in Las Vegas, about to go to dinner. Your dad and I were sitting in the living room of their suite waiting for your mother, who was in the bedroom having her hair done. We waited and waited. Finally your father said, 'I don't mind waiting for her—I never mind waiting for her—she's the most wonderful human being God ever put on this earth. No man ever had a better wife. She has looked after me, she has stuck by me—she's simply extraordinary. And you know something? I was never a good lay!' An almost celestial speech—and a hilarious punch line."

My parents' relationship was mysterious to me, but maybe that's the way most marriages look from a child's point of view. I have never been able to give a really satisfactory answer to the question of what their marriage was all about, but one and all agree that he adored, worshiped and idolized her. He called her doll or dollface and she always called him doll. He was always concerned about her health and happiness. He bought her many extravagant presents and always went where she wanted to go. I guess she loved him, too, but it confused me. How could you love someone, yet be so uncaring? Adoring my father as I did, there were times when I felt Mom thought only of herself—certainly moving from Roxbury falls in that category. She indulged her incredible spending habits. She would get a headache at the last minute and cancel a dinner party engagement. As she got older, she accompanied him less and less. He always wanted her with him—at charity dinners and on his many trips. When she refused, he was like a hurt, pathetic little boy. Not angry, just disappointed.

Still, I can't quarrel with success. Whatever the relationship was, it worked for them.

CHAPTER 23

On Valentine's Day, 1974, Daddy celebrated his eightieth and last birthday. I was thirty-nine at the time. The celebration turned into a week-long series of parties (one of which I gave at my home) that culminated in a two-day extravaganza at Frank Sinatra's "compound" in Palm Springs. Although he was thrilled with all the attention, gifts (Billy Wilder gave him *two* copies of *Life Begins at Forty*) and general gaiety, Daddy was not thrilled at all about being eighty years old. He felt his life was almost over, he was slowing down and he was less in demand. He could no longer memorize lines easily and he didn't have his normal energy—eighty meant *old*.

Over the last ten years I had seen his on-stage timing slow down a little. Except for that I didn't notice much change, though there were times when I thought I detected a loneliness about him. I asked Dad's confidant and close friend, Fred De Cordova, about this; he said:

"I believe that as time passed, his circle of friends decreased—not only through death, but I thought he withdrew in not wanting to make a lot of new friends, and he would see only those in whom he had some interest—primarily a business interest. During the last twenty years of his life I don't ever recall him saying, 'Let's get a gang together and . . .' Once he reached the later years the razzle-dazzle didn't interest him and I think he was happy to stay home in the evenings. As old friends died or moved away he had little interest in replacing them.

"I think he was the happiest when he was in Palm Springs with three or four close friends, playing gin rummy or golf, going to the Beachcomber for dinner or staying home and enjoying Mrs. King's cooking. He was comfortable there, and relaxed. There was no drive in him to shine. He did that on the stage.

"When we use the word 'lonely'—lonely paints a picture of someone miserable, of someone alone with no one calling. I don't mean that kind of lonely. He was a lone man but not a lonely man. He didn't need to be surrounded with people. Also, as he grew older he harked back to the past—I guess we all do. Perhaps that's a kind of loneliness. Again, I don't mean he lived in the past. Professionally, he was always planning his next show, but his conversation frequently began, 'Remember the fun we had at . . .' or 'the time we went to . . .' or 'the night someone said . . .' as opposed to 'Next week why don't we . . .'

"I think loneliness perhaps was happiness for him. His being a lone person—there was no sadness in that. People who made a move to know him or to try to make friends with him—in his later years—unless they had been a part of his past, he just couldn't have cared less."

Daddy continued to do what he always did. His schedule didn't change, it didn't even slow down. He played Vegas, performed at charity functions, played concerts, did a TV special, played golf, went to baseball games, dropped in on friends, spent time with his grandchildren and me—all the regular activities. Except, once in a while he complained he wasn't feeling well. I attributed it to his age and his hypochondria. "Daddy," I said, somewhat impatiently, "you're imagining things. There's nothing wrong with you. Go to the club, have lunch with George, tell some jokes, play a few holes—you'll be fine."

Rex Kennamer disagrees with me about his hypochondria: "In the late 1950's he had a very bad attack of pancreatitis—in no way connected with the later cancer—and from that time on he was a mild diabetic. So it was sensible of your dad to be conscious of his health. I have a feeling, like a lot of things your dad did, he kind of made it into a joke. He was health-conscious, but I don't call that being a hypochondriac. A diabetic who has to control his diabetes with diet is knowledgeable and pays attention to it and takes care of himself. I don't call that being hypochondriacal."

One hot day in August Daddy wanted to go to the ballgame. He called me. Although I tended to be a fair-weather Dodgers fan, Daddy was a loyal one, even when they were losing. This summer they were indeed in the basement, but he wanted

450

to go to a game anyway. He hadn't been feeling well, which made him grouchy, and he thought an afternoon at Dodger Stadium would cheer him up. So did I.

You've heard of Murphy's Law? Well, this was one of those days. It began when I was late picking him up. He grumbled. Then I hit traffic that further delayed us, so when we finally arrived it was the middle of the second inning. The Dodgers were losing. Five innings later they were still losing. Now I think when a baseball game is exciting it's the most exciting sport of all, but when it's dull it's really dull. This one was extra dull. Daddy was miserable and bored. "Let's go," he said, "my stomach hurts." I attributed that to the hot dog and Coke he had eaten—along with his bad mood.

"Okay," I agreed, and we left. "Let's get home quickly, I want to go to bed," he said. There are many ways of going home from the stadium and as we walked to the parking lot I tried to figure out which would be fastest. I had lived in Los Angeles for thirty-nine years and had driven for twenty-three of them. You would think I knew my way around. I certainly thought I did, so I decided on the Golden State Freeway to the Ventura Freeway, then across Coldwater Canyon. That way we would avoid most surface street traffic. Clever. I didn't realize I had never taken the Golden State before, and I somehow managed to get hopelessly lost. We drove and drove, Daddy every so often asking if I knew where I was going. "Yes," I kept saying. When an hour had gone by,

451

I had to admit my folly. But now I had gotten off and on at least three different freeways. From annoyed he had passed angry and was well on his way to furious.

"You always think you're so smart, don't you? If you were so smart you'd stop at a gas station and ask someone," he yelled. He was right of course. I stopped, got directions and while Daddy sat in the car tight-lipped, I filled the by now empty gas tank. When I finally let him off at his house we didn't even say goodbye to each other.

It turned out to be the last ballgame he ever saw.

No one at that time suspected there was anything really the matter. But during the summer and early fall the pains had become increasingly worse. He complained more frequently about his stomach and lack of appetite. He visited his doctor almost daily, and was put through a series of tests, all of which proved negative. I continued telling him, "Go to Hillcrest, it's all in your head." My impatient attitude probably proved helpful—I may have partly convinced him that he really wasn't ill. Actually, I believed what I said. I had no idea until . . .

On October 19 Daddy went to Dallas to work at a promotion dinner for Neiman-Marcus. He rehearsed in the afternoon and everything went perfectly. But that evening as he was warming up, he found, to his consternation, that his right hand was numb, and he couldn't hold the bow. A local doctor diagnosed his condition as a minor stroke, and ordered him to go to the hospital. He insisted he was all right except for his hand, and could do the show without playing his violin. The following morning, after talking to Rex Kennamer, he flew home and on Kennamer's orders was met at the airport by an ambulance which was to take him directly to Cedars of Lebanon Hospital. Daddy agreed reluctantly to the ambulance, but refused a wheelchair or any other kind of help, and on the way to the hospital insisted they stop at a diner because he was hungry and wanted a doughnut and coffee.

After four days of extensive testing he was released. The strength had returned to his hand and the tests again proved negative. In fact, he had cancer of the pancreas and we didn't know it. According to Dr. Kennamer, "Today we'd be able to diagnose it—we'd do a CAT scan and we'd know it immediately. But in those days that was an almost impossible diagnosis to make. You didn't make it till the very end." Later, after Dad's death, Dr. Kennamer told me he had suspected it, but didn't want to put him through long and painful procedures when there was nothing that could be done anyway. I have always been grateful to Rex.

Daddy came home from the hospital to face one of the busiest periods of his life. His schedule from then through the spring of the next year was crowded with commitments. He was in good spirits for a week or so and then the pains returned, still intermittently but more severely. He began taking medication. What was wrong? Was it really just in his head?

Al Gordon, one of Daddy's writers, remembers, "Irving Fein called me up and said, 'We don't know what's wrong with Jack. He's upset, he can't eat—you've got to get him to a psychiatrist.' I guess he thought I could talk to him better than the others. So I called him up and suggested he see a psychiatrist. Jack said, 'What am I going to tell him?'

"I said, 'I don't know. Maybe they *are* miracle workers. You don't feel good. Nobody knows what it is. You're going to do a TV special and a picture, *The Sunshine Boys*—maybe it's upsetting you.' I suggested a friend of mine, a Dr. Loman.

"Jack said, 'All right, have him call me.'

"Later I spoke to Dr. Loman. 'What happened?' I asked.

" 'I talked to the man for an hour and a half and he was as sane as anybody I ever knew—it wasn't in his head.' "

By the middle of November Daddy was deteriorating, taking great quantities of sedatives and painkillers, and sleeping most of the day. Yet he still had his moments. He accepted a plaque at an award dinner, and after receiving a standing ovation he spoke and told jokes for over twenty minutes. He practiced the violin almost daily. He and the writers and Irving were making plans for the future: starring with Walter Matthau in *The Sunshine Boys*, a TV special, dates in Vegas.

Perhaps I buried my head in the sand. Perhaps I was too busy with my own life. Perhaps I didn't want to know the truth, to face reality. I had no inkling that he was dying. I saw him frequently and knew he wasn't always feeling tip-top, but I attributed it to age. I didn't know then about all the medication. We spoke on the phone daily, we went to the Ice Capades, we even did a long magazine photo session in late November—the last pictures he had taken. Mom never said a word to me about his condition. To this day, I have no idea how much even she knew or suspected at that time.

On December 12 I took my children to Mammoth Lakes for a ten-day ski trip. In mid-afternoon before we left, I called my parents. Daddy was taking a nap so I spoke to Mom, saying, "See you for Christmas. Tell Daddy goodbye for me."

I never said goodbye to him.

We returned on the evening of the twenty-second and immediately went out to buy our Christmas tree. By the time we got home it was too late to call—and as far as I knew, there was no reason to. The children and I decorated the tree; getting in the holiday spirit, stringing popcorn, singing Christmas carols, drinking eggnog and generally feeling festive. Early the next morning we piled in the car and went out to do the marketing and our last-minute shopping. We were gone almost all day. When we walked in the back door laden down with packages the phone was ringing. It was

Mom. "You'd better come right over. Your dad's in a coma. He's dying."

What did she mean? A coma? Dying? Not Daddy. She couldn't mean it. My daddy couldn't die. He was never going to die. I didn't understand.

I drove to Charing Cross in a daze. Daddy's door was closed. Mom was lying on the sofa in the upstairs sitting room. She told me that he had slipped into a coma the previous day and that it was now a matter of a day or two or maybe just hours.

The next three days are a blur in my memory. I don't remember even crying. It didn't seem possible, as though it was happening to someone else. When I went in to see him, which I did frequently during the next two days, he was always sleeping peacefully.

We went about our routine almost as if nothing had changed. Bobby was then ten years old, Joanna nine. Mom, Michael, Maria and I decided not to spoil their Christmas. Besides, I don't think we knew what else to do—it all seemed unreal. Perhaps "surreal" would be a better description. So we celebrated Christmas Eve as we had always done; with Hickey and his wife, Babe and Clem, and Miss Vallance. The Christmas tree stood at the end of the gallery, decorated with the same ornaments, the same lights and on top the same sparkling star with "Merry Christmas" lit up in the center that had been on our tree ever since I could remember. The gifts were piled underneath.

In the dining room the buffet table was laden with turkey, stuffing, cranberry sauce and all the typical holiday foods. The huge dining table was adorned with pine cones, red candles, a Santa Claus centerpiece and the Christmas tree china at each place setting. We tried our best to carry on through dinner, to behave normally. We talked of our ski trip, laughed at some of the mishaps, discussed recent gossip and trivia, speculated about our presents. We stuffed ourselves on the delicious dinner and dessert, which at the children's request was profiteroles au chocolat. Everything just as usual, but for one thing—Daddy's place at the head of the table was empty.

After dinner we gathered around the tree and opened our presents. Every year they got better and this was the best yet. Mike received a stereo for his room at college, Maria's tiny package contained diamond studs for her pierced ears, Bobby's gift was a train set, Joanna's a dollhouse. Mine was a breathtaking gold and diamond chain from Tiffany's. We were all thrilled with our presents and everthing was just as usual, but for one thing—the gifts marked for Daddy remained unopened.

On Christmas day the news about my father's condition spread around town. By mid-afternoon friends began to arrive. By five the house was crowded, and remained so, with people coming and going, for the next three or four days. It was one continuous party—the longest I've ever been to.

Leonard Gershe remembers "a strange kind of

457

festival that was going on—out of love for him and for your mother. People wanted to be *there*, wanted to be part of something important that was happening to him, no matter how sad it was. It was to say goodbye, to be counted as one of his friends. To be one of his friends was a great honor.

"Jack, in his time, was very much like what Jimmy Stewart is now—a folk legend. The people adored him. He could do nothing wrong. Jack Benny, above all others—nobody was as beloved. This was shown by his friends, his peers who came."

Billy and Audrey Wilder remember, "In kind of a weird way, when your father was dying at the house, it was like an Irish wake. It's never happened before. It was kind of a—if such a thing could happen—a joyous kind of memory. It was extraordinary.

"Do you remember when Jack Lemmon spilled the bottle of red wine? He was still drinking in those days. [I do remember. The carpet was white, and the red stain remained until the house was sold—ten years later!] People were drawn to be there—it was not macabre—there was nothing sad about it. It was kind of like a purgatory. People came there to cleanse themselves and they felt so close to him very suddenly. People came and went and came back again. It was like waiting for the birth of a child—people coming to the hospital and waiting. There was very little sleep there, right? It was a continuous gathering. It was very moving, very touching. So

458

many people came—people who had not seen him for years.

"We've all been to see people who were dying. You do your duty. This was just the opposite of that—you couldn't keep the people away."

In spite of the sadness, what I remember most vividly is the camaraderie and the laughter—as Billy and Audrey said, it was almost a "man-of-the-year" celebration. People told funny stories and anecdotes about him, talked of their close friendship and recalled hilarious incidents. Many of my friends were there as well. I played hostess: greeting the guests, seeing to it that they had plenty of food and drink, entering into the party atmosphere, listening and laughing, and sharing stories.

The party spirit continued until the next afternoon about two when Rex told me Daddy was near the end. Then I went up to his room and sat on his bed. He looked very peaceful. Occasionally, during the next few hours, his friends came in to kiss him goodbye: Danny Kaye, Janet and Freddie De Cordova, Dolores Hope, others . . .

I stayed with him, never leaving his bed, stroking his face, talking to him and telling him again and again how much I loved him. I have no idea how long I sat there—five hours? Nine hours? I don't know. I just remember when Rex touched me on the shoulder and said, "Joanie, he's gone."

I hope Daddy heard me.

The funeral took place at Hillside Memorial Cemetery. There seemed to be thousands of people, but perhaps there were only a few hundred. It's all foggy in my mind, disjointed and dreamlike. I remember George Burns beginning a eulogy and breaking down, unable to continue. Then Bob Hope speaking so eloquently, ending with, "For a man who was the undisputed master of comedy timing, you would have to say that this was the only time Jack Benny's timing was all wrong. He left us too soon. He only gave us eighty years. God keep him, enjoy him. We did for eighty years."

And I remember particularly a moment of humor. As the service ended, I was standing at the side of the family room looking at Daddy's coffin, quietly crying, when I heard the funeral director reading a list of speakers and contributors. It was like a list of movie credits or the crawl at the end of a TV show. I started to giggle. Then he read the list of pallbearers. When he came to Leonard Gershe he pronounced it Gershay. Walter Matthau became Walter Matthew. By Ronald *Ree*-gun I was laughing. But with Gregor Piatigorsky he completely fell apart, tried it three times, each time incorrectly, and finally gave up. He couldn't even continue with the rest of the list. In the midst of tragedy it was a hilarious moment of black comedy.

Lenny Gershe said, "I say this with great love and affection. Jack would have adored it. It's what he would have wanted—this kind of celebration

460

and humor. He would have thought, 'Enjoy it, enjoy me.' "

His fame set him a world apart. I still have trouble sorting it out. There was Daddy and there was Jack Benny. They were the same person and they weren't. I talked about this phenomenon recently with a friend, who said, "I understand. What you mean is he was a celebrity out there but when he came home he was just your father. That's not unusual. It would be the same if your dad was the mayor of the town you lived in, or a prominent doctor, or the commanding general of the army base."

"No," I said. "That's not what I mean. What you say is true in part—when he was at home he *was* just my dad. But even the dad at home wrote the show, had celebrity friends and talked about his career. He was always, and in any milieu, Jack Benny." Unlike a mayor who is a celebrity in his city, or a neurosurgeon famous within his profession, my father was recognized by all, asked for autographs and fawned over. In fact during the radio days his fame was overwhelming. I recently met a gentleman who told me that when he was a child he lived in the Washington Square area of New York City. He recalled, "It was before air-conditioning and when the weather was warm everyone had their windows open and I would be out walking or running up the street or playing in the park with my friends. It didn't matter how far or fast I went, I knew I would never miss a

461

word of Jack Benny. Everyone's radio was tuned in to that show."

On the same note, but a funny one: a 1936 movie magazine poll listed the most recognizable voices in America as (1) Jack Benny, (2) President Roosevelt, (3) Bing Crosby. Surely Daddy read or was told about that poll. Surely he had to know how famous his voice was, and yet he always identified himself on the telephone, even to his best friends. He would say, "Hello, this is Jack Benny," as if he were a stranger. It made his friends crazy. "Jack, I knew it was you before you finished 'hello,' " was the usual reply. It didn't stop him. He continued the habit all his life.

I hadn't realized his fame had spread to non-English-speaking countries as well. One night in Paris very, very late, about four in the morning, a group of us wound up at a Russian nightclub. A band of violinists was serenading us and when they were about to take a break one of our group, Radie Harris, approached the leader and in her high school French tried to explain that Monsieur Benny was a famous radio artiste and violinist in America. A glint of recognition showed in his eyes.

The musicians left, Daddy paid the bill. We were standing on the sidewalk, looking at the beautiful sky as dawn approached, waiting for a taxi, when all of a sudden the musicians appeared. They nodded to Daddy, and broke into "Love in Bloom." It was a glorious moment.

But that's still not it—I learned to take his fame

462

in stride—that's not the difference I'm talking about.

My son Michael remembers something about this: "I always knew Granddad was a celebrity, that he was famous—but I never really felt the full impact of how much of a celebrity he was until after he died. Maria and I sat down and read some of the letters that were pouring in to my mother and grandmother, and it was then that I first realized how much he had affected other people's lives. There was one letter that stands out in my memory. This woman was an invalid and she wrote that all week long she just waited for Sunday night to hear his radio show. It was the highlight of her week. It was the one thing in life she had always looked forward to."

My daughter Maria recalls: "One day—I must have been twelve or thirteen—I was bicycling on South Beverly Drive, on my way to the dentist, when I heard a man yelling, 'Maria, Maria.' I looked over, and there was Granddaddy strolling down the street. My first reaction was one of surprise that he had recognized me, knowing that he usually had his head in the clouds. My second was, 'That's Jack Benny,' and I was impressed. The star, Jack Benny, had said hello to me!

"It was an odd feeling—the Jack Benny–Granddad thing. I wish I could explain it, but I can't."

When people talk to me about Daddy in superlatives, when they tell me, "Your father was an institution," I find myself thinking, Daddy?

Famous, yes, but an institution? Really? It's too much. That's not my daddy, that's a bigger-than-life person. My father wasn't bigger than life, but that "institution" was. That's what's hard to sort out. That's the difference.

About a year ago I was in Palm Beach for the first time staying at the Breakers and one evening I went exploring. Partway down one of the myriad corridors was a multiwindow photo display advertising the wares of a local photographer. The first group included pictures of President and Mrs. Kennedy, the Duke and Duchess of Windsor, Winston Churchill and other assorted important guests who had at one time or another stayed at the hotel. Then I came to the second window. The whole side wall was covered with pictures of my father! How odd, I thought, to be in a strange city in a strange hotel, and there's Daddy.

Also about this time, a friend and I walked into a new restaurant in Beverly Hills called, believe it or not, the Beverly Hills Restaurant. One side wall was covered with assorted posters, the other with blown-up photographs. At first I paid little attention—just a glance, as we were busy gossiping. We were shown to a booth against the photo wall where we ordered drinks, looked at the menu and continued our conversation. At some point I looked up and there, directly above our table, hung a huge picture. "Oh, my God," I exclaimed, "that's my pool!" Actually, the photo was of Daddy, sitting in a little rowboat in the pool. The boat was white with "Joanie" in red-lettered script on the side, and in the background you could see the pool furniture and pool house, but it was Ollie, the octopus, that grabbed my attention, even before I noticed Daddy and the boat. That photograph must have been taken in 1936 when we first moved into the Roxbury house because I have no recollection of the rowboat.

How odd, I thought, to be in a strange restaurant, and there, right next to me is not only my house, my pool, my dad, but even a boat with my name on it.

That's the difference, too!

Fred De Cordova was, next to George Burns, my father's closest friend and confidant, and I just can't end this without these lovely words from him: "The part I liked most about him, if I had to select one thing, was that he cared about his friends. Not, like some celebrities, by sending planes for them or extravagant gifts, but by a phone call or a visit. All his life, I think, he cared more about people than he cared whether people loved him.

"He was a more solitary man than people who are stars tend to be. Many people I've worked with carry a large entourage, and make sure that the entourage precedes them to alert everyone who is coming next. On the Johnny Carson show, for example, the guest stars are frequently preceded by their hairdresser, makeup man, publicist, piano player and assorted hangers-on, who announce whosits will be here in fifteen minutes. Jack just walked in.

"His good humor was pretty constant. That's not to say he didn't have a temper. He did. One time he turned on me in front of an audience during the filming of the show. His anger took the form of rather biting sarcasm. We didn't speak afterward and I went home in a sulk. At that time I was still unmarried and living with my mother. The following morning flowers arrived, not for me, but for my mother . . . with a nice note that read, 'Please apologize to your son and tell him never to be angry with an aging Jew.' He was never afraid to apologize when he thought he had hurt someone.

"No, he was not an intellectual giant. No, he was not without flaws. No, he was not the funniest man in person. No, he had some anger. He had faults, but none of them, I thought, serious faults, and all covered up by the fact that he was so dear to those he loved.

"He wasn't perfect . . . but he was as close as anyone I'm ever going to meet or ever have met."

When Daddy died I was thirty-nine years old. How ironic. On television and in the newspaper obituaries, whenever I was mentioned as a "survivor," I was referred to as "his adopted daughter, Joan." I tried very hard not to let it bother me. The fact of my adoption certainly never had before—it was simply a fact. But after all these years of love and caring, I read "adopted daughter" as if I weren't really his child, but rather some kid he felt sorry for and took in. Yes, it bothered me—a lot—and for the very first time. Daddy was gone and the press made me feel as though I was an afterthought. Why couldn't they have said "his daughter, Joan"?

I never wept for him. There was no reason to. I still see Daddy frequently on television and hear his voice on the radio, or on one of my many tapes. I miss his footstep, his cigar, our phone conversations, the trips, the drop-in visits, but those things aren't so very important. What's important is that he's still very much alive for me. He's just out of town playing a long engagement.

How could I be sad—I can only be happy for him. He lived eighty full, happy, successful years. He had a wife and daughter who loved him. He had hundreds of loyal friends and thousands of adoring fans. He had recently finished a gig and was about to star in a film. He didn't get old and doddering, grow deaf or blind or lose his memory. Not him. He went out a star. Yes, I wish he could have lived forever, but since that couldn't be, I have to disagree with Bob Hope. His timing didn't desert him. It was perfect right to the end. He left a legacy few men have equaled in any profession. One of gentleness, kindness, simplicity, generosity and loyalty.

As for me, I think you'll agree I led a charmed, enchanted life. From those early Sunday Nights at Seven through a lifetime of love and laughter.

But I think Daddy should have the last word . . .

After attending high school for only one term, one of the ironies of my life is that in 1959 they put up a beautiful new school in Waukegan. It is named the Jack Benny Junior High School. I went there for the dedication ceremonies, and made a short speech. It was the proudest moment of my life. I even received a diploma. It was fifty years late, but I'm glad I finally got out of high school. What I regret is that I don't have the education to go with the diploma. Now that it is too late, I realize how much I missed, both in my lack of general knowledge, particularly in history and the arts, and in such habits of mind as concentration and logical reasoning.

Maybe it was due to the lack of ability to reason things out that I never deliberately planned to be a miserly character on the show. Nor did I scheme out any of the other pieces of business and material that were so successful—not even the famous feud with Fred Allen. I have found that when you go after something in cold blood, it becomes contrived. As I've said, it's always the audience that tells you what to do. It was the people who told me they wanted stingy jokes, violin jokes and "39" jokes.

Everything good that happened to me happened by accident. I think it was like this in my whole life. I am not an aggressive person. I am not one of those men who knows where he's going when he's a young man. I was not filled with ambition nor fired by a drive toward a clear-cut goal. I never knew exactly where I was going.

My whole life—it is as if I were a passenger on a train. I don't want to be on the train, but I have no strong desire to get off, either. I don't know where the train is going, but meanwhile I will count the telephone poles and watch the scenery and see what the other passengers have in mind. And then when the train arrives at the last station, I get off. I look around. I like the place where I am. I don't know exactly how I got here, but I'm glad to be here just the same.